ALBERTA

ALBERTA

✳

ROBERT KROETSCH

Afterword by Rudy Wiebe
Photo Essay by Harry Savage

NEWEST PRESS, EDMONTON

Canadian Cataloguing in Publication Data

Kroetsch, Robert, 1927-
  Alberta

  ISBN 0-920897-31-2

  1. Alberta–Description and travel–1951-1980. * 2. Alberta–
Description and travel–1981- I. Title
FC3667.3.K76 1993   917.123   C93-091178-4
F1076.K76 1993

CREDITS:
Book Design: Bob Young/BOOKENDS DESIGNWORKS
Cover Photograph: Harry Savage
Map: Mostly Maps
Photo of Robert Kroetsch and Rudy Wiebe: Isabel Hamilton
Editor for the Press: Mort Ross
Financial Assistance: NeWest Press gratefully acknowledges the financial
assistance of The Alberta Foundation for the Arts, The Canada Council, and
The NeWest Institute for Western Canadian Studies.

Printed and bound in Canada by Kromar Printing Ltd.

NeWest Publishers Limited
Suite 310, 10359 – 82 Avenue
Edmonton, Alberta T6E 1Z9

for all my cousins

ALSO BY ROBERT KROETSCH

NOVELS

But We Are Exiles
The Words of My Roaring
The Studhorse Man
Gone Indian
Badlands
What the Crow Said
Alibi
The Puppeteer

POETRY

The Ledger
Seed Catalogue
The Sad Phoenician
Completed Field Notes

CRITICISM

The "Crow" Journals
The Lovely Treachery of Words

CONTENTS

Many thousands of people in the Eastern
Provinces, the United States of America, and
the older countries of Europe, are every year
seriously contemplating emigration. And the
first great problem to be solved by capitalists,
by parents with rising families, by young men
of bone, sinew and courage, anxious to better
their fortunes, is –

WHERE SHALL WE GO?

Let all such persons carefully study this
pamphlet, which is written not by speculators,
but by actual settlers engaged in the general
callings of life; who having found a most
desirable country, are convinced that, so
soon as its scenery, great fertility, genial
climate, abundant minerals and vast capabilities
are known, its speedy settlement will be assured.

– *District of Alberta; information for
intending settlers.* Compiled by the
Calgary Agricultural Society, J. G.
Fitzgerald, Secretary. Ottawa, 1884.

NORTHWEST TERRITORIES

Fort Smith

WOOD BUFFALO

NATIONAL

PARK

Bistcho
Lake

to Hay River
and Yellowknife

Zama
City

Hay

ASSUMPTION IR

58

High Level

35

Fort
Vermillion

88

Rainbow
Lake

BRITISH COLUMBIA

Churchaga

Peace

River

HIGHWAY

MACKENZIE

Manning

64

Grimshaw

Dunvegan

Peace

River

Peace River

2

49

McLennan

2

Grande
Prairie

Beaverlodge

34

FORESTRY

TRUNK

ROAD

River

43

Smoky

Little

Smoky

Smoky River

Grande Cache

WILLMORE

WILDERNESS
PARK

JASPER

NATIONAL

PARK

Jasper

40

YELLOWHEAD

HIGHWAY

Hinton

47

Robb

Cadomin

Miette
Hot
Springs

Yellowhead Pass

Edson

16

Athabasca

River

Pembina

River

Wabasca

River

BICENTENNIAL

HIGHWAY

Red Earth
Creek

Utikuma
Lake

Lesser
Slave Lake

SWAN
HILLS

Swan Hills

33

44

Slave Lake

Calling
Lake

Athabasca

63

2

18

North

Saskatchewan

Fort
Saskatchewan

ELK ISLAND
NATIONAL PARK

St.Albert

Spruce Grove

39

Edmonton

Ledue

Wetaskiwin

Camroac

55

Lac La Biche

Cold
Lake

36

Moose
Lake

28

St. Paul

Frog
Lake

45

Mundare

Vermilion

Lloydminster

14

Tar Island

Fort McMurray

Clearwater R

Athabasca

63

Lake
Athabasca

Ft.
Chipewyan

Lake
Claire

Slave River

SASKATCHEWAN

22

20

2

Pentoka

53

Edberg

63

Heisler

Dirudmeat
Lake

13

Wainwright

Battle

River

13

Provost

Rocky
Mountain
House

11

Lacombe

Sylvan
Lake

54

Red Deer

Stettler

56

Sullivan
Lake

Consort

BUFFALO

Innisfail

Olds

27

Hanna

9

36

Red

TRAIL

Mt Columbia 3747 m
Highest point in Alberta

Peyto L.

NATIONAL
Lake
Louise

Kickinghorse Pass

Banff

Athabasca
Falls

Maligne
Lake

Athabasca Glacier

93

BANFF

R O C K Y

FORESTRY

TRUNK

ROAD

22

Crossfield

Drumheller

Deer

River

Empress

Lake
Minnewanka

BIG HILL SPRINGS
PROV. PARK

Morley

KANANASKIS

COUNTRY

40

Calgary

1

21

TRANS-

CANADA

Cluny

DINASAUR
PROV. PARK

Jenner

Brooks

HIGHWAY

Saskatchewan R.

M O U N T A I N S

Turner
Valley

High
River

23

Bow

River

South

Mt Livingstone 2423 m

The
Gap

Oldman
River
dam

LIVINGSTONE RANGE

Crowsnest Pass

Coleman

Frank
Blairmore

Pincher
Creek

6

Cowley

5

Oldman

Oldman River

Fort
Macleod

3

Coaldale

Taber

Medicine
Hat

CYPRESS HILLS
PROV. PARK

Lethbridge

4

61

ALBERTA

0   50   100 km

WATERTON LAKES
NATIONAL PARK

Cardston

Chief
Mountain

62

MILK RIVER
RIDGE

Milk
River

WRITING-ON-STONE
PROV. PARK

Milk   River

41

UNITED STATES

Inge Wilson / Mostly Maps

ALBERTA,
TWENTY-FIVE YEARS AFTER ALBERTA:

ROBERT KROETSCH

IN A PIG'S EYE

The young woman standing beside me at the barn window had never in her life seen a real live pig. Lauralyn Chow was born and raised in Edmonton and practises law in Calgary; she writes gentle, comic stories about cultural misunderstanding. But she had never seen a pig.

"It's looking me right in the eye," she said, delighted.

Is it truly possible, I wondered, listening to her wonder, to be an Albertan and never to have seen a living hog? What happened to the Alberta of my childhood?

We were on the farm owned by Aritha van Herk's parents, near the village of Edberg, in central Alberta, just south of the Battle River and Driedmeat Lake.

"My shoes are heavy with mud," Lauralyn said, delighted again. "Is this what you call gumbo?"

We were twenty-three writers on a tour. We were in Alberta, and our intention was to find Alberta. "What are we talking about when we talk about place?" Fred Wah had asked, one winter afternoon over a beer. And there we were on an April day, twenty creative writing students from the University of Calgary, their instructors, the poet Fred Wah and the novelist Aritha van Herk, and I. We were on the road, travelling in three vans.

Mrs. van Herk, gracious, elegant, eloquent, had prepared a lunch that was a feast. We left our twenty-three pairs of stained and muddy shoes at the back door and crowded into the van Herks's spotless new kitchen. We heaped our plates with Dutch-style open-faced sandwiches and homemade pickles and squares of cake. We crowded into the living room and filled the chairs and the sofa and the floor with our presence. We ate heartily and went for seconds. But the talk was still of the beauty of hogs. And the question of turning hogs into poetry.

Brian Stanko, guarding a rock he had found on the van Herk farm, a granite fragment he would deliver to a poet in Drumheller, quoted the opening sentence of Aritha's famous first novel, *Judith:* "Pig shit and wet greasy straw were piled high in the wheelbarrow."

The optimistic energy that abides in Alberta's two and a half million citizens was there in the van Herk house in the persons of twenty student writers. The group included undergraduates, a graduate student, an architect, two lawyers, a philosopher, teachers, administrators, a bill collector, busy mothers whose husbands were at home looking after the kids. The group included people born in Texas, in Winnipeg, in Japan, in India, in small Saskatchewan towns, in Africa, in something called Toronto. There were even two writers who were born in Calgary.

We were all Albertans. That was agreed upon and taken for granted. The catch was: where to find Alberta?

*

WALKING ON (DINOSAUR) EGGS

We were on the road again.

We went in our three vans to Drumheller and the magnificent Royal Tyrrell Museum of Palaeontology, set on the edge of the badlands of the Red Deer River.

The Tyrrell Museum opened in September 1985, and each year

attracts up to a half million visitors. Both an exhibition and research centre, it concentrates on the study of ancient life through fossils. Its display of two hundred dinosaur specimens, the largest collection to be found anywhere under one roof, is alive with slide shows, hands-on experiments, and the exciting talk that goes with discovery and astonishment.

If pigs wouldn't give us the answer, perhaps dinosaurs would.

And, instead of going there to talk with the distinguished palaeontologist, Philip Currie, we went to talk with the poet who was to receive the rock from the van Herk farm.

Monty Reid is one of the finest poets anywhere. He interrupted his work at the museum to talk to us about dinosaurs. Dinosaurs he explained are, in a way, a kind of fiction. We do of course find their skeletons in the steep, exposed slopes of the badlands. But the stories we tell of their lives, the descriptions we give of their bodies, the supposed causes of their disappearance, keep changing as we make new discoveries.

A major search commenced in June 1987 when a young woman, Wendy Sloboda, scouting in Devil's Coulee, in the Milk River region of southern Alberta, made the uncanny guess that what she was looking at were fossilized shell fragments of dinosaur eggs. Philip Currie quickly organized an expedition. On the last day of the search, in the last ten minutes of the search, when it seemed that nothing was to be found, the technician Kevin Aulenback came running into camp and "babbling" that he had found not only eggs, but a nest of eggs, whole nests of eggs, and even some eggs with "babies" in them.

And he had. He and Currie's team made the major palaeontological discovery of the past half century. By understanding how dinosaurs nested and hatched their young, and how the young grew to huge sizes so rapidly, we might yet understand how life comes and goes on our small planet. And we might begin to know why three-quarters of the existing species, half the existing genera, disappeared abruptly, some sixty-seven million years ago.

The catastrophe theorists argue for the impact of a huge asteroid or the radiation from an exploding sun or a recurring cloud of comets (we may run into it every twenty-six million years). The gradualist theorists argue for the development of seasonal climates (many shallow seas were drained by the shifting of the continents) or the massive eruptions of volcanoes.

We talked there in the museum, with Monty Reid, and we learned that to understand a place you go and take a close look, then you think for a long time about the fragments that constitute your perceptions. And then you guess at what the story might be.

Fred Wah is one of those gifted guessers. He tells himself a changing and ongoing story by constantly rebuilding his house. And he was one of our leaders, there on the road again – with not a motel in sight.

And yet we were all pleased. We were sure we would get the hang of it. The young writer and editor Ashok Mathur, on a computer in one of our vans, began as we drove to write an account of the day's events; time is a variable ingredient in the mix called place.

He and his nineteen fellow students students had it figured out. They would tell twenty stories.

*

STARTING OUT BY GOING BACK

Spring came and went; July came down wet and green on a southern Alberta that is usually brown by midsummer.

Rudy Wiebe and Aritha van Herk and I, on a wet July day, went to the Calgary Stampede. We pretended we would look at the ways in which Alberta has changed since I toured the province in 1967, at the time when I was writing *Alberta*.

The 1988 Winter Olympics did indeed transform Calgary, giving its spirit and its image a lift. But the Stampede was there long before the Olympics; it will still be there when the next Olympics come round.

We were three novelists looking at the Alberta we write out of, exploring the province we grew up in. How does one get from experience to a story of that experience? And again, how does one get back from the story to the experience?

There, that day at the Stampede, we went to the World Champion Blacksmiths' Competition, where we delighted in the ring of hammers, the glow of forges, the utilitarian beauty of a newly shaped horseshoe. We went and looked at the immense beauty of draft horses; we studied the new breeds of cows that have come into Alberta – the American Brahman, with its large ears, its hump, its pronounced dewlap, is a storybook addition to the Alberta landscape.

And we did find something else that was new. We attended the Cowboy Poetry Reading.

The Stampede auction ring was cut in half by a curtain, to make a small amphitheatre. There was sawdust on the floor; there were rows of steep seats in a half circle around the performers. Cowboy hats and tight jeans and red silk shirts filled the air with color and movement.

And the featured poets filled the air with expectation. Doug Richards, from the Devil's Head Ranch. Gordon Colliar, from the M Ranch. Donna Alm, from the Porcupine Hills. Jim Baker from Willow Creek. Doris Daley from Granum. Rob Chisholm from the 3 Walking Sticks Ranch.

That's how it was. Person and place had a way of connecting. And the poems were about those places, about local events. Often, the poems told stories. Sometimes the poets broke into song. And the tall tale jostled with humorous self-deprecating love laments, or just plain bitching about doing the chores.

Maybe those poems made us go to the chuckwagon races. Or maybe we had gone to all the other events, Rudy and Aritha and I, waiting for the races to start.

Chuckwagon races are surely one of the great spectacles of North America, and the Calgary Stampede offers the best example of a sport that finds its champions among Alberta drivers and Alberta teams.

The mud was ankle-deep on the track, the night we braved the weather. The famous drivers, George Normand, Ray Mitsuing, Jerry Bremner, Tom Glass, were all in fine form – and splattered with mud. The four-horse teams ran neck and neck from the starting barrels to the finish line.

Tom Glass of High River, that night, was on his way to his third championship, and a fifty-thousand dollar prize.

We went to the casino, after the races. We played roulette. Or rather, I played roulette; I was the only one betting. Rudy told me to put my money on twenty-four. I put it on twenty-three.

Twenty-four came up the winning number.

✳

"THEMES"

A few blocks away from the Calgary Stampede, on a gracious old street that in large part survived the oil boom that transformed so much of Calgary, I found John and Kay Snow at home.

I had talked with them twenty-five years earlier.

John retired from banking in 1971, at the age of sixty. A painter most of his life, he is now as busy as ever. His current project is a huge mural, twelve feet by eighteen feet, for an open-to-the-weather, right-on-the-street wall.

The Arts 17 Society has commissioned a series of murals for Seventeenth Avenue, and in the process contributed to the passion for the arts in Calgary. Gary Olson's magnificent cow graces the wall of a liquor vendor. Sandy Haeseker's big dog makes the whole street seem like home.

John took me into his studio to see the panels that will constitute his lithograph become mural. "Themes" offers, powerfully and gently, a bowl of flowers, a jug, a table, and a window onto a prairie landscape. A Korean artist now living in Calgary, Sam Kwon, will help John mount the mural.

Kay Snow, retired from the University of Calgary and busy with writing projects that include a major biography of the artist Max Bates and numerous letters to governmental ministers, was her usual dynamic self. She spoke me a letter, right there over a Scotch and soda.

Art has to get out of the museums and go public, Kay said. But then she went on to lament that Calgary is the only city of its size on the continent that doesn't have a civic art galley.

Calgary does, however, she added, have a superb symphony. And Michael Dobbin, the director of Alberta Theatre Projects, stages original and daring plays in the Martha Cohen Theatre.

Musicians anywhere have difficulty getting new work performed. What Kay didn't volunteer was that she and John in 1982 founded an association called New Works Calgary and sponsored the first concert, a performance of new works by Calgary composers. Now the thriving association concentrates mostly on chamber music, and mostly on first performances.

There in the two-storey wooden Snow house, with a raspberry patch out back and an apple tree and Calgary's modernist skyline out front, I dared ask what the oil boom did for Calgary.

Kay's spoken letter to a friend who has been inexplicably absent went on. She told me that the LRT has transformed downtown Calgary. She told me the university has *finally* found a gifted president.

On the matter of Calgary's architecture she gave a mixed report. The macho impulse – my building is taller than yours – has fortunately spent itself. But the balcony craze is no great substitute, with rows of new balconies crammed with bicycles, packing cases, and garbage. "I begin to crave cupids all over the place," Kay said. "Anything to get away from all the squares."

I think the pun was intentional.

"And, fortunately," she said, "the inner city is being rediscovered, along with the virtue of back lanes. If only people didn't build all those monstrous houses with the double garage as the main architectural feature . . . ."

I dared to ask her about the province at large.

Premier Lougheed and his Conservatives, she explained, tried to diversify the economy and didn't succeed – go look at the magnesium plant in High River. Magnesium, she repeated. Magnesium. But she had high praise for the Lougheed government's establishment of the Tyrrell Museum, and Kananaskis Country, and Head-Smashed-In Buffalo Jump Interpretive Centre. She also gave the Lougheed government high marks for building homes where old people can be independent, and full of zip and vinegar.

I asked her about the current premier.

"I hear he's an accomplished golfer," Kay said.

*

LOOKING FOR GAP POND

We got stuck.

We had set out to visit Kananaskis Country. Rudy was driving. Aritha was reading the map.

Kananaskis Country may well be Alberta's gift to itself for hosting the 1988 Winter Olympic Games. That area of over four thousand square kilometres adjacent to Banff National Park is a gift and a temptation as well: a place to hike, a place to ski, a place to loaf, a place to hide, a place to dream.

We had with us a pamphlet called "Kananaskis Country at a Glance" and that pamphlet said: "Kananaskis Country's spectacular terrain ranges from rolling foothills and montane forests, to the ice and rock of the high alpine. . . . Kananaskis Village offers world class resort hotel accommodation and amenities. . . ."

As I said, Rudy was driving. Aritha was reading the map. I was reading the pamphlet.

When we saw the sign that said Willow Creek we knew we had missed a turn. We had been instructed by an old man sitting in a pick-up in a light, insistent rain to take a detour. We were south of

Kananaskis Country. And we were headed south.

Rudy swung the car off the road, down onto a grassy slope, toward a rancher's fence. The light, insistent rain had obviously been falling for hours or days. We sat looking down over a tongue of prairie that came up into the foothills. Into the Porcupine Hills. And they do look like porcupines, the grass-sloped hills with their caps of spiky trees.

We studied the map. We changed our plans. Rudy tried to back the car up the grassy slope and onto the gravel road from which we had so recklessly departed. The car wouldn't move.

We were in a U-Drive. Aritha and I got out to push. By the time I was completely spattered with mud, Aritha, calmly, sanely, asked Rudy if by any chance he had the handbrake set. He did.

After that we found Highway 22 and drove south and stopped at the provincial government campsite just north of the Highway 517 turnoff.

We stopped simply so that I might wash some of the mud off my clothes in the clean, racing water of the Oldman River. And we discovered the cottonwoods that grow along riverbanks in southern Alberta; on the top of the cutbank above the river we found black-eyed Susans, wolf willow, cinquefoil, prairie sage, gopher holes and striped gophers; at the river's edge we found patches of orange lichens aglow on tilted rock outcrops.

"Lucky you got muddy," Rudy said to me.

We had set out to find Gap Pond, a pond near the place where the Oldman River emerges from a gap in the Livingstone Range of the Rockies. That supposed place, now, was immediately to the west of us. Almost above us.

And we did find the gap, if not the pond. We drove toward what seemed a solid wall of mountain and just that suddenly we were into a gap and through it.

Somewhere inside there, inside the gap, we found not a pond but rather Daisy Creek. We came upon a cowboy and his helper at the roadside, unloading two saddle horses and a packhorse out of a four-horse trailer.

The cowboy was Jim Whyte, from Okotoks. We talked while he saddled up, tightened cinches, then loaded four blue salt blocks onto the packhorse saddle. His dog, Griz, a heeler, had earned his name by chasing grizzlies out of a camp, but at the moment he was trading insults with a squirrel.

Seventeen ranchers share a communal pasture up in the mountains above this road. The pasture, from 15 June to 15 October, is grazing land for 820 yearlings. Jim was wearing leather chaps for a good reason; he would be riding through lodgepole pine for the first part of his three-hour trip. "The cows will be salt hungry," he said.

The cowgirl came toward us. She had gone a short distance, testing her mount. "This horse needs some training. Right now it's half horse, half knothead."

The two riders with their packhorse rode toward what seemed solid forest and disappeared into a gap.

Aritha and Rudy and I drove on. We saw a coyote and three mule deer in a matter of minutes. Then we stopped in Crowsnest Pass to look at the places where Rudy, in his student years, worked as assistant to a trucker who delivered Pepsi.

Rudy Wiebe, a teenager then, his tall, hard body jangling cases of Pepsi down the narrow stairs and into dark cellars, remembered the back entrances to no end of rickety stores and small cafés and old hotels.

There in that long, high, narrow coalmining valley, he was our guide. And he knew the stories as well as the delivery route, stories of bootleg rum, of miners who forgot the colour of day.

We walked across rusted railway tracks to look at coking ovens.

We found abandoned tipples. We saw slag heaps that had not yet allowed the return of poplars and grass.

Aritha directed us into back alleys and showed us the old miners' shacks, with smaller one-room shacks behind them, places that were let to bachelor miners. Places that came back vividly to life in her novel, *No Fixed Address*.

We talked of the dangerous work in the mines, the seams of coal tilted and broken by geological change. We talked of the hard lives of the immigrant families that came to the Crowsnest Pass on the promise of easy wealth.

There is a new Interpretive Centre at the site of the infamous Frank Slide; that awesome place where, at 4:10 in the morning on 29 April 1903, ninety million tons of limestone crashed from Turtle Mountain, onto the town and the dreams of the mining town of Frank. And it happened in less than one hundred seconds.

The Interpretive Centre recovers, eloquently, the stories of the dead and of the survivors. But there is in the valley another memorial to the miners and the difficulties of their lives and deaths.

A short distance east of the Frank Slide and across the highway is the Hillcrest Cemetery.

We went to that cemetery. We stood mute before the two mass graves, neat in their white picket fences, that mark the greatest tragedy in Canadian mining history. In the Hillcrest mine, in 1914, 189 miners died in a sudden explosion. Their bodies were hurriedly given over to those two mass graves, there on a mountain hillside.

＊

DAM IT ALL

Outside the pass we drove east. Out of the mountains. Back again toward open prairie.

We came to the site of the Oldman River Dam project. We drove out onto the huge earth-fill dam; we looked down into an empty valley, a truly vast valley, that will fill with water.

Fire and water. Alberta, still, is an elemental world. The advent of diesel-powered locomotives put an end to the Crowsnest coal industry. Now water is the name of the game. The demands for water, agricultural, industrial, recreational, urban, are relentlessly on the increase; the supply that flows down off the eastern slope of the Rockies remains fixed.

The environment is under pressure, and with it the varieties of life that, over the past century, over the previous thousands of years, over the preceding millions of years, shaped themselves to fit that environment.

Milton Born With A Tooth, leader of the Peigan Lonefighter Society, argues for one kind of future. Alberta's Public Works minister, Ken Kowalski, argues for another kind.

Albertans like to say they live in next year country.

*

McINTYRE RANCHING CO. LTD.

Rudy and I said goodby to Aritha and drove to Lethbridge to visit with the artist, Isabel Hamilton.

Isabel and Rudy were chosen in 1991 by the Arctic Awareness organizers of the Polar Continental Shelf Program to spend time in the Western Arctic. On Herschel Island, just off the northern coast of the Yukon, Isabel quickly discovered that even in July her watercolour paper wouldn't dry. She would have to be resourceful.

When at home she likes to paint on her kitchen floor, kneeling on a pillow, reaching out over large sheets of watercolour paper. There in the Arctic, she quickly learned to sketch and photograph while huddled in a parka on a gravel beach, the bright sea ice moving before her eyes, glaciers at her back.

Isabel is a watercolour artist with a special interest in landscapes. And in faces and flowers. Somehow those interests add up to a singular vision.

One of her hobbies is raising orchids; her greenhouse is a tropical contrast to her interest in the Arctic.

Isabel feels that now, approaching the age of sixty-five, she is "just getting rolling as an artist." She began to paint as a child in Trail, B.C. But she went off to university and studied psychology, then raised a family, before beginning to paint seriously. In 1963 she attended the famous Emma Lake summer school in Saskatchewan, where she worked with artists Ken Lochead, Art McKay, and Ernie Lindner. Further, at the University of Regina, watching the distinguished Canadian sculptor, Marilyn Levine, destroy ceramic pots that weren't exactly what the artist wanted, Isabel learned how patience and persistence and self-understanding are basic to art.

The Alberta Art Foundation recently purchased two of her paintings, *Summer Storm* and *Coulees in Winter, Old Man River*. Perhaps it was her special knowledge of local landscapes that led to her offering to take us for a drive to the southern border of Alberta.

Ranching is basic to the Alberta economy; it is also basic to Albertans' image of themselves. We drove, Isabel and Rudy and I, down toward the Montana border. Approaching the Milk River Ridge on Highway 62, we came to a sign that read, McIntyre Ranching Co. Ltd., 1894.

The McIntyre family, toward the end of the last century, drove cattle up the Chisholm Trail from Texas to Utah, then from Utah into southern Alberta.

Today the ranch is owned by the Thrall family. Ralph A. Thrall III, the present ranch foreman, is a third-generation rancher. Ralph was a professional golfer for a year. "I got my golfing thing out of the way," he said. "I started cowboying full-time in 1987."

Now he is foreman on the largest deeded ranch in Alberta. Further, the McIntyre ranch contains within its boundaries the largest area of native grasses to be found untouched in North America. Of the ranch's eighty-nine square miles, seventy-nine remain in native grasses.

The herd lives off grass during the winter, thanks in part to the chi-nooks that might in a matter of hours turn the snow cover to running water. The native grasses retain more protein than do cultivated grass-es; as a result they are ideal for winter feeding. Further, the ranch area includes something like forty developed springs and another twenty that aren't developed.

"This ranch," Ralph said, "is a grass operation more than a cattle operation."

The McIntyres had seen the grass destroyed by overgrazing in the U.S. They came into Canada resolved not to let that happen on their ranch. The Thralls have reinforced that concern.

The McIntyre Ranch produces approximately twenty-five hun-dred calves each spring. This includes 150 purebred Horned Herefords and 150 purebred Red Angus. From the purebred stock the ranchers develop the stock that will be the hybrid that is basic to the ranch.

"Our bull power," Ralph said, "is something like 150. We try to maintain a ratio of one bull to twenty cows. Of course some of the bulls aren't doing the job."

The cows on the ranch are naturally serviced, not artificially inseminated. A bull, Ralph explained, like the cows, has to have good sound feet. The cows are grass fed and "they travel a lot out there." The bulls have to do a lot of keeping up.

As any Albertan is likely to tell you, grass-fed beef has a different colour, a different flavour. It's simply the best.

Raising cattle today is in many ways a scientific operation. For instance, the cowhands take the birth weight, the weaning weight, the monthly weight, and the yearling weight of each purebred born on the ranch. They use computers to study the rate of development of each calf into a yearling. Overfeeding produces a variety of problems, including liver problems. A grass-fed calf gains an average of two and a half pounds a day, as compared with a feedlot calf that will gain four pounds a day.

Two cowboys strolled up from the bunkhouse to join us where we talked on the Thralls's front porch. The older of the cowhands tried to exchange his stained cowboy hat for Rudy's black Stetson, but Rudy was not about to do any dickering with a horse-trader. Somewhere in the large ranch house Mrs. Thrall was reminding Ralph that he was wanted on the phone.

Isabel and Rudy and I got permission to drive onto one of the ranch's trails.

No hunting has been allowed on the McIntyre since 1908. Ralph estimates a ranch population of three hundred to five hundred antelope, along with one- to two-thousand deer, including white-tailed and mule.

We drove along a prairie trail, stopping often to marvel. From a cliff top we looked down over limestone hoodoos into a long, green coulee and counted seventeen deer. We climbed a high hill to look out toward the mountain skyline and especially the dominating presence of Chief Mountain. We stopped to watch a herd of bulls that were certainly, that day, "not doing the job." We stopped at a small lake to watch a raft of ducks feeding and to listen to the Canada geese.

The flowers and plants of my Alberta childhood were everywhere around us: lupine, vetch, pasture sage, yarrow, saskatoons, chokecherries. The varieties of native plants, here, number up to four hundred. Hawks and eagles ride the updrafts high above a landscape that is a kind of memory going back to the last Ice Age.

But Isabel was not about to let Alberta rest on its laurels. "Writing-on-Stone Provincial Park. It's even more spectacular than this. Just east of here. The next time you visit we'll go there."

And we certainly will.

*

THE JENNER RODEO

That same afternoon, in Lethbridge, we talked with Isabel's son-in-law, a farmer.

Geordie Peat and his wife Sharon farm two thousand acres near Skiff, Alberta. In the crop year 1991 they had an exceptional crop, an astonishing crop – a wheat crop that went seventy bushels to the acre. And they just about broke even.

The family farm in Alberta is in crisis. "We have diversified all right," Geordie said. "We live in town in the winter so my wife can teach school."

Geordie farms during the summer; during the winter he looks after the children while his wife works. Small towns have two basic problems, he explained; they depend on expensive road systems and they require expensive educational systems. Both systems are hard to come by, in rural Alberta. "The agricultural specialists tell us to get bigger as farmers. But a big new combine costs as much as a quarter million dollars. The technology has become so expensive that no crop can pay for it."

Early in the morning, Rudy and I drove east from Lethbridge through irrigation fields and crops of hay, of sugar beets. Groups of workers moved through row crops, shrouded in a morning mist.

We stopped in the town of Coaldale, where Rudy spent much of his childhood. He showed me the small white house where he lived on a quiet, treed street, a child on the way to speaking for the Mennonite communities that, escaping from the U.S.S.R., came here to work and farm. Nearby, Joy Kogawa was growing into the writerhood that would make her the voice of the Japanese-Canadians who did not seek to come here but were sent, exiled from the Canadian West Coast during World War II.

Coaldale, now, is a bedroom town; it is an adjunct to Lethbridge. And this, too, is a part of the new Alberta; people living in small towns drive to work in the cities, Edmonton, Calgary, Lethbridge, Red Deer. The result, in those towns, is a hybrid lifestyle that is flexible, various, attached to the Alberta past by campers and hockey arenas, yet shaped by the urban worlds that it loves to hate.

We drove east to Taber and there swung north on Highway 36. Alberta, at one time mapped by its rivers, is mapped more recently by highways. Its terrain varies from shortgrass country to boreal forest, from semi-desert landscapes to the high country of the Rocky Mountains. Alberta is a good deal larger than France. Alberta's highways and forestry roads and gravel roads and dirt roads and mountain trails and bush trails and prairie trails seem to excite an incredible variety of machines into motion.

Rudy and I stopped beside the road while two houses went by. We stopped to let the landscape stand still while we looked, listened, inhaled, stretched, and strolled.

The art of peeing in an open prairie landscape is something that must be learned in childhood.

We stopped again, just short of the bridge that crosses the Oldman River south of Vauxhall. I had noticed a great blue heron, feeding in the shallows. We were surprised by a large flock of white pelicans, feeding while they floated down the river, under the high, bare banks. As we watched, a dozen of the pelicans lifted their black-tipped white wings and slowly climbed into the air, then flew, glided, flew in a single column toward an upstream bend in the river.

Just north of the bridge, out on the bald prairie, we in turn did the surprising. We surprised a herd of pronghorn antelope by stopping our car. A dozen of the antelope were lying down; the others were still grazing. When we stopped, those that were lying in the grass stood up, walked a short distance, squatted and humped at once to urinate abundantly, then turned to watch as Rudy and I got out of our car. Cars speeding by did not disturb them; they were uneasy about our curiosity.

The sight of a herd of antelope, turning to run, stopping to watch, turning to run again, showing their white rumps, is one of the great sights offered by the prairies. Perhaps no animal on earth, except for the cheetah, is faster than the pronghorn.

We found gopher holes that had been dug into by badgers. Rudy pointed out a teepee ring on a hillside – a ring of stones that marked a place where Blackfoot or Cree must have watched a herd of antelope, a herd of buffalo.

Perhaps it was those stones that made us decide to look for the place where the Cree leader Big Bear had his first major vision.

Going north, we crossed the Trans-Canada Highway. We found a road that would take us east. We were on our way to the eastern boundary of Alberta. We wanted to look in on Big Bear and on k. d. lang. But then we were distracted, or tempted, again; we read a sign and couldn't resist; we hung a left. We swung off the highway to see if we could find the Jenner Rodeo.

Jenner itself seems to have no more than two families in residence. The rodeo grounds are a few miles north of Jenner. You drop down in the valley of the Red Deer River, just a few miles below the famous badlands of the World Heritage Site, Dinosaur Provincial Park.

The rodeo was about to begin its second day, there on the south bank of the river, on a sagebrush flat. We paid our money and found a place where we could park the car and started walking. Prickly pear cacti concealed in the grass. Greasewood. Cowpies both dry and fresh. The reassuring smell of sweat and horse manure and sage in the early afternoon air.

The bleachers face north towards the rodeo grounds; north of the grounds and across the river are the eroded buttes and coulees of the Red Deer River badlands.

The signs on the judges' booth above the chutes were various and intriguing: Table Rock Roping Club, Top Brass Charolais, Jenner Field Transport, Patricia Hotel.

The cowboy music on the loudspeaker system stopped in midsong. A raspy voice introduced the colour party. Five young women carrying flags rode into the corral. Someone introduced as Sandra sang "O Canada," and somehow, listening to her awkwardness there on that sagebrush flat under those eroded river hills, I understood the song as I had never understood it before. I pretended it was the blinding sun, there that hot, windless day, that brought tears to my eyes.

Then the announcer for the Chinook Rodeo Association introduced the competitors and we were watching the first event, the bull-riding.

The first announcement: "Monte Freimark of Buffalo out of chute number two, on Gizmo."

It was not Monte's best day. He stayed on Gizmo for two seconds.

"Put your hands together, folks. That was a nice try."

We applauded.

They were working five chutes, so the action was fast. Marvin Smith came out on Short Circuit. Six riders in quick succession, the winners mostly the bulls: Sun Tan, Mr. Frost, Lucky Dollar, Top Gun.

And then it was time for calf roping.

The calf. The rider, a length of cord held in his mouth. The lariat, swinging fast over the rider's head. The calf snapped up short, the horse stopping, the lariat taut between the calf and the saddle horn, the roper in his cowboy boots racing, trying to throw and tie the calf.

"Got himself a big calf there, a longhorn cross."

Ed Mandel of Monarch threw up his hands, the job done.

"The calf is on the ground. The horse is still working."

The next calf came into the arena, the rider hard behind him. The thrown lariat.

The calf still running.

"No money today, folks, but your applause is always received."

And we applauded again. I like that kind of generosity.

There are bleachers on the Jenner rodeo grounds, but you can go put your face against the wire fence if you like. No one is going to shoo you away. You can hear the event and smell it too, along with seeing it.

I talked with the rodeo clown, Clint Dolan, a young Aussie.

"I've rodeoed in three countries," he said. "Australia, New Zealand, and Canada." And at twenty-three he has been rodeoing for six years. "There's an Aussie or a Kiwi in every rodeo here these days," he said proudly.

We were seated at a picnic bench in front of the bleachers. He was having a Pepsi and a hamburger during the saddle bronc event.

While we talked, little kids came up to marvel at the clown's makeup and ragged clothing, and to ask for his autograph.

Clint was from north Queensland."We catch wild bulls in Australia," he said. "A lot of people don't believe us but we throw them by the tail. When they come around to charge you, just pull."

I nodded.

"This is my full-time job," he said. "In Australia we rodeo all year – don't have to stop for winter." He paused to remember. "My second weekend in Canada. Man was it cold. Snowed during the rodeo." He shivered a little, there under that hot afternoon sun.

Three children all at once were tugging at his ragged sleeves, but listening too.

"You're not allowed to run a rodeo without a bullfighter," Clint said, acknowledging his audience with a clown's smile. "Most dangerous job there is."

We children were entranced.

"Bullriders only get onto one bull a day. The clown has to be out there to distract the bull after every rider –" The clown was stuck for the right word. "Gets off," he said.

We nodded. We wanted him to tell us more stories.

"At home in Australia, I faced up to 120 bulls a day."

The bulldogging event had begun. Not the bull riding, the bull-dogging.

The announcer was explaining as a bulldogger got up out of the dirt, "He got one of them Charolais crosses."

The next bulldogger came out with his hazer, galloped up beside a running steer and leapt from his saddle, caught the steer by the horns; the two of them fell to the ground, the cowboy trying to turn the steer onto its back.

The announcer's voice: "Now that's what I call bulldogging. That steer did go to the ground, didn't he?"

Again, behind us, there was applause.

The applause seemed to stir Clint to some more primal obligation. He had bulls to distract, lives to save.

I went and stood in line for a long time for a hamburger and a Coke; you could watch the events while you stood in line, so waiting wasn't so bad. And you could taste rodeo in that burger. I wiped my fingers on the legs of my jeans and went to press my face to the wire of the arena fence.

The novice bronc riding event had begun. I chanced to be standing by an old bronc rider, Bob Gilbert.

Bob was in a talking mood. An old friend of his walked across the grass, through the sagebrush, to bring him a bandana advertising the Jenner Rodeo. Bob talked while he knotted the new bandana around his neck.

"I like to get up close. One of these bronc riders – you watch how he spurs, you pretty much know what his score is going to be."

I watched the next rider. I heard the creaking of leather, pounding of hoofs in soft ground, the puffing and farting of the horse, the gasps of the young rider. He was off the horse, showing daylight beneath his new chaps, then plowing into the ground behind the horse's hoofs, one second before the required eight.

"You see?" Bob said.

I was nodding again.

"These kids are right from the ranches," Bob said. "This is where they get their start."

I was watching the young rider as he tried to limp out of the corral and look stoic at the same time.

"They're teaching these young guys," Bob said. "You see what happens, you spur back and then you don't bring your feet forward fast enough. The horse comes down on its front hoofs and you go over its head." He was pointing as two riders herded the riderless bronc out of the arena. "Or you take too short a shank and the horse pulls you over."

"You were on the circuit?" I asked.

Now it was Bob who nodded. "Last time I got bucked off was at the Hay Lakes Rodeo. Smoky Ward from Brooks had rodeo stock. I worked with the stock. My entries were paid." He straightened his new bandana. "I also done a lot of team roping."

Walking toward our car, Rudy and I stopped to talk with a young bronc rider who was sitting in the doorway of his 1972 Chevrolet, his pants down around his cowboy boots, a bag of ice on his swollen right knee.

"You okay?" I said.

The young rider had his pants down but he had not taken off his hat or his spurs. His face was sun-reddened and wet with sweat, but the sweat was from pain, not from the sun.

Two young riders joined us briefly, then turned away to throw saddles and chaps into the trunk of the Chevrolet.

"You guys leaving?" I asked.

"Fernie, B.C., last night," one of the young riders explained. "Calgary before that. Today, Jenner. Tomorrow Buck Lake. We're doing pretty good."

"Sort of like writing a travel piece," I said.

The seated rider lifted the bag of ice and tried to flex his knee.

Somewhere behind us, or over our heads, the announcer was cajoling the audience.

"Put your hands together and make some noise."

✳

FINDING BIG BEAR

We drove off The Buffalo Trail and entered the town of Empress. As we drove onto the empty Main Street, Rudy casually mentioned that when he was researching his novel, *The Temptations of Big Bear*, he stopped one evening in Empress with his wife and children in a van and asked if he could camp on the low hilltop he had noticed while entering town. "Don't stay there," the service station attendant told him, "That's Pecker Point. You'll be bothered there by couples all night."

We drove around town, looking for coffee. We noticed a road that hadn't been in existence when Rudy did his research.

The railway line from Empress, Alberta, to Leader, Saskatchewan, has been abandoned. Someone had turned a section of railway bed into a gravel road.

Rudy knew the old railway bridge crossed over the South Saskatchewan near the place where the young man who was about to become a great Cree leader had his first major vision. Rudy and I decided to see how far we could drive on the old railway bed.

It was a Saturday. The road was not in use. We drove past cacti in yellow flower, past tumbleweed in delicate bloom, past a herd of cattle and fields of hay.

We drove just a little ways into the Province of Saskatchewan before we entered through a gash in a hill and saw before us and below us the wide valley of the South Saskatchewan River, then, off to our left and below us, the wide and closing junction of two rivers, the South Saskatchewan and the Red Deer.

Moving toward each other, the two rivers moved also through sagebrush flats, through great green patches of cottonwood, through open prairie valley that was dotted with cattle.

Directly ahead of us the railway bridge reached in a long, straight and mathematical line toward the far edge of the valley. And there across the valley from us, in a graceful line above the reach of the bridge, was Bull's Forehead Hill.

It was on that hill, sometime in the early 1840s, that a young Cree in his teens, a boy about to initiated in manhood, had the vision that earned him the name, Big Bear.

Rudy and I walked slowly out toward the middle of the bridge. The tracks that were gone from the railway bed had not yet been removed from the bridge. We walked, that sunny, hot day, hearing the cattle below us, the crows below us, and as we walked Rudy was talking both to himself and to me.

To have a vision you had to stand in the sun all day, slowly turning to face the sun, not drinking water unless rain fell on your face; and you prayed for a vision.

You would lie down and sleep at night, there on the spot where you stood; you would rise next morning with the sun, and face the sun all day, and you would sleep again that night, under the stars or rain, and rise again the morning after that, if necessary; and you would go on fasting and praying. And you would learn to wait.

If you were strong, you resisted the spirits that came first and early and easily. You went on waiting. You found the courage to wait. You waited until the greatest spirits agreed to come to your fasting and your praying.

The greatest of the great spirits was the grizzly.

The young Cree who waited there on Bull's Forehead Hill was coming into manhood at a time when the Plains Indian cultures were in their prime; those Indians had reshaped their lives and beliefs around the acquisition of the horse; the horse, new hunting techniques, the enormous prairie buffalo herds, had made the Plains Indians prosperous, powerful, secure.

The greatest spirit on the plains was that of the plains grizzly. It was that spirit that agreed to come to the young man who fasted and waited and prayed on Bull's Forehead Hill.

Along with his name, Big Bear received two outstanding powers: the power of war that would make him a leader as warrior and hunter in his youth; the power to understand the future, a power that would make him a leader of his people in his old age.

Did Big Bear, could he, at the time of that vision, see the future that would reduce the plains tribes to disease and poverty, to a life of deprivation and humiliation? Did he know, there on that hill, no doubt hearing buffalo in the valley below, that in his own lifetime those same herds would be destroyed to the edge of extinction?

Rudy Wiebe, the novelist who recovered for us at least something of the greatness that was Big Bear, standing there in the middle of that abandoned bridge, his black Stetson shading his face, fell silent. Then he pointed down at the scattering of cattle far below us, in the long reach of river valley.

"They almost look like buffalo," he said.

✳

LISTENING FOR K. D. LANG

I wanted to see the country that is home to country singer k. d. lang.

Leaving Empress, Rudy and I came upon a sign that read: M.D. of Acadia 614 people. And the municipality, unrolling to all horizons, looked so deserted we wondered where those 614 people might be. But within a few minutes we encountered the road construction that is as inevitable as a dry wind in the Alberta summer.

We were stopped by a flagperson. Since we happened to be the only car waiting for the pilot car, we were at the front of the line. I noticed that all the operators of heavy equipment working on the stretch of torn-up road ahead of us were women, and I asked the flagperson if there was a reason why.

"Because you no longer need bull strength to operate those machines."

I thought I was being courteous when I suggested she should be an operator.

"I was," she said. "Until I lost my driver's licence for impaired driving."

"You need a driver's licence to operate a packer out there?"

She looked at me disdainfully. "It's a highway, ain't it?"

"Right now it looks like a dust storm."

We were both still while a huge machine rumbled us into silence.

"Don't worry," the flagperson said, watching the dust clear. "I'll get my licence back. Our next job is in Yellowknife. I'll be driving by then."

Rudy was driving. We drove through the humps and hollows of knob and kettle country where ranchers were making hay. We had entered Paintearth county. Then we saw a sign that said, Consort, Population 679. Populations were going up.

Consort is a three-elevator town. When I was a child in Heisler, ours was a five-elevator town, and that in a town with a population of 211. We have ways, on the prairies, of measuring status. I should confess that Heisler, now, is a two-elevator town.

Consort's main street slopes down toward the valley of a creek. Rudy and I asked a young woman running a service station if the creek had a name.

"What creek?" she said.

"That creek down there." I pointed.

"I've never seen any water down there." The young woman returned my credit card. "But I've only been here five years. I'm from Veteran, farther west."

Farther west by twenty-six kilometres.

On the skyline across the valley that might not have a creek or a name, just beyond the end of Consort's main street, the oil pumps outnumber the grain elevators by a long shot.

Consort is a comfortable town with treed streets and, as if by magic, watered lawns. There were campers and vans and half-tons parked in front of tidy wooden houses. The trees were a pleasant surprise, after the open prairies. Manitoba maples. Poplars. Caragana hedges.

The main street is bright and pretty close to empty on a summer day. And there were the usual signs: Consort Dining Lounge Chinese & Western Cuisine, IDA Drug Mart. The usual banks and grocery stores.

k. d. lang's father was a druggist in Consort, her mother a teacher.

Rudy and I went into C. J.'s Cafe for coffee. I asked the waitress if she had known k. d. lang.

The waitress shook her head. "I'm from Coronation." She pointed in the direction of a neighbouring town. She poured me a cup of coffee, letting me stew, before she pointed again and she said, "That woman over there went to school with her."

Cathy Matheson, it turned out, went from grade one through grade nine with Kathy Lang. It was Cathy's coffee break. Rudy and I joined her and her friend and I ordered pie to go with my coffee. Cathy said yes, she would talk about her classmate.

"Did she sing then?" I asked.

"She sang for everything in school. Christmas concerts. Graduations. Some of the school dances."

"Well. . . ." I was trying to frame a question. "What was she like?"

"She was definitely one of a kind."

For some reason, I was stuck for questions. I'm a k. d. lang fan.

"She liked being around lots of people," Cathy said, helping out.

"She was popular, you're saying."

"She was the centre of attention. Most of the time."

"Did that bother people?"

"People liked her. Most of the time."

So I asked, "When didn't they like her?"

It turned out that people liked k.d. lang a lot until she made her famous or infamous remarks about the eating of beef. The eating of cow.

"Her stand about meat went down hard here," Cathy said.

Consort is ranching country. When k.d. lang was a young performer in Consort she played with a rancher's son from out by Sounding Lake. He played banjo and sang with k.d. They played mostly country. He was as shy as she was open.

"She went on cattle drives," Cathy said.

"So she wasn't always singing. Or I suppose you could sing on a cattle drive."

"She liked playing basketball. One time twenty-six of us went to Nova Scotia to play basketball. We had a good time."

"Does she come back here?"

"She comes back often to be with her mother."

"Do you listen to her music?"

"I have some of her tapes."

I was eating the most incredible piece of coconut cream pie I had ever tasted; it was hard to concentrate.

"How do you feel," I said, "listening to her tapes?"

"The sound of her voice makes it sound like she's still here."

"You know," I said, "I heard there's a sign outside town, calling Consort the home of k.d. lang. We didn't see it."

"They took it down," Cathy said.

"Did that have anything to do with her lifestyle?"

I waited.

"Her lifestyle was no surprise. It never bothered anybody."

"Her beef about beef did?"

"After that the sign was always being scribbled over. It cost too much to keep it clean."

"She made her mark," I said.

Cathy had hardly moved, where she sat. She had careful, gentle eyes. "k. d. always said she was going to make something of herself."

I had licked my pie plate clean. "I'm just wondering," I said, "who made this coconut cream pie. It's got to be what I'd call perfect."

Cathy's friend had not said a word until then. "Cathy made it," she said.

"Why didn't you tell me?" I almost cried out.

"That would be bragging, wouldn't it?" the friend said.

Cathy's hands were gently at rest around her empty coffee cup.

"You should try her apple pie," Cathy's friend said. "That's even better."

✳

EPISODES TOWARD A CITY

1

First we got lost. We were looking for Sounding Lake, expecting to find a lake.

And then we found what used to be Sounding Lake. On one side of the road is a long, stony shoreline, a fringe of willows, behind that a fringe of poplars. But there is no water in Sounding Lake. The lake is bone dry. Ranchers have built barbed wire fences out over the old lake bottom.

Across the road from the lake we found what seemed to be a remnant of the vanished lake. But that remnant was so shallow that snipes and other wading birds, landing on the bright sheen, stood motionless. They looked surprised, puzzled, as if, expecting to land in water, they had landed instead on a mirror.

2

The Yellowhead Highway. That name too has its way of luring you on.

Driving the Yellowhead – that too is a kind of getting lost. One gets lost in the ease of the drive.

The Yellowhead is built for speed, for efficiency. You could swoop across Alberta, feeling yourself a bird. The curves on that long, twinned highway are engineered to make you hurry. You don't ask where you are going; going is what you are there to do.

3

Rudy and I stopped at the Ukrainian Cultural Heritage Village. There, fifty kilometres east of Edmonton, you see how Ukrainian immigrants adapted to a new land in the years between 1892 and the Great Depression. Thatch-roofed houses, onion-domed churches, the Alberta Provincial Police post from the town of Andrew, the livery barn from Radway, and many other buildings come alive when their staff members, dressed in the clothing of the time, welcome you not as a visitor but as a citizen of the time. Even the gardens and the fences and the muddy roads are authentic.

Those old buildings and wooden sidewalks and the cows getting out through a gate left open, they slowed us down. We had time for perogies and strawberry ice cream.

4

To drive from the Ukrainian Cultural Heritage Village into the city of Edmonton is to begin to understand the journey that has shaped the lives of many Albertans, not only those of Ukrainian background. They migrate, Albertans. They migrate out to the interior valleys or the coastal towns of British Columbia. Having complained about Toronto, they go there. Like the birds that so abound in Alberta, they migrate south in the winter, looking for a warmer sun. But mostly they migrate from rural areas and smaller towns into Alberta's cities.

There at the invisible portals of the cities, they take on second lives. They are doubled in just that way, Albertans; they are, like those actors in the Ukrainian Cultural Heritage Village, able to inhabit at once two time zones of the mind.

5

Festival is the word, in Festival City:

Edmonton Teen Festival of the Arts
Edmonton International Children's Festival
International Jazz City Festival
International Street Performers Festival
Heritage Festival
Edmonton Folk Music Festival
Local Heroes Film Festival

6

The Fringe. A festival of theatre. North America's biggest and first. They come from around the world, the troupes, the performers. The theatre groups. The mummers. The one-person shows. The singers and musicians. The standup comedians. The jugglers. The magicians. The children's shows and the medieval pageantry and the latest in gadgetry and illusion and the oldest in hoopla noise and bravado. One and all, they show up for the opening parade, bringing their group names with them: Three Dead Trolls in a Baggie. Theatre of the New Heart. Bad Boy Productions. English Suitcase Theatre Co. And for nine full ("BANG! KAPOW!") days the shows go on:

SENSIBLE FOOTWEAR MAKE OUT
THIS SHOW ONLY COSTS FIVE BUCKS
HAMLET DOES HAMLET
ONE MORNING I REALIZED I WAS LICKING THE KITCHEN FLOOR:
    A HUMOROUS LOOK AT DEPRESSION
SEVEN CENTURIES OF GUITAR

Theatre Immersion. Theatre itself as theatre: and the biggest hit of the whole one thousand performances is The Fringe Itself, the crowded streets of Old Strathcona, the instant reviews over cappucci-

no, the greeting of old friends, the finding of new friends, the hulla-
baloo of midnight bars, the eternal quest for a ticket to the best yet
ever show.

A kind of getting lost.

*

THE NEWEST ROAD TO THE OLDEST TOWN

We headed north on a road that didn't exit when last I visited the
Peace River country. If you don't like gas stations and fast food places,
Alberta has the solution. If you like those signs that read, NO SERVICES
ON THIS ROAD or NEXT GAS 160 KILOMETRES, then Alberta offers your
kind of challenge.

We gassed up in Red Earth Creek, 160 kilometres north of the
town of Slave Lake, another 250 kilometres north of Edmonton. We
filled our tank, cleaned our windows, and that was the last time we
were to see a gas station – or a house – for approximately two hundred
kilometres.

Rudy and I were on a new gravel road, Highway 88, the
Bicentennial Highway that runs north from Lesser Slave Lake, through
bush, to Fort Vermilion.

Approaching the Tall Cree Indian Reserve, we saw the first houses we had seen in hours. During that time we had met three trucks but
no cars. We drove almost forlornly through the beautiful Buffalo Head
Hills and into Fort Vermilion.

Fort Vermilion, the oldest white settlement in what is now
Alberta, dates back to 1788. The new gravel road – the shortcut to
Fort Vermilion – got there two hundred years later.

We went directly to the banks of the Peace River. To rest our
eyes. To throw a few stones at the water. To enjoy whatever it is that
North is.

Rudy, within a few minutes, picked up a piece of petrified wood, then found the jaw of an animal skull. I found, as reward for my long search, a rusted hammer that someone had dropped or thrown away.

Alexander Mackenzie might have poked along that same river-bank in 1792 on his way to the Pacific. Except that Mackenzie wasn't much given to poking along. He did however comment on a garden kept at what was then called Boyer's Post.

Charles Boyer of the North West Company recognized the agri-cultural possibilities of this area. Farmers, ever since, have been trying to improve on his garden. The settlement on the north side of the river, known as Buttertown, was for a long time a Métis dairy farming area. Today the local farmers are mostly raising crops, not milk cows.

Twenty-five years earlier I had talked with the people at the sub-station of the Beaverlodge Experimental Farm, there on the outskirts of Fort Vermilion. Rudy and I went to talk with George Clayton, the sci-entist in charge today.

While farmers in southern Alberta are moving off their farms, competition is still strong for homesteads in this area. The provincial government uses a draw system for the granting of homesteads. When new land is made available for farming, in quarter-section units, forty at a time, approximately one hundred farmers put in applications.

Don't rush to homestead. Developing a bush quarter costs some-thing like twenty-five thousand dollars.

These grey wooded soils are proving to be just as productive as the black soils of the Edmonton area. A crop seeded here will ripen in ten fewer days than a crop seeded near Edmonton, this thanks to the day-length in Fort Vermilion. During some parts of the summer a crop in that northern climate grows for twenty-two hours a day.

The average wheat crop in the Fort Vermilion area is thirty bushels per acre. There is very little hay produced here, mostly because the farmers often have jobs in logging or oil and gas, and only a few have schedules that will let them keep livestock. But a community pasture in the area is one of the most productive in Alberta.

George Clayton directs his staff in a long search for sustainable cropping practices. One of those is zero tillage, especially for crops like wheat, barley, oats, and peas. Summer fallowing is an expensive farming technique. But getting farmers to believe that land doesn't have to be left idle and worked over and over has proven to be difficult.

Dr. Clayton has had exceptional success with the introduction of peas as a crop. He took us out into a field to look at experimental plots where he is growing and testing sixty-five varieties of peas, peas in their various adaptations from all over North America and Europe. The plots looked like the dream of a gardener gone exquisitely mad.

"Will these soils last?" I asked. "What will farming do to this area?"

"We can improve the soils here, by the right kind of farming." Dr. Clayton picked up a handful of soil and showed us the rich organic matter. "We can add matter instead of losing it. We can grow crops that add nitrogen."

He was determined that the family farm can survive. And thrive.

*

ZAMA CITY OR BUST OR BOTH

Zama City. That's what it said, there on our map at the end of a road that reached into the north and the west from High Level. The letter zed, the end of the road. We couldn't resist.

There are two hundred people in Zama City, but not one house. There is a brand new school. Zama City is a community based on an oil field that is out in bush and muskeg. The citizens of Zama City live in trailers. No one, so far, has built a house in Zama City. But almost everyone here has a satellite dish.

A busy young man who somehow finds time to stop and talk, Hakan Sahin is responsible for much of what happens in the way of business in Zama City. His garage and service station and general store have become unofficial post office, and unofficial bank; his is the only store in the community.

Hakan, when I met him, was seated in his office playing a game on his computer.

Hakan Sahin's father was from Turkey. Mr. Sahin and his brother were working for a trucking company in Montreal, until one evening in 1976 when they read an ad in a newspaper asking for workers to work in an oil camp in northern Alberta.

The two brothers went to Zama City and very soon started their own trucking company. They went into the business of collecting crude oil from wells out in the bush and hauling it to collection centres. They called their company Zama Transport, but in 1982 they changed the name to ATA.

Hakan jokes about the name now. Some people, he says, believe the three letters stand for Awful Truckers' Association. Others believe it stands for Alberta Turks' Association. In fact it has something to do with the first three letters of Ataturk's name; ATA means grand, or father.

Hakan and I went to the bunkhouse where he and his drivers live. Or rather, we went to the cookhouse; he disappeared into his room and came to the dining hall with three photograph albums.

We looked at pictures of an oil truck stuck in Alberta muskeg; we looked at pictures of handsome men and beautiful women on Turkish beaches.

Hakan's father is in Turkey now. Hakan's uncle has bought a motel in B.C. Hakan came to join his father in Zama City at the age of fifteen; now he has a degree in computer engineering from the University of Alberta. And now he and his brother run ATA.

The demand for oil trucks has declined since the pipeline came into the area. Now Hakan and his brother concentrate on their grocery store and garage. And Hakan's brother, on the day of our visit, was in Turkey, trying to get permission from Canadian Immigration to bring his new bride to Zama City.

Hakan's father, Mr. Sahin, is in Turkey, but he lives on in Zama City as a legend.

We looked at photographs, Hakan and I. His father is famous for having kept trucks operating when the thermometer fell to minus sixty centigrade – back then, when he couldn't afford a new window for the driver's side of his own truck. When a pipe wrench or tire wrench might snap like a stick of wood if used outside in that iron cold. And fixing tires, those days, took just about as much time as hauling oil.

Hakan admitted, apologetically, that the weather in Zama City isn't what it used to be. For six years now, minus thirty-five has been the coldest day of the winter. How can you become a hero in such weather?

"But the mud," he added, defending himself. "The mud in summer is worse than any cold in winter. At least in the cold your truck doesn't sink out of sight. In the muskeg, in summer, you can't decide whether the mud or the mosquitoes will get you first." He paused to consider. "And the sour gas," he went on. "When you empty a tanker, what you have left is sour gas. H_2S. One sniff and you might be paralysed."

The nearest doctor is a long ways off. A nurse comes in to visit Zama City once a week.

A lot of people, Hakan explained, have a love-hate relationship with Zama. And perhaps that includes Hakan. He would like, one day, to make films. For now he runs the family business, and keeps a frontier town buzzing with his investment and his energy.

The oil patch, he said, is a twenty-four-hour business. No holidays. The phone has been on line since 1976. "We don't own an Office Closed sign."

And that was lucky for Rudy and me. We had a flat tire before we were half an hour away from Zama City. We limped back on a small wheel.

Hakan wasn't surprised to see us.

"You see," he said, "the oil company grader throws all the garbage and junk and bits of iron back into the middle of the road. They graded yesterday."

✳

"ASSUMPTION IS NOT AN INDIAN NAME"

Driving south from Zama, on a labyrinthine network of oil company roads, Rudy and I found the entrance to the Assumption Reserve – the reserve of the Dene Tha' (Chateh).

We went to the band offices, in an old wooden building across a muddy road from the Catholic church. We skidded in the mud, driving up a low grade. We ran through the pelting rain, Rudy and I; we left our shoes inside the door and went up the stairs in our stockinged feet, past an array of posters advertising rodeos, writing contests, self-help programs. We were introduced to the band's manager, Steve Didzena.

A handsome, articulate, driven young man, Steve was educated at the University of Calgary. But he was also went to school here on the reservation; he was, for nine years, a student in the Mission school, and even though his family was eight miles away, he wasn't allowed to visit his parents, except on special occasions. In the Mission school, the nuns spoke French among themselves, taught the students in English, and would not allow the students to speak their own language. If you spoke the Athabascan language that is related to the language of the Apache, the Navaho, and the Sarcee, "you got your ear twisted or the shit beat out of you."

To this day, Steve said, he can't talk with his parents. The child-parent bond is gone.

Further, the students had to sing and pray in Latin, without understanding a word of what they were saying. When church regulations changed in 1961, young Steve was surprised to find out what he had been saying for years. And, he said, "to be saved you still have to go see this gentleman in black."

Of the eight hundred people at Assumption, three have jobs in the white world that surrounds them. When the oil rigs moved in around 1965, the Dene people knew nothing about royalties. They were told they were being protected, but in fact they were being pushed aside so that "development" could proceed. Everything was based on a trust relationship, and the Dene realized too late that the forces that were supposed to be looking after their interests could not be trusted. They got almost no benefits from oil. They are in danger now of getting almost no benefits from their timber resources. They applied for a licence to establish a hunting lodge. The government gave the licence to a non-native.

We sat talking in Steve's crowded office, interrupted often by telephone calls or by people popping in at his door. Water dripped into a waste paper can placed strategically behind Steve's chair.

"Confidence," he said. "Determination. Pride. Self-respect. We have to have these to have self-government. The parents, here, are often illiterate. They don't instill drive in their children." He continued. "Alcohol is a devastating drug here. It kills more people than do the diseases. People freeze to death, because of drinking. They drown. They have vehicle accidents. The nearest bars are sixty to seventy miles away, and people drive home drunk." He answered the phone again, spoke briefly, hung up. "A lot of young men," he said, "go to jail because they can't pay fines."

And then he added, abruptly, "Assumption is not an Indian name."

Steve is a registered trapper. He travels regularly to his trapline in B.C., a trip by skidoo that takes him seven and a half hours. "To trap is therapy for me," he said, "a continuing of a tradition." And he joked about eating "uncultured" meat – moose, bear, mallards, canvasbacks, pintails. "In the spring when the coots are nesting we like to go out and gather a few eggs. They're a delicacy, very rich." And then he laughed again. "Eat too many and you get the shits." He talked more about trapping. "What's the difference between a leghold trap and raising cows in a pen and then slaughtering them?"

Steve is married and has four children. The reservation has a day school now.

I asked him where he would like to live, if he wasn't so busy at Assumption.

His face lit up. "Bragg Creek. Down by Calgary. On the Sarcee Reserve. Or Morley. Have you been there? Now that is paradise."

✳

ABOVE IT ALL

"Alberta," Toshiko Ichiyoshi said, "is a perfect place for ballooning. In Tokyo I have to drive two hours before I find enough space for a landing. Here I drive for five minutes."

Precise, thoughtful, the famous balloonist paused for a moment before she spoke again. Toshiko Ichiyoshi, competing in 1991 on the south island of Japan, became International Ladies' Champion. She has competed in the U.S., England, Sweden, France, and Germany, as well as in Japan. She was in Grande Prairie, Alberta, to balloon in the Pacific Rim competitions.

Toshiko Ichiyoshi went on talking in her careful, quiet way. "It is very huge here. And so open. Japan has many mountains, many houses."

She and I and Rudy and the organizer of the competition, Dan Balisky of Grande Prairie, along with a crowd of balloonists, were lingering over breakfast, waiting for an unlikely July fog to lift off the nearby fields.

Rudy asked if ballooning is dangerous.

"Very dangerous," Toshiko said. "Ten years ago I flew over Mount Fuji. The turbulence can be terrible there. Even airplanes have difficulty. I was caught in an updraft. I went up sixty-five hundred metres. I needed oxygen."

She stopped.

"Well?" Rudy said.

"Ballooning is not a physical sport. It is a mental sport."

"How do you mean?" Rudy wanted to know.

Toshiko thought for a while. She said she couldn't find the words. She didn't have the English words. She raised her delicate hands to her face.

"Navigation skills," Dan Balisky said. He has held Albertan and Canadian and North American championships. "Navigation skills. Speed doesn't matter. We like that."

"Why do you balloon?" Rudy asked Toshiko.

She smiled. "To get away from Tokyo. To be alone."

"What do you do when you aren't ballooning?"

"I sell women's clothing. T-shirts. Swim wear. Underwear."

Rudy and I glanced at each other, remembering the heroine of Aritha van Herk's novel, *No Fixed Address;* the woman who sold women's underwear, then at the end of the novel disappeared.

＊

DOWN TO EARTH

Rudy was telling me the one about this farmer, he was driving his team up the big hill from the Peace River bridge, and he had a heavy load on his wagon. He also had rawhide harness on his horses. Rawhide harness stretches when it gets wet. Well sir, sure enough, he was no sooner across the river than he got caught in a sudden thunder shower. And, what with the horses pulling hard, the hill a steep one, the harness began to stretch.

The team was halfway up the hill before the farmer realized his loaded wagon was still sitting down there in the valley.

Alberta weather being what it is, before the farmer could figure out what to do, the sun came out. That northern summer sun. Hot. And that harness began to dry. And as it began to dry it began to shrink. And the loaded wagon began to move.

Anyways, to make a long story short, that farmer had to cut his team loose, or that damned wagon, charging up the hill, would have killed both horses.

Euphemia McNaught, the distinguished Albertan sculptor and landscape artist, was born near Brantford, Ontario, in 1901. As a child she caught scarlet fever from an Indian family working on a farm next to her parents' place. A while later she caught smallpox.

But the young child was nothing if not hardy. When her parents decided to homestead in the Peace River Country, she had the experience, at the age of seven, of going west to homestead.

The family shipped a half-carload of settlers' effects to Edson, Alberta. There they bought enough groceries to last four to six months – rice, sago, beans, tapioca, dried fruit. "Concentrated foods," Euphemia said.

They also bought a team of oxen, Josh and Jerry, and eight Andalusian hens. Carrying a tent in their wagon, and leading three heifers, they struck out on the Edson trail north, a trail that would take them over three hundred miles beyond the railway. "It was a two-week trip either way on that trail. Horses didn't do well in the mud. Their hoofs were like suction cups. Oxen have cloven hoofs."

They arrived in the Beaverlodge country on a day in the latter part of June. Euphemia's father located a post and four holes and said to his family, "If I read this right, we're home."

And he was right.

On an earlier trip of exploration, her father had taken a homestead on a low ridge. He wanted his land to have good drainage and a southwest exposure. He had located land that was partly spruce with not much poplar; there was a small lake on the land, ensuring a water supply; there was enough natural prairie so that he could break sod immediately without having to brush.

Euphemia and her older sister Isabel, born in 1899, still live on that land and still delight in the lake.

They live together in a delightful house on a low hill. Isabel gets on with her journal keeping. Euphemia works at her art each day.

Rudy and I sat in their kitchen for three hours and talked. And listened. And drank tea and ate salmon sandwiches and cake. And talked. And listened.

Euphemia's journey toward being a distinguished Alberta artist was in numerous ways a long one. As a child of five in Ontario she one day impressed her family by drawing a picture of her sister after a bath. "My first drawing was a nude," Euphemia said.

Isabel broke in to add, "The trouble was that in our family we weren't musical and we felt very badly. So we tried a hand at drawing."

And Isabel herself does some drawing as well as writing. But it was her younger sister who had the abiding passion to draw. And there on the Peace River homestead, at the age of nine, Euphemia made a drawing of a chestnut roan that signalled what was to become a lifelong fascination with the figure of the horse. Fortuitously, just at that time, "A man who wanted to get on the right side of one of my sisters bought me a very good box of paints."

That love-struck man, however his strategy might have worked or failed, had helped launch Euphemia McNaught on the road to success.

Not that life was all farming and painting in the Peace River Country. "We just lived for basketball," Euphemia said. And play basketball they did. All the games were out of doors, on bare courts. Each district had its basketball club. "They were quite the social events, those games."

Euphemia went away to Normal School in Calgary. "I was just an average student. My spelling was atrocious. But at Normal School I got just a little bit of recognition in the art department."

Behind her modesty was the fact that she was encouraged to go back to Ontario – this time as an art student. She taught school for two years while living in her parents' home; she saved one thousand dollars and went to Ontario. Four years later, in 1929, she graduated from the Ontario College of Art.

Isabel had gone east to live with her younger sister. Isabel's first job, in 1925, was selling telephones. She lasted one day at that job. Then she got a job painting flowers onto lampshades in an art novelty studio.

In 1929, when Euphemia graduated, the two sisters and another young woman decided to motor back home to Alberta from Toronto.

They pooled their money and bought a Model-T.

Since they didn't know how to get out of Toronto by road, they followed a streetcar that was headed west. "Streetcars went quite a ways those days." At the end of the streetcar line, they were on their own.

They drove to Niagara, the three women. They drove through Michigan – Euphemia remembers stopping to buy a beaded belt on an Indian reserve in Michigan. They were less fortunate in Chicago – they wanted to stop to visit a relative but were out of Chicago by the time they had figured out how to get off the road. They followed the Yellowstone Highway – "we could keep track of it because it was pretty well marked." Since they couldn't afford hotels, they tented "in primitive campgrounds all the way along." They hit a lot of gravel roads and had a lot of flat tires. "You had to take the rim off and patch the tire." Except that one time they were fortunate enough to have a flat in front of a firehall.

The trip took two weeks.

After that there was no stopping the young artist. She had worked with J. E. H. MacDonald in lettering and design and sculpture. Once back home, she "ruined two or three kettles trying to do some casting" and decided that sculpture didn't pay; she would stay home and paint.

And, with the exception of the odd job – Arthur Lismer persuaded her to teach at the Ontario Ladies' College for two years – stay home and paint she did.

And the world, as did Rudy and I, beat a path to her door, in order to admire her Peace River Country landscapes, her drawings and paintings of horses and the people who like horses.

Isabel interrupted our praise. "That's her strong point – horses."

They keep five horses and a pony on their farm, the two sisters. "We just like them," Euphemia said.

And she likes the landscape too.

"It's just as well we enjoy the scenery that we have," Euphemia said.

Isabel looked up from her teacup. "There are trumpeter swans on the lake. Six young ones this year."

"Yes," Euphemia said, "we enjoy the water in the summer, the ice in the winter."

I asked about the skating, on the lake.

Isabel shook her head. "We didn't get any in last year."

They are busy and then some, Isabel and Euphemia. They didn't have time to skate last winter. They did find time for some cross-country skiing.

Rudy and I were rushing away; we had to get to Strawberry Creek, near Edmonton, where Tena Wiebe was preparing to host an international group called Futurists. Besides, in the course of two weeks we had driven five thousand kilometres. Perhaps, like all travellers, we had got to the point where we wanted, simply, to go home.

"Artists," Euphemia said, "never retire. They just work until they starve to death or die."

There at the door of her house she was, in her quick, kindly way, offering us more cake.

✳

POSTSCRIPT: HEISLER (it rhymes with Chrysler), THE PREMIER
    VILLAGE

My hometown, Heisler, is called The Premier Village, not because it is
first among villages, but rather because its streets are named after the
premiers of Alberta. Here is a town with a future. As the Province of
Alberta adds more names to its list of premiers, Heisler will have to add
more streets. This is next-year country with a twist. Imagine having to
cast a vote when the name of the leader of the winning party is about
to become the name of one of your streets.

      And not only is Heisler caught up in provincial politics. When I
attended the Heisler Homecoming in August 1992, that village was in
the riding of the deputy prime minister of Canada, Don Mazankowski.

      The Homecoming began with a large and boisterous parade down
the village's Main Street (the only street not named after a premier).

      Behind two kilted bagpipers followed a Mountie in his regalia
that included a red coat and spurs. Then came four flagbearers, one of
them Heisler's most distinguished soldier, Irwin Kroetsch, who saw
action for six years with the Loyal Edmonton Regiment during World
War II, at Irwin's side his grandson, behind the flagbearers the lieu-
tenant-governor, Gordon Towers, and his wife. And behind the lieu-
tenant-governor's car came Don Mazankowski and his wife, seated in
the rumble seat of a Model-T.

      What followed was an eloquent and beautiful portrait of an
Alberta village. Floats and more floats. The Heisler School that I
attended, our old inkwell desks up there on the flatbed, a student
dressed as a teacher, teaching the alphabet to inattentive students who
were busy throwing candy out to the crowd. The 4-H Club. The Sea
Cadets' band, boys and girls the size of their instruments, from Premier
Getty's base, nearby Stettler. Then a number of antique cars. Then a
float sponsored by Wellers' Hog Herding Services. Then a car sponsored by the Heisler Hotel and Bar. The floats kept coming. The

Troyer Cattle Company. A statue of the Blessed Virgin, representing
St. Martin's Catholic Church, on a flower bedecked platform pulled by
a garden tractor. Then a team of horses pulling an old-fashioned sickle
mower for making hay, then a team pulling a hayrake of the kind I
drove for hours on days in dry slough bottoms, tripping the rake by
foot, making windrows that could be raked into piles that could be
bucked onto a stack. The Heisler Fire Department parading the newest
of its trucks. And from almost every float and car, a veritable hailstorm
of candy.

"A nice day but a bit hot," a lady under a straw hat told me, as
we overcame our reserve and scrambled for the wrapped candies that
hit the pavement around our feet.

More floats and still more floats. A flowering. An abundance.
The whole of the Spring Lake Baseball Team, boisterous and rowdy,
arch rivals to the Heisler Cardinals. The Heisler Hemmers' Club, represented by young girls dressed as old ladies. The Martz Hardware display. The float of Paintearth Mine – a huge strip mine that provides
coal for the local power plant on the Battle River and some of the jobs
that keep the village alive. Clowns on stilts that seemed half the
height of a grain elevator. Beneath them, jugglers. A group of thirteen
saddlehorses, each rider splendid in western garb, each silk shirt shining gold or green. Ponies pulling an old-fashioned buggy of the kind
many of us in the audience drove to school in. Magnificent draft horses, mostly Belgians and Percherons. More antique cars. The car of the
Battle River Tourist Association. And then the Senior Citizens of
Heisler with their prize-winning float, Nora Kroetsch seated on the rear
of the float in an outhouse, the door open, and over the door a sign,
The Parliament Building.

Mazankowski – Maz to his friends – has many admirers in
Heisler. But that admiration is accompanied by a sense of humour.

"How you doin' there, buddy?" Maz said to my cousin Delmond,
the former mayor.

Another cousin of mine, George Weller, leaned close to me and said, "I went to school with Don in Sedgewick. Most of the time he looked around, joked, and sat with his legs crossed and didn't study. I studied the way I was told to study. Look at the difference."

My cousin George, I should add, is a retired electrical contractor.

It took the parade over half an hour to pass by, there that sunny morning on the first day of a two-day celebration. Somehow it was the best parade I have ever seen.

Over a thousand people had returned from far places to a village of two hundred. Another couple of hundred had come in from the surrounding farms and ranches and mines.

We were into a wonderful frenzy of handshaking and hugging. And talking. Talking and talking. Remembering.

"1937? You better believe I remember 1937. It was a pigweed year."

Recognizing. "I haven't seen you since that night we hit the ditch, driving back from that New Year's dance in Galahad. You haven't changed one iota."

Not recognizing. "I wouldn't have guessed in a million years if the Fankhanel girls hadn't told me, 'That fellow with the grey beard, that's Bobby Kroetsch.' "

We had a few beers. We ate lunch at the CWL Booth, set up in the village utility building, hammers and saws and fan belts and snow shovels and jumper cables around us on the walls, more kinds of home-made pies on the tables than a Chinese emperor could have asked for.

We went to the formal opening of the village's new park, named the Irene Parlby Park by His Honour the Lieutenant Governor in memory of the great Alberta politician, Irene Parlby, one of the pioneers in the Alberta feminist movement, one of the genuine reformers in Alberta politics.

We ate a catered beef supper that night, in the community hall;

we ate a huge meal that should have sent us all to our tents and campers and motel rooms to sleep. Instead we went outside the hall to the dance that was getting underway.

You could have, as they say in Heisler, knocked me over with a feather.

It used to be a basic rule in Alberta that you could drink as much as you liked, as long as the government collected its tax, and you didn't have any fun.

There were one thousand people in the street, having one hell of a good time. A band, set up on a flatbed, could be heard four miles outside town. There was a beer garden, set up right there in the street, next to the gyrating dancers. There was a real Mountie, without a red coat, in attendance; he was strolling around, keeping an eye open mind you, but apparently enjoying himself.

Inside the community hall a second band was playing. The kind of band we used to call an orchestra. Piano. Saxophone. Drums. A fiddle. None of that electric guitar stuff. That orchestra was playing two-steps. One of my three sisters told me I had to dance. My daughter Meg and her partner and something like thirty of her cousins, close and distant, were out at the street dance. The hall was jammed, you could hardly find room to get to the dance floor.

Next morning by 9:00 A.M. the women of the community were in that same hall serving a Royal Purple Pancake Breakfast. And the line-up of customers went all the way down the street to the new library.

The old phone exchange opened officially as a library during that Homecoming, there on Main Street in Heisler. I went in, to pay a courtesy call and to offer to send the library some of my books.

I couldn't resist having a peek at the shelves under the letter K – writers are like that.

There were none of my books, so far, on the brand-new, wooden, unpainted shelves of Heisler's first public library.

May Neameyer saw me come out of the library door and maybe

she read my face. Maybe she had already checked the shelves, who knows.

She grew up on a farm near ours and later became the book buyer for Woodward's in Edmonton. We met once in a while, in front of her bookshelves. The Neameyers were a bookish family that somehow got themselves onto a prairie homestead. May saw my face and she, as discreetly as possible, told me why I wasn't on the shelves. She did that by telling me a little story that ended, "And when your first novel came out, Mrs. Fankhanel told my mother, 'Bob comes from a nice family and I don't think he should write books like that.' "

It was a beautiful morning. We were scheduled to play softball, soft pitch, my mother's family, the Wellers, against the Bendfeld family.

I was asked to play right field.

When I was a boy in Heisler, and we chose up sides to play ball, the worst player around was, naturally enough, chosen last. And he or she was expected to play right field.

While I was out there in right field that morning, I had a lot of time to think. The game was measured by time, not by innings – we were to play for one and a half hours.

Our team spent a lot of time in the field and I spent a lot of time thinking.

While I was standing out there in the hot sunshine, smelling the freshly cut grass and listening to the joking and the teasing and the laughter, the shouts of encouragement and the occasional crack of a ball off a bat – I got to thinking back.

I remembered that as a kid I played field fairly often – left field, not right. I had a good eye and I could run; I could get under a fly ball. I wasn't ashamed to use both hands to make the catch. But my peg to home plate was terrible.

Maybe that did it, I thought – maybe that was one of the things that turned me into a writer – my playing far out in the field.   The playing, and the watching that went with it. The listening, out there.

The wanting to enter the game while fearing that someone might hit the ball in my direction. The being isolated, out there in the prairie wind and the summer light; my striking up a conversation with a nearby gopher as I watched the pitched ball. . . . The caring so much, so enduringly, for the movements of small creatures, for the ongoing game, for all the shouting and the laughter that are some of the various names of love.

1. THE SUMMER WORLD: AN INTRODUCTION

Spring is not seen, but heard, in Alberta. Drive off the four-lane highway, off the asphalt and onto a gravel road, and stop at the edge of a slough to listen.

How strange to a visitor in this land-locked province, the gulls crying over a stubble field. Here is no ship's wake; the Franklin's gulls, their proud heads black in the springtime, follow the tractor and tandem disc, picking cutworms and wireworms out of the freshly turned earth.

Listen for the music of a western meadowlark as he sings his territory from a telephone pole. If you are quiet enough, and if the frogs will be quiet with you, from half a mile down the barbed-wire fence, you'll hear a sung reply.

Listen to the harsh impatience of crows nesting in the poplars at the wheatfield's edge. Listen to the trilled hoarse oka-*lee*-a of the red-winged blackbirds, colonizing the willows between the poplars and the cattails at the edge of the slough. Listen to the chuck of paired pintails and teals and mallards as they watch, then tip down to the succulent mud beneath the slough's stilled surface.

The Great Central Plains meet the Rocky Mountains in Alberta, the boreal forest meets the semi-arid southern prairies. Here, in a cross-roads of nature that is larger than France and Switzerland combined, over 320 species of bird life either pause in their migration or stop to nest. Listening, you might hear the song of an oriole, the killdeer's call, the hell-diver's sudden racket, the bugled surprise of whistling swans.

Do not look to the leaves for a sign that winter is over. The birches and balm of Gilead are slow to turn green. The prairie beans wait for the trees. The gardeners' flowers all bloom as if at a given sig-nal – lilacs, tulips, roses, columbines together on a sparkling morning.

But then it is summer.

THE LAND AND THE WEATHER

To celebrate one hundred years of Canadian history, the town of St. Paul built a landing-pad for flying saucers. In Alberta, the uncertainties of the past and the certainties of the future have found a meeting-place. Albertans have little doubt that when the millennium arrives, whatever its form, it will arrive in their province. The only question open to debate is: Will it make itself manifest first in Edmonton or in Calgary?

A certain giddiness characterizes an Albertan, a certain confident heady willingness to top whatever was said before, whether he is mixing politics and religion in one sentence, talking football and oil stocks in one breath, telling of the trout he caught and the moose that turned out to be a horse – or simply remarking on the prospects for next year's crop.

I might add that the word *giddy* derives from *god*; it suggests a frenzy that is divine in origin. Some say this condition is encouraged by the salubrious effect of Pacific air strained through the teeth of the Rockies and mixed with an Arctic cold front; others, less inclined to praise temperature extremes, attribute it to a slight deficiency in the oxygen supply combined with the decreased gravitational pull.

At any rate, Albertans are in an excellent position to look down on the rest of Canada. Not only do they have no sales tax, rat-free slums, and an ombudsman who was formerly a policeman; but, more important, their elevation is such that they live with their heads quite literally in the clouds.

Mount Columbia, on the Banff-Jasper Highway, at 12,294 feet, is the highest point in the province; the slope is both eastward and northward, so that Lake Athabasca in the northeast corner, at 699 feet, is part of the Mackenzie River lowlands.

But all the cities are situated well over two thousand feet above sea level; the densely populated part of Alberta is on the highest of the three steppes making up that region of Canada that is given the misleading title the Prairie Provinces.

This living on a height of land explains the suspicion found among quite a number in the province, especially political leaders, that they are nearer heaven than thou. It also explains a certain tendency to pass off as gospel truth what those from the lower regions might dismiss as tall tales. Albertans bow to no one; the multitudes of their own number who flee over the Continental Divide and down to Vancouver and the Okanagan Valley are so many sheep who deserve the misery of endless rain and a too long summer.

It must be conceded that Alberta has no rain forest, or at least has not had one for the last million years. And palm trees are admittedly scarce. But almost anything else can be found within its borders. Stretching north, as it does, from the 49th parallel for 756 miles, averaging 300 miles in width, the province confronts the fortunate visitor with a multitude of landscapes.

It is the high altitude that has won for Alberta the accolade "Sunny Alberta," for altitude and the consequent clear air make for week after week of crisp star-filled nights, and days so dry (if slightly windy) that every object seems starkly etched on the horizon. Calgary, for instance, averages 2,200 hours of sunshine a year; Edmonton, 1,250 feet lower, averages 2,000 hours. It is this kind of perfect flying weather, incidentally, that helped make Alberta a pioneer in the development of Canadian aviation.

Latitude, surprisingly, is of less importance than elevation in creating Alberta's climate. At best it makes for such long summer days that the Alberta Council for Standard Time, during a recent plebiscite, campaigned with the solemn warning that daylight saving time "will mean putting reluctant youngsters to bed in bright sunlight, or letting them stay up beyond their normal bedtime. What will this do to their marks . . . or their health?"

Needless to add, Alberta's youngsters alone in the nation were saved from the malevolence of daylight saving time.

The third factor in the creation of Alberta's weather is the Rocky Mountains, which cut off the flow of moist Pacific air. Man cannot live by sun alone, and few places in the world are so much at the mercy of a few inches of rain as is Sunny Alberta.

Rain determines the vegetation, the soil, the drainage features. And through these, through the kinds of agricultural activity that result, it determines a good deal about the people.

Summer in Alberta is, for most Albertans, an incredibly close race with the elements, for the growing season is hardly longer than the growing time of the cereal crops that are basic to the agricultural economy. But just the right amount of rain at just the right time means a bumper crop of wheat and oats and barley, good pasture, fat herds of the famous Alberta beef – and prosperity for the whole province. For the world it means a supply of the scarce high-protein wheat that can only be produced in an area of limited rainfall.

Alberta has recently taken to advertising itself as the Oil Province. It boasts that 67.8 percent of its 1.5 million people are urban dwellers (that is, they live in centres of 1,000 people or over). Edmonton rises like Camelot on the far horizon. Calgary has the Rockies as a background. But to most visitors, the province is first a checkerboard of prospering farms. Few of man's accomplishments are impressive when seen from a jetliner at thirty thousand feet, but the immensity and precision of the cultivated Canadian parklands is a view that rivals the natural splendor of mountains and oceans.

Before the First World War, hundreds of thousands of people came west to the idyllic promise of free land and another chance at fulfilment. Coastal dwellers remembered the Old World; to these settlers on the inland prairies, any remembered world was distant indeed. It was the future that became the inspiration and the obsession.

Then, in the 1930s, these same settlers experienced drought and the Great Depression. The Canadian prairies were hit as hard as, or harder than, any region in the world. The drylanders, like the buffalo-hunting Indians before them, had bet on a one-crop economy. In the experience of starvation and suffering and poverty, a whole society found a new common denominator, the ambition to be fulfilled was replaced by the need simply to survive. Out of this recognition, or resignation, came a religious fundamentalism and a political upheaval that were fused in the Alberta election of 1935. The soil and the wind and the absence of rain had made an agricultural society aware of new dimensions of daily despair and ultimate hope: in that fateful year, in that year of decision for contemporary Alberta, it was significantly to the Book of Revelation that political leader William Aberhart turned for deliverance.

Depression was followed by war. Then, in 1947, an unexpected prosperity was grafted onto the Depression mentality. When Imperial No. 1 blew in near Leduc on 13 February 1947, oil became the panacea the leader had prophesied and the people had waited for. From beneath the soil rather than from heaven came black gold.

Today the evolution of the earth's surface has brought back optimism and an aggressive concern for the good life to a people who are reluctant to believe in evolution. But Alberta thrives on its paradoxes. Western hospitality combines with a finely honed sense of how to trim expenses. Openness combines with reserve. And the visible world of Alberta makes manifest this delight in contradictions: the wind carries dust before it brings rain.

A Blood chief flashes along a landscaped highway, rocking his horse in a trailer toward a civic parade. Farm boys in new cars on a Sunday afternoon cruise the dirt roads, leaning from open windows to shoot wheat-fattened gophers. Roughnecks working on frozen muskeg drill down to coral reefs that grew in tropical seas. And perhaps most surprising to the visitor: rivers that are the milky green of glaciers flow eastward across the scorched, bald prairies.

It is these unforgettably beautiful rivers of Alberta, cascading down from the Rockies, that carve the province into its natural regions.

In the south, the Oldman and the Bow flow together to become the South Saskatchewan, and all of them sprout tall cottonwoods in the shortgrass country of Blackfoot memories and cattle and wheat. In the parklands the North Saskatchewan and its tributaries cut deep into a world of poplar groves and derricks and high red elevators and grain-fed beef. In the north the Peace River carries a farming community deep into the boreal forest; the Athabasca lures suburbanites into a world of trappers and fishermen with the Eldorado promise of its sand-locked oil.

It is these cool rivers on a dry steppe that give uniqueness and form to a province that seems, according to a map, to have been shaped chiefly by pen and ruler. And the people's uniqueness is further quarried from other extremes. The hard sun and the promise of rain above, the mysteries of Devonian shoals below: these have locked a people between dream and nightmare. Two views of existence contend here: for some, life is controlled by an apocalyptic vision with the end and judgment always nigh; for others, especially for those who build cities and plan conservation and create schools, Alberta is no longer a promise but a fact. Theirs is the historical view; and for them, man must make his own and continuing destiny.

The land and the weather, then, the blizzards and the drought and the green forests and the yellow fields, have urged upon a people a sense of the immensity of what is and what might be. To the timid among them, this very immensity is the source of alarm and caution. To the brave, it brings a new and exciting sense of possibility and freedom.

The young did not know the Depression. And now in this beautiful, rich, sad, and comic province a creative energy is contending with doubt. Especially in Edmonton and Calgary, one has the sense of a new and vital and sophisticated society about to seize the day. Now and finally in Alberta, the future has a sufficient past out of which it can grow and flourish.

THE PEOPLE AND THE MELTED POT

Alberta became a province in 1905. The population in 1901 was 73,000; in 1911 it was 375,000. The ranchers and businessmen and policemen and coal miners and lumbermen and, above all else, the homesteaders had transformed the buffalo country into a prospering province that awaited only the discovery of the oil beneath its surface to make it wealthy. The future was their abiding goal; but in the names they gave to their towns, and rivers, and mountains, they recognized the past.

Names like Peace River, Red Deer, Manyberries, Pipestone, Smoky River, and Seven Persons are translations from the Cree and Blackfoot tongues. A number of names have been kept without translation. Okotoks is Blackfoot for "lots of stones"; Ponoka translates as "elk." Wabamun is Cree for "mirror"; Pembina, a lovely name, means "cranberry." Athabasca is also Cree, meaning "where there are reeds"— a reference to the muddy river delta. Finding an English spelling of that word has not been easy. Peter Pond, on his map of 1790, tried "Araubaska"; another attempt comes out as "Athepescow."

Further, the white settlers often used names that reminded them of distant homes. Edmonton had its namesake in England, though the English city has now been swallowed up by London. Tomahawk's first citizens came from Tomahawk, Wisconsin. Lord Strathcona named Banff after a town near his birth-place in Scotland. Colonel Macleod of the N.W.M.P. named Calgary after his cousins' ancestral estate on a Scottish island, a place he'd visited shortly before coming west. The Blackfoot name for Calgary was *mokk-inistsis-in-aka-apewis*, or, if you prefer the Cree, *o-toos-kwa-nik*, meaning Elbow House.

Many towns were named after the people who helped create them. Cardston is named after Charles Ora Card, the son-in-law of Brigham Young, who led a group of Mormon families from Utah to

Alberta. Lloydminster is named after the Reverend George Lloyd who helped found a British colony on what turned out to be the Alberta-Saskatchewan border. Trochu was founded by Colonel Trochu, a man who came to Alberta to farm when he and a number of cavalry officers left the French army because of religious troubles. Most of them returned to France when the First World War broke out, and many were killed in action.

And then there are unique names. Yellowhead was named after a fur-trader, François Decoigne, who was nicknamed Tête-Jaune, or Yellowhead, because of the colour of his hair. Taber, situated in a Mormon area, is the first part of the word "tabernacle." Early voyageurs mistook the pine trees of the Cypress Hills for cypress. Bruderheim translates from the German as "brethren's home." It was named by twenty Moravian families who came from Russia in 1893-94 to take up homesteads. Whitemud was the source of white mud used by traders as whitewash. The Kicking Horse Pass was named when Dr. Hector, the geologist with Captain Palliser, was kicked by a horse. The citizens of Camrose, stuck for a name, simply opened the British Postal Guide and liked the sound of Camrose, Pembrokeshire, Wales.

As might be guessed, not all names proved to be satisfactory. The residents of Waterhole had occasion to move their town a short distance and, in the process, changed the name to Fairview. A ranching centre with the earthy name of Pisscow seems to have been stricken from all records. The burghers of Soda Lake, in 1907, felt a surge of dissatisfaction with their permanent address and changed it to Hairy Hill.

Alberta itself was so named by the marquis of Lorne when he was governor general of Canada. He named the future province as an honour to his wife, H.R.H. Princess Louise Caroline Alberta, the fourth daughter of Queen Victoria. Appropriately, the present governor general of Canada is Roland Michener, born in Alberta in a town that was named in honour of Father Lacombe. The name Michener has already been given to a housing park at the University of Alberta.

Today's urban dwellers lived, only yesterday, in or near one of Alberta's 260 small towns and villages. Summer here means the flowering of sale bills across the land. In restaurant windows, in bus depots, on power-line poles, on the fences of weathered stripping that hide vacant lots on main streets, on wires strung from wall to wall across the middle of general stores – the cheap blue or yellow bills announce that more farmers are "making sale." The smudged black print gives the road to the farm: one and a quarter miles north Rocky Rapids, or four north, one east and one and a half north of Drayton Valley. The auctioneer announces that:

> Having received instructions from John Eklund who is giving up farm-ing, I will sell by public auction the following items listed: John Deere Model 65 combine, Massey ten foot cultivator, Pollard two-wheel rake, one-bottom breaking plow, Surge milking machine, eleven head three-year Angus cows and nine calves at foot, seven Holstein heifer calves, one stock saddle and blanket, approximately 1,500 bus. Parkland barley, Winchester 12-gauge hammer pump shotgun, two chests drawers, chesterfield and chair like new. . . .

Small farmers, no matter how hard they work, no matter how good the soil, cannot survive the economics of modern farming.

In Alberta in 1941, there was an all-time high of 93,200 farms. Since then the number of farm families has decreased by some twenty-four thousand. Each year the farms become bigger and more valuable. Now the average farm is 607 acres. In the Hanna district, where much of the topsoil blew away in the thirties, the average farm is over twenty-seven hundred acres. Where once a homesteader needed a breaking plough, a team of horses or oxen, and ten dollars with which to file his claim to 160 acres, a would-be farmer now must be a one-man corporation. The cost of land, livestock, and machinery is such that at best one son in a farm family can expect to become a farmer; the others must move off the land.

They go, with the young from the shrinking towns, into the cities, taking with them memories of the little community centres in which they were deeply rooted. It is not only the natural world, then, that has shaped Albertans.

These small towns were established in the time of horse travel; they are, as a result, ten to fifteen miles apart. Driving across the prairie, you see first a row of three to eight grain elevators along the railway track. As your car bumps off the highway and over the track, you see two church steeples: one is Roman Catholic, the other is United Church, or Presbyterian, or Anglican, or Lutheran. There is somewhere in town a third church: Church of the Nazarene, Kingdom Hall of the Jehovah's Witnesses, Pentecostal Assembly, or The Gospel Tabernacle. The evangelist rejects the substantial architecture that for him symbolizes the failure of the older churches, whose priests and ministers, he feels, are overly educated and have lost sight of harsh prairie reality, the literal meaning of the Bible, and the imminent end of the world. In some towns, especially in the central and northern parts of the province, there is a fourth church, characterized by five domes, the centre dome surprisingly large on the small, square stuccoed building, the bell set off from the church in a square tower of its own. If some of the church is painted blue, it is probably of the Greek Orthodox Church; if not blue, it is of the Greek rite of the Catholic Church.

Then you swing onto main street. At the corner stands a fairly old hotel; each of these towns has at least one – the Queen's, the Commercial, the Rex. The owner in order to sell beer in his beer parlour must have rooms for rent; both drinks and rooms are a bargain. But if you are hungry, go across the street to the general store for a box of crackers and a ring of bologna.

It is one of the ironies of Alberta that the people, being so much a part of an agricultural world, eat in their homes or at community get-togethers a delicious and abundant variety of meats, vegetables, and desserts yet go into a restaurant and eat a meal which a starving man should pronounce inedible. Instead of saying grace over your soup you tilt the ketchup bottle and hit its bottom with the palm of your hand. You conclude by drinking a cup of what is probably coffee while scraping the canned filling off the bottom crust of a piece of pie.

If you want to see a small town or small city at its best, try to take in an annual event such as a sports day, or a local rodeo, or a district fair. The Jay Walkers' Jamboree in the small city of Camrose is a fine place to begin.

On that day all traffic is barred from the main street and dozens of booths cater to visitors. The Church of God ladies serve delicious homemade pies. The Loyal Order of Moose raffles off a pig. CFCW, "Your Rodeo Radio Station," plays country music from a trailer all day, insisting loudly that "Country Music is Canada." Five self-conscious, long-haired local boys in the back of a pick-up truck turn up their electric guitars and sing of their unhappy love, while four Hutterite girls in long skirts and headscarves watch quietly, each of them now and then touching her face to a cone of candy floss. The Woman's Christian Temperance Union wages its ceaseless war from a booth outside the town's most popular beer parlour. Children line up to ride a Ferris wheel, or a merry-go-round, or a string of ponies that walk all day in a circle while the owner sells tickets from the window of his truck. The newest pieces of farm machinery, fiercely green and yellow and red, look like something out of science fiction. Men and women in Klondike outfits stroll from store to store, their arms full of bags and packages.

But if you get to a small town when there is no public celebration in progress, I recommend two beers in the local beer parlour. It is customary that you order two glasses per person, on the sane theory that you can't fly on one wing so why make the waiter walk across the floor twice? Thus, for thirty cents per person, you become members of the community; and the prairie beer parlour is as much *the* community centre as is any pub in Christendom. Here the real news is passed along – the news about those absent, that is – business deals are once again very nearly transacted, friendships are made and daily renewed, the weather is forecast (A: "She's going to rain within the week." B: "She's going to be drier than the summer of '32."), yields per acre are compared and elaborated upon, makes of farm machinery are put to the rigid test of long debate, bad winters and other calamities are rejoiced in, shopping-lists are mislaid, local lakes are stocked with huge perch and jacks, past hangovers become heroic feats of endurance, white-tails and mule deer and mallards and grouse tumble before the unerring aim, tons of gravel and wheat are hauled, politicians are exposed as a bunch of thieves and idlers, the genuinely great men of this nation are rescued from oblivion, world affairs are set straight by the wave of a hand – and stories are told by the hour. And here, believe me, is bred a kind of democracy that insists vehemently that all men are equal, even if a good liar does get more than his share of red-eye – that sustaining combination of food and drink that is made simply by pouring a little tomato juice into your third glass of beer.

In the past fifteen years, forty of the forty-eight counties and municipal districts in Alberta have shown a decrease in population. Projected figures indicate that such counties as Wheatland, Ponoka, Forty Mile, Paintearth, Smoky Lake, and Vermilion River will go on losing population for the next fifteen years. One consequence is that some small towns must simply become ghost towns. But another and principal consequence of this large and continuing movement of people is the breaking down of family and ethnic ties. The young man who goes to the city gets a job on the basis of his particular qualifications, he marries a girl on on the basis of proximity, not memory, he buys a house on the basis of his income, not because it is near his parents.

These small towns and farming communities were frequently established as ethnic communities, for the early settlers more often than not came in groups. Even today, a look into any local graveyard will quickly give you some insight into a community's national origins.

The province today is forty-five percent Anglo-Saxon in origin. By a nice twist of fate, the Scotch and the Irish, after centuries of heroically resisting the Angles and the Saxons, are now lumped with them statistically. These same statistics show that in the 1961 census the remaining people of Alberta gave their national origins as follows: German 183,314, Ukrainian 105,923, Scandinavian 95,879, French 83,319, Dutch 55,530, Polish 40,539, Indian and Eskimo 28,554, Russian 17,952, Hungarian 15,293, Italian 15,025, Jewish 4,353.

Politicians tend to wax sentimental over the fact that the United States is a melting pot while Canada preserves its national groups. I have lived in Iowa, New York, and North Carolina; I would insist that Alberta is as much a melting pot as any one of those states might be. And for a number of reasons, the Alberta melting pot has pretty much melted.

First, the major flow of immigrants was cut off by the commencement of the First World War. Granted, quite a number of the Netherlanders, the Italians, and the Hungarians arrived in Alberta after the Second World War. But the great majority, the migrating generation, arrived before 1914; and since then as many as three generations have been born in Alberta.

Second, Alberta is a province in which fifty-five percent of the people are under twenty-five years of age. These young people were born not so much into ethnic communities as into prosperity, travel, and TV. For them ethnic means a certain kind of folk song.

Third, the statistics offered by the census-takers fail to indicate that a large percentage of the immigrants came not directly from the Old World, but from a pioneer experience in Ontario, the American Midwest, or the Maritimes. These three regions, in the above order, provided a predominant number of the social and political and cultural leaders in the new province.

The process of losing ethnic backgrounds is pretty much over in

Alberta; the process of recovering those backgrounds has begun. Young Albertans have become so remarkably alike that at least there is some consolation in knowing your grandfather was different. A regular forest of family trees is sprouting across the province. Old-timers are kept so busy remembering the pioneering experience and talking into tape recorders that being retired is harder than working. Recipes for ethnic dishes are bootlegged into family histories from old cookbooks. Elderly women run the risk of having their shawls and brooches snatched off them and carted away to the new local museum. Camera crews turn up regularly at funerals.

This is not to deny the complexities and genuine pleasures of ethnic ties, nor am I suggesting that prejudice does not exist in Alberta. The *Edmonton Journal*, responding to Prime Minister Pearson's appeal for bicultural awareness, ran on its front page the headline: MORE PARLEY-VOO. The Government of Alberta, in hiring, insists on knowing a person's national origins. In public schools a child can arouse the ire of some of his teachers by insisting that he is "Canadian." Priests and ministers are often assigned to rural churches on the basis of their names rather than their qualifications. A government official told me he knows that in certain industries a considerable bias exists against either hiring or promoting persons of eastern and southern European origin. And I might add that the most anti-French human being I ever met was a drunk editor of the University of Alberta's newspaper, the *Gateway*.

Yet the fact remains that at best most of us are "ethnic" only once or twice a year. If you have a German ancestor up your family tree, or if you're just plain hungry, show up in Heisler on the last Sunday of October for a feed of sausage, sauerkraut, mashed potatoes and gravy, creamed corn, apple sauce, dill pickles, salads, homemade buns, and lemon or raisin or apple pie. The farmers who make the sausage work from a recipe that has been handed from father to son since back in the 1830s when the first immigrant fattened his first hog in the Western Ontario bush. If you like beer, get there Saturday night. If you prefer celebrations that last longer, get yourself invited to a Ukrainian wedding.

Marrying and burying customs tend to endure, yet marriage is possibly the greatest leveller in Alberta. In checking at random a daily newspaper, I found seven forthcoming marriages announced. In four of those seven marriages, one but not both of the individuals had a Ukrainian name. (Opinions differ, but in my own opinion a wedding is still superior to a funeral for a family get-together.)

The shortage of skilled labour also helps to break down Canada's notorious "vertical mosaic." The assistant personnel manager of an Edmonton factory told me she has in the past few years hired people of fifty-two national origins. I asked if national origins made a difference in whether a man got a job. The only concern, she insisted, was whether he was a skilled or unskilled worker. Canada in general has neglected to train its own citizens in required skills. Her company not only was hiring skilled workers, but would help them enter Canada from any part of the world.

Geography and history have done a remarkable job of creating in western Canada a unique subculture. I remember meeting an elderly couple in a London bed-and-breakfast place on Gower Street. Both had been born and had spent their lives in Alberta, yet both had grown up calling themselves not Canadian but English. They were on their first visit "home." And "home" was proving so incredibly alien to them that they were cutting their visit short to get back to the foothills west of Calgary.

Unlike Ontario, there was in Alberta no charter group that might absorb or alienate the newcomer. In a few short years all the settlers arrived in a virgin and unpeopled land. (Riel's magnificent dream of a Métis nation died at the end of a rope in 1885.) The English and Irish settlers who went out onto the prairies had to undergo a more difficult process of adjustment than the few settlers from Quebec or the many from Ontario. The families from the Ukraine had a more difficult time of it than the German- or Scandinavian-Americans from Minnesota and the Dakotas, who had already undergone the change of language and become acquainted with the climate and the methods of farming. But all were coming into a vacuum created by the destruction of the buffalo and those who depended upon them, and each newcomer, instead of feeling he was being assimilated, felt instead that he was helping to create what Alberta was to become.

People alive today remember clearly the creation of Alberta not as history but as experience. Mrs. George Campbell has not appeared in the history books; she has the kind of uniqueness that makes us say of people that they are typical. She is eighty years old now; when I last visited her she was out by the caragana hedge behind her ranch house, picking up an armful of wood for her kitchen stove. "It looks like rain," she said, for a strong wind was blowing from the west across the valley of the Battle River. Within an hour, incidentally, rain lashed at the windows. We sat in comfort at her kitchen table, each nursing a mug of coffee, looking at an album of snapshots of her own and her sons' favourite horses.

Mrs. Campbell confessed to me that she hadn't ridden in a long time. "How long?" I asked. "Three years," she lamented, her bright blue eyes alert and mischievous. She pointed to another snapshot. "In that race my horse headed for a fence and I had to choke him down. I went back on the track and beat the other twenty-two horses."

In pioneer days the horsemanship and beauty of Mrs. Campbell were famous from Duhamel to Alliance, from Sedgewick to Hastings Coulee. A horse race was a part of every picnic, field day, or sports day in that time when people still owned and took pride in horses. Mrs. Campbell was the only woman jockey in the local area and, win or lose, men competed after a race for the privilege of caring for her horse, for she was as attractive as she was petite, spirited, and proud. The other ladies were aghast, however, because she rode astride. When the race was over the dancing began, and Mrs. Campbell's popularity was as great at a dance as it was on a racetrack.

She was born Edna Viola Walter in Livingston, Montana. In 1897 her father, John H. Walter, took his family through the mountains and an Indian reservation to settle in Kalispell, Montana. On that wagon trip they were stopped at least half a dozen times by young Flathead hunters on horseback. Each time her father politely asked how far it was to Kalispell. Each time he got a different answer. But the wagon was allowed to proceed, and John Walter's little daughter remembered vividly the fleet saddlehorses and the scanty clothing of the Flatheads.

In 1901, when his daughter was fourteen, John Walter again pulled up stakes, this time to join the thousands of Americans from the Midwest who were rushing to homestead in western Canada. A flood had taken out the railway bridge near Lethbridge, and the train ("the narrow-gauge") had to detour through Medicine Hat. When the Walters finally got to Wetaskiwin they bought horses and a wagon and drove the seventy-five miles to a homestead.

Their first tent was torn to shreds by a hailstorm. Then her father put up a room of poles – they didn't deserve to be called logs – and these were "chinked and mudded." Mrs. Campbell reminded me that logs were used to build cabins, sawn lumber was used to build shacks. Two stoves back to back and sharing one stove-pipe heated most cabins in the winter; theirs was so small they had to set a heater on top of the stove. A bedroom was made by pulling a curtain across one end of the room on a wire. Again, in larger families it was necessary to build a platform just higher than people's heads across one end of the room; in the evening six or seven children climbed up a ladder and slept snug and cozy all in a row on the planks.

During that first winter the "Spring Lake Germans" were arriving – thirty-eight young men from Minnesota who had sold their farms and come into Canada to homestead. These men preceded their families.

Heather Brae was the last hotel on the sleigh trip; they arrived at the Walter homestead having driven forty-five miles leading their cattle, and were thawed out in the warmth and hospitality of the Walter cabin. One morning after a blizzard Mr. Walter went outside to chase a cow away from in front of his little barn, only to discover that the cow, leaning against the door, was frozen stiff.

When spring came and the land thawed, the Walters added a sod house to their cabin. Even today many farmers have to work around those old sod heaps in the middle of a field, but they were warm, dry, and windproof for many years.

Homesteaders like the Walters had been preceded by ranchers. Among the ranchers who were losing open range to the farmers were George and Victor Campbell, two brothers who had emigrated from Ontario to the Dakotas, then to Alberta. George tempered the loss of pasture by proposing marriage to the farmer's lovely daughter.

The young couple had no house; George had not built the usual shack, an outbuilding which was supposed to become, a few years later, a shed or blacksmith shop. Rather, he moved his bride into a log cabin belonging to Gabriel Dumont's nephew, Pascal. George had earlier met Gabriel, the buffalo hunter and brilliant lieutenant of Louis Riel. By this time, 1905, Pascal Dumont's career as a young buffalo hunter had ended, and the Métis were retreating from this prime buffalo country to reservations – or homesteads of their own.

Pascal Dumont's cabin was located on a spring-fed slough just one mile north of what was later to become my father's homestead. In my youth it was a forbidden place where ducks and slough-pumpers (bitterns) throve, where cattle watered, and where children might drown. Today a gravel road borders one side, a wheatfield the other. But for a bride of eighteen in 1905 the site meant a log home with a dirt roof full of spiders and a floor of sawn logs that was full of garter snakes. Here Mrs. Campbell gave birth to her two oldest sons, who today as bachelors live with her in her tall ranch house.

The young Mrs. Campbell attempted to paper the wall around her baby's crib, only to find, one day, a snake crawling out between two sheets of paper. One morning she reached up to fix a curtain and discovered a snake hanging from the curtain rod. Another time her husband called her out of the house to help with a sick cow; she returned to her sleeping baby to see the heads of curious snakes literally growing everywhere out of cracks in the old floor. To cap it all, one evening her husband had to use a shotgun to kill a stoat in a corner of the principal room of their dwelling.

But the pleasures outweighed the tribulations. Summer was full of picnics and races, especially around the beginning of July. The settlers from Ontario celebrated 1 July ; the settlers from America still celebrated 4 July. In the winter there was time for the long sleigh rides to neighbours' houses, and time for card parties followed by long nights of dancing. "We went to dances – that's what shortened me," Mrs. Campbell said, her face glowing in its frame of pure white hair. "Someone always had a fiddle. The women brought sandwiches and cakes. We ran out of prairie chickens, but in the fall you could get up to twenty-three ducks with one shot."

In the winter, also, when the snow was right, they chased coyotes on horseback with hounds. Mrs. Campbell remembers a neighbour who trained his hounds by locking them and a coyote in one room of his two-room shack. "He was a bachelor," Mrs. Campbell added.

She had begun to ride at the age of five, getting on a horse by climbing up the corner post of a barbed-wire fence. An English lord was their neighbour in Montana, and when he rode by to get his mail, not condescending to speak to any of "us commoners," little Edna Walter loved to mount her own pony and, as she put it, "get a little attention."

Her husband became a horse rancher, maintaining a herd of 150 head. One of the Dumont boys was a hand on the Campbell ranch for years. Homesteaders needed horses badly. The cayuses – wild range horses – driven up by ranchers from Montana were crossed with registered stallions and produced a tough, strong breed that was in demand across the prairies. The First World War created a new market for horses. But when George Campbell died in 1941, the market was beginning to decline; a few years later the last of the herd was allowed to go wild. Lloyd, one of the sons, keeps old Beetlebaum, a descendant of those tough horses, but now the Campbell boys raise cattle and wheat.

Mrs. Campbell feels she is getting too old for the saddle; parked in front of her gate is a Model-A with snow chains on the hind wheels. The law has taken away her right to drive on the roads. But the R.C.M.P. – once great horsemen themselves – don't stop her from driving on her own land, and on a sunny afternoon she and an old friend climb into the Model-A and go for a spin, bouncing along the Battle River, on sod that has never known a plough. They bump through dried-up creeks and the red-shale coulees, they stop to open a gate in a barbed-wire fence – for her neighbours such as the Dietrichs and the Mavises and the Strausses and the Bruces are also Ontario folk who settled finally along this river, where the land was too wild for the sodbusters. She and her friend may stop to pick enough saskatoons for a fresh pie or to examine a stone that was once an Indian's hammer for killing buffalo. They may drive past the shaft and rusted iron rails of a deserted coal mine, or find a new and oddly beautiful rock for her rock collection. They talk for hours, remembering in astonishing detail the births and marriages and deaths of the many families that came into this lovely harsh country after Pascal Dumont was forced to leave. They sit in silence, fiercely loving the muddy little river and its raw, eroded clay banks, the stands of poplar and spruce in a ravine, the rich grass waving in the wind. Every fence and field and building already has its story. The Bruce boy from just down the road became bronc-riding champion of the world. Out in Hastings' pasture is a circle of rocks where a teepee stood. A gang of rustlers from across the river used that Indian trail. One of the Dietrich brothers has a garden full of arrowheads.

The Campbell house itself once belonged to Archie Morrison, who was carrying a gun on his breaking-plough and accidently shot himself, then smeared a horse red with his own blood as he tried vainly to mount it.

As Mrs. Campbell swings the old Model-A toward her house and its barns and corrals, as she deftly dodges a badger hole, I suspect that, finally, she and her friend talk of open range and horses – and of races lost and won.

Many of the people who entered Alberta at the turn of the century were to become founders of large families, and Alberta today is characterized by such large family groups that a particular community is often associated with two or three family names. One of these is the Shandro district, which began with the migration of two Ukrainian-speaking brothers from the foothills of the Carpathian Mountains in Austria to Alberta, as a result of Sir Clifford Sifton's immigration plan.

Stefan and Nikon Shandro and their families arrived in South Edmonton on Victoria Day, 1899; indeed, "Victoria" was the only English word they were able to make out in the celebration that went on about them. Together they bought a wagon and horses from an Indian and drove out along the south bank of the North Saskatchewan, stopping periodically to turn over a spadeful of earth, looking for black loam such as they had known in the Old Country.

Within a year the two brothers were joined on their homesteads by a nephew, Wasyl, and Sidori, another of their four remaining brothers.

A homestead could be registered for ten dollars, but before the homesteader had clear title he had to bring so many acres under cultivation and own so many head of livestock. To do this, many of the men in the new settlement had to go out working until their farms began to produce, and some of them walked as far as the Lethbridge collieries. One of Stefan's sons, Andrew, got a job at four dollars a month on a farm near Fort Saskatchewan, where he quickly learned English.

Andrew Shandro, in 1909, became postmaster, and the new district was named after him. He lived near the river and in that same year acquired a ferry for the Saskatchewan crossing that joined the new community to the old Red River oxcart trail from Fort Garry, Manitoba, to St. Albert, Alberta. More than once he had walked the hundred miles to Edmonton, picked up provisions for himself and others, built a raft, and floated the provisions down river to the crossing; he later became instrumental in establishing a river-boat service that ran from Edmonton to Shandro Landing.

In 1913, at the age of twenty-seven, he was elected to the provincial legislature, the first Canadian of Central European origin to be elected to a government office in Canada. In 1917 he joined the army and rose to the rank of lieutenant. In spite of all these activities, Andrew Shandro managed to become a prosperous farmer, specializing in livestock and especially Percheron horses.

In the thirties his son Thomas became a teacher, earning the sum of $950 a year. Thomas had a successful career as a basketball player, later became a newspaper reporter on the Edmonton *Bulletin*, and then a cofounder of two radio stations, founder and manager of Shandro Agencies Limited (general insurance), and an elder of the Grace United Church in Edmonton. It was Thomas who remembered the tales told by Nikon and who began to record the family history, tracing the name back to Shand, the surname of three Irish brothers who went up the Danube in the eighteenth century to build a flour mill. Shandros had been Shandroffs and Shandrovs – sons of Shand.

He discovered that the original four Shandros who immigrated to Canada had had a total of forty-eight children. Stefan, who married twice, himself had had twenty. At one time the community of Shandro had a baseball team of fourteen players made up entirely of Shandro boys. In 1931 a basketball team made up of five Shandros won the rural championship of Alberta. While there were, in 1967, only nine

Shandro families in the district of Shandro, Thomas conceived the notion of holding a family reunion as a centennial project.

On 21 May 1967, sixty-eight years after the original two brothers arrived in South Edmonton, 356 of approximately 550 surviving descendants from across Canada gathered in Shandro, Alberta, to meet each other, to gossip about the 149 families in the family tree, to eat *nachenka* (a corn dish) and *studenets* (a headcheese), to see the million-dollar Shandro bridge that has replaced Andrew Shandro's ferry, and to hear letters of greeting from, among others, Prime Minister Pearson.

The touring crowd, guided by the R.C.M.P., visited the Greek Orthodox Church, the site of which had been selected by Stefan's wife, Anastasia, when she cut two willows and made a cross. They acted out the erection of a lean-to on the site of the first homestead and remembered that, while waiting for the first *bworday* (sod house) to be built, Anna, wife of Nikon, gave birth to John, the first Shandro to be Canadian-born. They found that John's son is now a lawyer, that in the Shandro family there are twelve teachers, a medical doctor, a number of doctoral candidates, and many successful businessmen.

While the fifth generation blew out sixty-eight candles and waited for the huge birthday cake to be cut with a *toporatz* – a combination hatchet and cane – C.B.C. television crews toiled diligently, newspaper reporters took notes, historians took pictures, radio commentators spoke into microphones, and visiting politicians spoke over loud speakers.

As a culmination to the celebration, everyone went together to the Shandro Historical Village and Pioneer Museum to marvel at the quaint costumes, handicrafts, utensils, and machinery of their ancestors, one of whom, Mrs. Wasyl Shandro, only survivor of the first generation, was present to marvel in turn at her Canadian descendants.

But a people – the Campbells or the Shandros – define themselves often through their heroes. In Alberta, the heroes are usually men who have begun slowly to take on the dimensions of legend – men like Peter Pond, David Thompson, Poundmaker, Crowfoot, Father Lacombe, Rev. George McDougall, Kootenai Brown, John Ware, or Twelve-Foot Davis. Yet a man very much of this century seems most to have embodied the fears and aspirations of the people of this province.

William Aberhart is still a name about which few Albertans can be objective. I can only hope that my own ambiguity of response is illuminating. The man deserves a major biography; fortunately we have at least a chapter in John A. Irving's brilliant but neglected study *The Social Credit Movement in Alberta*.

Aberhart was a big man, heavily built and tall, with exceptional energy, a jovial manner, an immensely powerful and pleasing voice, expressive large hands, and a large head that to women was handsome, to men suggestive of intelligence. He was a deeply religious man with an almost compulsive will to dominate. Like many another visitor to the Alberta Legislative Building, I have paused long before his portrait.

Aberhart was born in Ontario; as a farm boy he was more responsive to evangelical revival meetings than to the Egmondville Presbyterian Church to which his parents took him. At the age of thirty-one he interrupted a successful career as a schoolteacher to move west, arriving in Calgary at Easter in 1910. He was quickly made principal of an important high school. But, more relevant to his destiny, in 1918 a group of sincere young men formed the Calgary Prophetic Bible Conference, and here Aberhart began to lecture on biblical prophecy and the second coming of Christ. He was gaining recognition. In 1925 he began to broadcast his talks over a Calgary radio station, CFCN, "The Voice of the Prairies." Money and letters of praise began to flow in. (Irving reports that ultimately 350,000 people were listening for the magnificent and assuring voice each Sunday afternoon.) To propound his Christian fundamentalism he also established a magazine, *Prophetic Voice*, and he started a Bible Institute course (of which the first graduate, another farm boy, this time from Saskatchewan, was Ernest Charles

Manning). In 1931 he wrote and produced a drama, *The Branding Irons of Anti-Christ.*

Much of Alberta is Bible Belt, as many an eastern-trained minister has learned to his despair. In Alberta the central theological issue is quite simply this: Does wine in the Bible mean wine or grape juice? This schism produces a province about equally divided between those who feel it's a sin to drink alcoholic beverages and those who feel it's a sin not to. Auxiliary questions multiply: Is it a sin to see a movie on Sunday? Is it a sin to see a movie at all? Is playing bridge worse than playing whist? Will you go to hell for bowling on the Sabbath? Is not the Sabbath Saturday?

In our Pythagorean longing for permanence we nowadays turn to statistics: the 1961 census shows that 31.5 percent of Albertans called themselves members of the United Church, 22.4 Roman Catholic, 11.7 Anglican, 9.2 Lutheran, 4.2 Presbyterian, and 3.6 Greek Orthodox. But in fact, many of the people who tell a census-taker they are members of an established church will, that night, attend a revival meeting. And during an election year, a political meeting, with its rhetoric and emotions and its neat categories of good and evil, can serve as a substitute.

Aberhart apparently had no interest in politics until the Great Depression began to have disastrous effects in Alberta. In 1932 one of his favourite students, in response to the hopeless economic conditions, committed suicide. Aberhart shortly thereafter began to read the Social Credit doctrines of Major C.H. Douglas.

By the time campaigning for the 1935 election began, Aberhart was a candidate for the premiership, leading his Social Credit candidates against the incumbent U.F.A. in a campaign that involved the entire population of Alberta in a combination political battle and religious crusade.

To weeping, praying, and applauding audiences, Bible Bill was suddenly an economic wizard, a martyr, a voice of prophecy crying in the wilderness, a lone brave man standing up against the eastern financiers, a saviour who promised redemption from the incredible woes of the Depression. I can do no better than quote from Professor Irving's book, for he interviewed many of the people who experienced conversion to the teachings and promise of the charismatic voice that was broadcast across the distressed province.

He quotes a lower-middle-class housewife in Calgary:

> The secret of Mr. Aberhart's appeal to us was his whole-heartedness and sincerity for religion. He loved us common people because of his religion. We felt he was a born leader, with something great to do in the world. It seemed to us as if God had picked Mr. Aberhart and then prepared an audience for him in Alberta first as a religious leader and then as leader of the Social Credit movement. The life of Mr. Aberhart in Alberta was a fulfilment of a Divine Plan.

A farmer in southern Alberta:

> Many times I have seen Mr. Aberhart walk into a crowded meeting. He would be detained at the back of the hall by people who wished to get near him. His progress would be impeded right up the aisle. Each one wanted to get the best view of him that could be obtained. The applause would be deafening. It was impressive to see that big man with the mischievous grin on his face climbing up on the platform. We felt he was the law – he was the only man who could give us a decent hope in the future – who could free us from the money barons of Eastern Canada. Who wouldn't gather around a man like that? Who wouldn't love him?

Finally, a farmer in the Edmonton area:

> One night I went to a Social Credit meeting in a town near us where Mr. Aberhart was speaking. A U.F.A. man began to throw questions at him and made a disturbance. I got real mad at this U.F.A. man for doing that, and I couldn't hold myself in. So I jumped up and led the meeting in prayer. I said, 'Let us pray for Mr. Aberhart. Let us pray for his soul.' As we prayed aloud, the U.F.A. man got frightened and shut up. There

we were, all down on our knees praying for Mr. Aberhart. We were a bunch of hard-working slaves – over-worked, over-tired, eyelids half closed from exhaustion and misery, children lying all about, under and over the benches. When we finished praying, tears were rolling down practically everybody's cheeks. Later on, I was surprised myself that I had led that meeting in prayer for Mr. Aberhart.

There were, of course, those who couldn't love him. I was eight years old in that frenzied summer; I can recall, as if it happened yesterday, not Aberhart's words, but his voice. My father, a die-hard Liberal, was under constant attack, for the Liberals were associated (perhaps rightly so) with the bankers and the financial "barons." Further, Aberhart seemed to promise every adult in the province a monthly cheque for twenty-five dollars (the original guaranteed basic income?), and my father would not be persuaded to that expectation.

Aberhart won the election hands down. To his followers it was not so much the work of voters as an act of God. Then, by a nice trick of history, the federal courts opposed and restricted his moves to restore the economy to some sort of vitality. Aberhart was again martyred, for attempting to use government intervention to manipulate economic responses – a theory that today is taken for granted. Even the university in his own province refused him an honorary degree.

But Aberhart, true redeemer that he was, even to himself, had singled out a chosen disciple; when the old master died in 1943, brilliant, articulate young Ernest Charles Manning took over – and almost overnight moved the party from the tradition of prairie radicalism to a reactionary position that reached its culmination in the right-wing shenanigans of Quebec's Réal Caouette. Social Credit became the agent of the forces it had opposed; but the shrewdness and mystic spell of Bible Bill had made Alberta safe for Social Crediters for many elections to come. For in his size and energy, in his hyperbolic humour, in his delight in talk and argument, in his longing for, and suspicion of, respectability, in his Christian humility and his will to excel and domi-

nate, in his distrust of the Ontario from which he came, in his antici-
pation of damnation for the wicked and rewards (both spiritual and
material) for the good – he was the embodiment of a people's dreams
and nightmares.

The province has had some fascinating premiers: men like A.C.
Rutherford, Arthur Sifton, and John Brownlee. But Aberhart was Mr.
Alberta.

2. START AT THE TOP: THE ROCKY MOUNTAINS

Mountains are the beginning and the end of all natural scenery.

– John Ruskin, *Modern Painters*

BANFF-JASPER: THE GLACIER ROUTE

Banff National Park became the foundation of Canada's national park system in 1885, when ten square miles were set aside to protect the medical hot springs that bubbled from Sulphur Mountain. The name of Holt City was changed to Laggan, then to Lake Louise Junction, and in 1892 that area was added to the park. Automobiles were kept out until 1916, to avoid disturbing the birds and animals in their natural habitat. Today the park comprises 2,564 square miles, and in the month of July as many as 137,000 automobiles enter through the east gate alone, carrying nearly 475,000 people. That's enough cars and people to turn Tunnel Mountain campground into a smog-ridden slum – and they do a bang-up job of it.

Most Canadians believe the crisis for our natural landscape is still somewhere in the future. Secure in this illusion, encouraged in it by well-meaning visitors who assure us the situation is worse in the States, we neglect to make parks of places like the Swan Hills in Alberta, or the Nahanni Valley in the Northwest Territories, or of any part of the Pacific coast. Canada can list a fairly substantial area of natural parks, but much of that area is in the huge and neglected Wood Buffalo Park, a park that is, according to rumour, to be traded in part to the Alberta government because it contains deposits of gypsum. The personal gain of a few wins out, and foresight fails us. Conservation is a concept slow to develop, and too often the frontier is gone, the wilderness is gone, before the plans are made. When I was a boy in Alberta our municipality killed off coyotes by placing poisoned horse meat in open areas such as frozen sloughs, not caring what other animals or birds ate the poison. We spent many Sunday afternoons shooting hawks and owls for imagined wrongs; we robbed eagles' nests. I remember also going east to southern Ontario for the first time, hoping to see the land where my great-grandfather had operated his water mill. No one had bothered to save a dozen square miles of that fabled and virgin forest.

On my favourite visit to Banff, my wife Jane and I travelled with John and Sheila Clendenning, a couple from southern California. As students together in graduate school we had, years earlier, promised ourselves a vacation together in the Rockies. Now we bought tents, sleeping bags, air mattresses, air pumps, coolers, Coleman stoves, candles, tin dishes, flashlights, gas lamps, axes, plastic buckets, coils of nylon line, fishing gear, hunting knives, canvas water-bags, dried foods – and having effected this economy, we set off to camp.

Since the Clendennings were coming from the west and we from the east, we met in Banff at 10:00 A.M. on a summer day at a place

where a stone bridge crosses the Bow River. It was a delightful beginning: we dashed off to Lake Minnewanka to fish for an hour, and
Sheila, perched on a rocky cliff, brought up two fighting trout from the
blue-green depths while a herd of Dall sheep watched her. We fished
on through a sudden rain squall, then went to the Cave and Basin to
laze around in the hot mineral waters. We strolled through the lush
Cascade Gardens behind the Park Administration Building, the carefully tended streams and rocks and flowers a subtle contrast to the
naked immensity of Cascade Mountain, looming over all from the far
end of the main street. We went to have a cocktail in the baronial
extravagance of the Banff Springs Hotel.

This hotel, reminiscent of a feudal castle stuffed with loot from
all over Europe, combines local stone from Mount Rundle with Gothic
design and Elizabethan echoes, with Jacobean and Georgian suites,
with Flemish cupboards and Queen Anne wing chairs, with Italian
Renaissance prints and Spanish ironwork. The flowers in the conserva-
tory lend a tropical fragrance to the tang of spruce and pine that comes
in off the mountains. Outside, the Bow River Falls are loud and cold
below the swimming pool and its warm mineral waters. The designer of
this hotel, by a small stroke of genius, brought all these elements into a
soothing harmony that has become world renowned.

There have been changes in Banff in recent seasons. John and
Sheila and Jane and I, finishing dinner, went to a small-town dance in
the Cascade Dance Hall. Now that hall is Josephine Tussaud's
Canadian Wax Museum. The process of becoming self-conscious has
gone too far when dance halls are turned into museums. But it has produced the excellent little park museum, with its informative displays of
the park's wildlife and minerals. And Luxton Museum, created as a
tribute to the Plains Indians, is in itself worth a visit to Banff: to see a
full-life model of the Stoney Chicken-Dance or a Swampy Cree dog-
team in its full regalia, to learn of Poundmaker, the chief who defeated
a Canadian army at Cutknife Hill, or to experience a little of the mystery of the Blackfoot Sun Dance.

But we dancers went home tired from our foxtrots and jitterbugging only to face the task of pumping up air mattresses in Tunnel Mountain campground. The children around us had now gone to bed; their elders sat gossiping by camp fires, listening to radios and trying to get something on their portable TVs.

Next morning we ate Sheila's two trout, then had breakfast in a downtown restaurant. We rode up Mount Norquay in the cable cars to see the view and to consult with the chipmunks. The town itself, even apart from its setting, is surely one of the prettiest in Canada, with its colourful stone, its ample use of attractive wood and logs, and its alpine architecture. Seen from seven thousand feet, dwarfed by Mount Rundle and the Sundance Range, it becomes a teasing pattern in the forested Bow Valley. The view and the friendly chipmunks confirmed a suspicion: we'd have to choose carefully from an abundance of possibilities. Already we felt short of time.

Sheila and Jane resolved to begin by spending a few hours in Banff's multitude of tempting shops. John and I countered with a plan for a ten-mile boat trip on the Bow River, followed by an invigorating hike, with a park naturalist as guide and instructor, up to the timberline and Bourgeau Lake, or at least to the glacial cirque.

Our wives offered to compromise by going for a horseback ride, for they'd read of several excellent trails. Now a stranger, a man who for some reason carried four cameras, told us quite bluntly that we'd missed the best thing of all: the Banff Indian Days. He'd got a few hundred feet of film of himself doing the Chicken-Dance with a Stoney squaw. We could at least go see the buffalo paddock, our wives concluded.

And we did.

It was the sight of a herd of buffalo that summoned John and me back to our true purpose. We'd gone broke to become campers; we were bound and determined to camp.

Shortly after lunch we rolled up our sleeping bags and took down our tents; we started out on a leisurely two-week camping trip to Jasper, 178 miles away through the heart of the glacier country. And we had made a wonderful choice.

Technically, the thirty-six miles from Banff to Lake Louise Junction are part of the Trans-Canada Highway; the Icefield Highway branches north there for Jasper. We camped first at Lake Louise, not in the immense and beautiful new campground, each site complete with a tent platform and a fireplace and surrounded by pine forest, but rather in the present picnic grounds near the château, for those grounds were then open to campers. As we climbed the long hill, the first sign we saw was PARADISE; and while it turned out to be Paradise Bungalows, we weren't disappointed. We canoed on Lake Louise, that haunting green lake set between a wall of glaciers at one end and a riot of poppies before a resort hotel at the other. The days became a confusion of joys. We fished in Consolation Valley, and found the place well named; we took our packed lunches and climbed a mountain to eat on the slopes of the Tower of Babel. We drank tea in English-looking tearooms set high in the wilderness. Wanting to learn more about the mountain world, we went at night to the Inglenook Cafeteria to eat fresh fruit and watch movies of the childhood of bears, of the metamorphosis of the dragonfly. In the morning we were up early, to hear the stillness of the mountains, to see Victoria Glacier reflected in the lake, the lawns and the poppies wearing their dew, the tiny red-breasted nuthatch flitting in the lower branches of the tall spruce. In front of the château is a reflecting globe, and one morning we watched a tourist walking around and around it, trying to photograph not the lake and the mountains themselves, but their reflections as they appeared in the globe.

John and I stroked our new beards and marvelled at human folly.

That night we walked into the château, simply because Sheila wanted to send a postcard to her Papa Joe. We adjourned to something called the Glacier Room to relax while she wrote, and in our relaxation we all began to smoke cigars over our ale, the two ladies drawing three looks of admiration to one of disapproval. Going upstairs to mail the postcard, we found a dance in progress. We joined the dancers, we sat and watched, we danced again; and then, in the exuberance born of mountain air, Sheila and I danced out of the blue ballroom with its fearfully sweet old music, out past gentle old ladies at oak writing-desks, out into the hallway of wonderfully overstuffed chairs, and past a grand piano; on we danced, along green carpets past room clerks and bell captains and photographic supplies, past the potted plants and arched windows that looked out onto the flag, and the lake, and the glacier that glowed in the moonlit night.

And we might have danced right up the red-carpeted staircase to the pinnacles of that unlikely French château perched there on a Canadian alpine lake, or into the swimming pool, had not a manager, in a patient Scotch accent, invited us to desist.

Our tents that night were touched with autumn frost. John, a California professor who grew up in West Virginia (pronounced "*West goddam Virginia*"), had never quite seen an August like that one, and he announced his disbelief with a loud rhetorical flourish to the hushed universe.

In the cold morning we raced from our sleeping bags to the big old roaring stoves in the campground shelter. An elderly gentleman busy frying bacon and eggs told us that some damned fools were making speeches in the camp last night. We drank the coffee he was generous enough to offer, and were silent enough to make up for our midnight.

My wife, that morning, patiently tucked me back into a sleeping bag; she went alone on a wonderful trail ride up to the Plain of the Six Glaciers. She brought me back a chunk of what she insisted was glacial ice, supposed to be excellent for an aching head and sore throat, and John used it to mix four martinis.

We started north again, and had the good fortune to run into rain. Our consciences eased, we left our tents dry and safe in our cars and drove into Jimmy Simpson's Num-Ti-Jah Lodge, just north of the Crowfoot Glacier, where Bow Lake gathers the melting waters from Bow Glacier to become the source of one of the most beautiful rivers in the Rocky Mountains.

We were assigned to the Bear's Den, a log cabin set in a tall forest, and while the rain poured and pounded we loafed in front of a fireplace, we read the books we were beginning to think we'd brought along in vain; we slept all afternoon, under thick, red woollen blankets, and then played whist by the fire at night, still listening to the rain.

Most of the glaciers face northward, and as a result, the drive south toward Banff is even more spectacular than that toward Jasper. But Peyto Lake and its source arrest all passers-by. As we stood on the lip of rock looking north into the Mistaya Valley with its range of mountains on either side, as we looked at the glacier that paints the lake a blue-green that is so nearly unique I cannot make a comparison, snow began to fall. At first it seemed only a momentary whim on the part of nature; as we started out on a short nature-trail it became an August mountain snowstorm, the flakes huge and wet, thickening the air, weighing the evergreens white.

We camped that night at Lower Waterfowl Lake. The campsites are well laid out in a dense forest on the edge of a lake, where the Mistaya (Indian for grizzly bear) enters from Upper Waterfowl Lake. Here Eskild Callesen is the benevolent ruler of a small empire of campers. Eddie arrives here himself on 15 June; one year Bow Lake was still frozen when he drove by to get to his domain. He closes this camp on 15 September; in 1966 he had to dig his way through four feet of snow to get to the highway. In between those dates, he holds court in a one-room shack that is his kitchen, bedroom, and office.

Eddie, at home and contented in these mountains, was born in Denmark. His father, like so many of another generation, came to Canada to work as a butcher for Burns in Calgary. Eddie took to the hills. He is proud of his job, and critical of the university students who come up here to work: this is a twenty-four-hour-a-day job, and they're always running off to parties.

Bears come wandering into camp during the spring and summer, before the berries are ripe on the mountains. One day a two-year-old tore up four tents, then came back the next day and opened a cooler containing six steaks, bacon, six bottles of whisky, and a bottle of wine. The bear ate a steak, then tore the top off the bottle of wine and drank it down while photographers came running from all corners of the camp. One of Eddie's jobs is to capture such animals in a barrel-like trap and haul them as much as fifty miles back into the mountains. He marks the offending bear's ear with a red ribbon; if that bear returns, which can happen, the ranger comes by and shoots it.

Eddie shows his visitors where to go to see a moose or a wolverine. He cautions them by telling of the man who wanted a picture of his little daughter feeding a coyote; the coyote accidentally split the girl's arm. And he gives advice to forlorn fishermen. "It goes by the moon, you know," Eddie can tell his visitors in four languages (and in one season they came from a dozen countries). "Won't bite just before or right after a full moon."

The spring before our visit, he and the ranger had used pack horses and two saddlehorses to stock Cirque Lake and Lake Chephren. The ranger had, he added, been kicked by a horse and was still recovering.

Next morning we four campers loaded ourselves with lunch and fishing equipment, and we made the delightful climb to the lakes. Cirque Lake is a little mountain tarn, a glacier-carved cirque that has filled with water. We fished for awhile between the logs that had jammed in the outlet of Chephren, working harder at keeping ourselves from falling into the water than at getting the fish out.

Very soon, Jane and Sheila were content to eat the best parts of the lunch and marvel at the scene, for Mount Chephren, at 10,710 feet, is exceptional even in this region of majesty, both for its classic beehive contours and for its reputation as a weather-breeder. John and I were beginning to despair as we descended fishless, and Chephren behind us was gathering a few wisps of cloud.

Next morning we fished the outlet of Upper Waterfowl Lake, standing in the swift cold water until we shivered from head to foot, then lying in the grass and sunshine, watching a young moose practise his swimming lessons out in the lake. His head rode comically above the water, but he crossed the lake with ease, and shook himself out of the water to watch brazenly our own comic antics.

The rain began in early afternoon; it proved to be so light that Jane and I drove to the outlet of Lower Waterfowl Lake to go for a walk along the river. As we started out, I noticed the fish jumping in the lake's outlet. Instead of walking we drove back to our tents for John and Sheila and our fishing gear.

For one hour we experienced what fishermen dream of. Rainbow and eastern brook and cut-throat trout hit our lines as if to drag us under, and in our excitement, as we waded over rocks in a swift current that was up to our knees, then up to our waists as we plunged on, they very nearly succeeded. Only Jane balked, when she found herself confronted with the task of taking her first rainbow off the hook. John and I were telling fish stories before the fishing was half done.

That night in camp, people came from California, from Minnesota and Manitoba and Iowa to peek into our frying pan. Well, at least they had licence plates from those far-away places. We were not unduly modest as we sat down to eat. And yet our immodesty hardly did justice to that mess of fresh trout.

Two days later, our early success not having been, to say the least, surpassed, we drove on north.

The one-mile hike up to Parker Ridge Viewpoint is an exciting introduction to the Columbia Icefields. We struck out, and on the way up the carefully maintained path we met a geologist. Or rather, we saw him just off the trail in a bed of fossils in the hillside, hammering and gesticulating and talking to himself. A young instructor from the University of Illinois, he was seeing his textbooks translated into geological evidence before his eyes; the geological history of Alberta and the world was written in the face of a mountain; the discoveries that a few feet of hillside offered were so great that we had to spend an hour listening to his delight.

And his delight was contagious. We climbed past fossils and snow to an alpine meadow blue with mountain forget-me-nots. Ahead of us the dazzling glare of the Saskatchewan Glacier met our shaded eyes. I hardly realized at the time that I was becoming addicted to high country – that special alpine world above the treeline.

Returning to our cars we drove on up over Sunwapta Summit (6,675 feet), the height of land between the waters flowing to Hudson Bay and those flowing to the Arctic. We had entered Jasper National Park and were about to camp within sight of Athabasca Glacier.

The Columbia Icefields, covering 150 square miles, went undiscovered until two English alpinists, J. Norman Collie and Hugh Stutfield, hit upon them in 1898. "A new world," Collie wrote, "was spread at our feet; to the westward stretched a vast icefield probably never seen before by human eye, and surrounded by entirely unknown, unnamed, and unclimbed peaks."

Three principal glaciers, the Columbia, the Saskatchewan, and the Athabasca, flow out and down from the central accumulation, or névé, situated above eighty-five hundred feet on the Continental Divide. Today a tourist can drive his car to the edge of Athabasca Glacier; he can ride up onto the ice itself in a snowmobile, getting some sense of the arctic desolation and the strange appeal of the white fields that flow for miles, like winter prairies, away from the Snow Dome, which is the point in the Rockies where three watersheds meet.

But the snowmobile, with its close-up of crevasses and seracs and mill holes, is only one approach. The Clendennings and Jane and I had a picnic on the glacier's toe. The Sunwapta River flows out of a small lake at the foot of Athabasca Glacier. Streams poured into the lake from holes in a towering wall of blue-green ice that dwarfed us almost out of sight; streams tumbled from beneath the ice, from its topmost edge. The glacier, now, is melting back faster than it is flowing forward. At its base are fields of waste rock that give some tiny notion of what our continent must have looked like as the last Ice Age retreated, as the first plants and animals pushed forward with the blind insistence of life.

We picnicked on a flat rock that had kept the sun from melting the ice beneath it – a perfect table. We spread our cheese and bread and cold meats upon it, cooled our last bottle of wine in water flowing across the ice. We put on our heavy sweaters. Not three yards away from our table, a crevasse big enough to swallow us all in one bite breathed out its cold breath. As hungry as we were, as chilly as the sunny air was, John insisted on proposing a toast: "To the miserable lying Los Angeles salesman who told me a six-dollar sleeping bag would keep me warm on a Rocky Mountain mountain."

We had yet to discover our favourite approach to the glacier. The campground is set on rocks in a stand of tall evergreens; its border is a stream that tumbles down Wilcox Pass. It was evening when we pitched our tents and built a fire; warmed by coffee and conversation, we hit on the idea of climbing up a short distance into the pass in the morning, for one last look at the glacier below.

We struck out at dawn, carrying only cameras and a thermos of water. We'd return in one hour and have breakfast, we agreed. One ridge led to another. We were quickly above the treeline; then we were on a point of rock with the glacier visible below us.

We had resolved to go no farther when three magnificent bighorn sheep came sauntering out of a rocky hollow. John and I opened our cameras. Instead of fleeing, the sheep posed. Then they climbed to another outcrop or ledge, to another pose, and we followed to photograph again. We were high enough now to come to a patch of ice; we followed the sheep across it. Tantalus, I believe, had less trouble resisting a temptation. Jane reminded us of our anticipated breakfast: oatmeal and raisins, eggs and toast and tea.

All three of the sheep were young rams. Now an old ram showed up, with a ewe; the ram's horns were immensely thick and curled in a complete circle. We had to take one more photograph, and to do so we had to cross another ridge.

When hunger finally won out, we were up in high country. We sat down to rest and talk by a stream in a rock crevice, on moss that was richly green, and so soft that to step on it was like walking on marshmallows.

First a rosy finch ventured near us. Then, a few minutes later, a golden eagle soared over and dropped suddenly toward its prey. But it was a distant roar that stirred us away from our stream; we leaped to a rock ridge in time to see snow smoking up from the Dome Glacier. This is the reconstituted glacier to the north of Athabasca; snow tumbles from the icefield above and refreezes together: we had heard the roar of the ice and snow falling.

Now we went to take the pictures we'd come for. From a high cliff we looked down on Athabasca Glacier, a tongue of ice flowing for six miles, up to one thousand feet in depth. It comes away from the main body of ice in a three-step ice-fall. Below its farthest reach, the marginal and terminal moraines show that once it covered the site of the present Information Bureau. To the left towers Mount Athabasca, its three peaks hung with smaller blue-green glaciers that wrinkle downward; the peak nearest the road is capped in dazzling white snow. Around the icefield rise at least sixteen peaks that are over eleven thousand feet, their walls of rock and ice all bare above the treeline.

Thirty feet of snow fall each year on the ice; and this icefield may well date back a million years to the beginning of the Quaternary period. We took pictures, John and I, braced against the wind on the cliff's edge. It was twelve noon. We started the long descent toward breakfast.

The Banff-Jasper road, for anyone who finds delight in driving an automobile, has little to rival it in all the rest of Alberta. My favourite stretches are the two descents from the Columbia Icefields. Going south, I like the beautifully engineered, outflung curve that drops down from the Parker Ridge Trail to the Weeping Wall. The swoop of road is exhilarating, a soaring-hawk experience, and in the evening the eastern cliffs, catching the sun, are yellow and Egyptian, turning rapidly to orange and back again to brown; the mountains in the west are shaded blue then purple, supremely alpine with their fields of protected snow. Anyone who remembers the difficult drive over the old road will especially enjoy this drive.

Going north from the icefields, the road is equally exciting, but quite different; after a winding descent it swings onto a river flat and drives straight out to Grizzly Creek. The Sunwapta River falls away from the foot of Athabasca Glacier into a deep gorge, earning the Indian name which means "turbulent water"; the road snakes down a shoulder of Wilcox Peak onto the braided river below Stutfield Glacier; then, while the river wanders through sand and gravel, the road leaps out straight and flat, surrounded by stark snow-capped mountains, leading down to a long valley of lakes and waterfalls and forests.

The Endless Chain Ridge directs the road toward Sunwapta Falls; after a short visit we drove on, the Clendennings and Jane and I, Mount Kerkeslin before us now, dominating the view, its bands of red strata conspicuous in the afternoon sun. We stopped again at the Athabasca Falls, stood in its columns of spray to see the rainbow in the narrow gorge, its rock-worn pot-holes and water-worn arches. But night too was falling, and we hurried on north to pitch our tents and build our fires in Wapiti Campground, just south of Jasper town. Sheila wanted to try a new recipe for flapjacks.

From here we drove back one day to Mount Edith Cavell and Angel Glacier. We were having tea in the chalet when a group of Australians came in off a touring bus. We listened to a discussion, not of glacial till or dog-tooth mountains, but of the relative virtues of Melbourne versus Sydney; a discussion, I take it, that had been going on for some weeks. After a while I found myself favouring Sydney. A lady, a Melbourne supporter, took her son and her binoculars outside for a few minutes. As they came back in, she said to the boy, "Now you can say you saw one."

Tea-time over, we ventured across the terminal moraine in front of the chalet and walked down into the great heaps of boulders and blocks that lie like rock chips before the monolithic grandeur of the mountain itself. Fascinated, we walked on and on, until we were climbing up onto the cones of ice below the hanging glacier, which resembles a huge angel spread out against the rock. We found deep holes in the bluish ice; holes that breathed out a blast of cold air, that carried up to us from far below the sounds of rushing water.

John and I pushed on across the ice to climb what looked like a hill, so that we could walk back to the tea-room along the ridge of a moraine. We had, apparently, missed a sign that told us to turn back. Unaware of this we began climbing upward toward the ridge; suddenly we realized we were working our way up the face of a cliff, finding a handhold, then a toehold. For an exhilarating and fearful five minutes we knew just a little of the pleasure a mountain climber must know, at once defying and conquering a vertical face of rock.

Our wives were less exhilarated. We returned from the great mountain under a little cloud of disapproval, and were reminded at least once that we were neither equipped nor trained to climb.

Fortunately for John and me, a bear had chosen that period of absence to visit our camp. Wapiti is a large campground set in a pine forest, near Mount Tekarra on the bank of the Athabasca River. Our tents were set up on well-spaced square platforms, and each site was provided with a fireplace and a pile of wood. The couple on the site next to the Clendennings' had that morning moved all the food out of their tent. "All we left in it was a little tin of cocoa," the lady was insisting as we drove up; a bear had walked into one side of the tent and out the other, taking nothing but the cocoa tin.

That night John and I found our wives more solicitous. And not without cause, for in the morning Sheila woke up to see light coming in through holes where a bear had simply touched their tent once with a paw.

That day my wife, who had smiled at the cocoa lady, left a can of blueberries on our table, intending to make blueberry muffins in the evening. We spent a busy morning at Miette Hot Springs, where four springs issue from fissures in the gorge of Sulphur Creek. The hottest spring is 129 degrees Fahrenheit.; the big pool is kept at 98 degrees. While we swam and soaked, a bighorn sheep performed on the rock cliff overlooking the creek. Leaving the water reluctantly, we strolled in the natural rock garden behind the pool building, watching the antics of the world's fattest chipmunks as they begged for still more food.

In the town of Jasper we shot a game of snooker in an old Alberta pool hall, our aggregate ignorance costing us a pretty penny before we finally cleared the table. We photographed the totem pole and ourselves beside it; the Raven Totem, centre of a happy world to many visitors with its Supernatural Raven, its Grizzly Bear Mother, its Frog Woman with six frogs decorating her forehead, another hanging from her lips.

We returned to our campground to find that the tin of blueberries had been opened by the bear's simply closing his claws on it. He'd drunk out the sweet juice, but had missed some of the berries. We did without muffins that night.

Next morning at daybreak, I heard what I took to be a man walking around our tent, and I wondered sleepily what he was doing; maybe he'd come to borrow our axe. Then a foot came to rest on the wooden platform holding our tent, and the whole platform sagged. I unzipped the little window at the back of the tent and found myself face to face with a six-hundred pound black bear. Without thinking I gave a shout that nearly frightened my sleeping wife out of her three pairs of pyjamas. "There's a bear out there," I said by way of apology, my language hardly appropriate to the occasion. My sceptical wife hadn't heard a thing; she put her face to the window. "There's a bear out there," she said.

Even more preposterously, I put on my boots and went outside to chase him away. Fortunately, it took me some time to lace my boots, and by the time I got out he had walked a few yards off. At least I could no longer hear his breathing. Now I followed after as he walked past the trap that had been set especially for him: a culvert on wheels and full of bones that he was supposed to crawl toward and seize, triggering a lid that locked him in the trap. He ignored this fine example of human ingenuity and walked up instead to a forty-five gallon steel drum for garbage that was supposedly suspended out of his reach. He swung a huge paw and gave that drum a swat; garbage came raining down all about him. He helped himself rather fastidiously to a breakfast of corn cobs and bacon rind, then ambled off down a hill toward the river to sleep somewhere until late afternoon.

We had only one night of our vacation left. Jane came up with the idea that we spend the last night in the Jasper Park Lodge. John and I put up only the most elementary resistance. For one last day, feeling just a little bit that we had let the bear intimidate us, we loafed in the rustic elegance of that beautiful lodge on the shore of Lac Beauvert, we swam in the swimming pool surrounded by pale-blue mountains, we dined off linen instead of paper napkins that were forever blowing away, we slept in cabins built of great logs on beds that needed no pumping up. And we talked already with a certain nostalgia of a breakfast we'd had at Wapiti when our fingers were so stiff with the cold we

could hardly eat. We remembered feeding half our fishing gear to the
rocks in Medicine Lake. And Sheila, who had lamented the hole in
their new tent, was becoming grateful to the bear for a tale she would
tell on camping trips outside Los Angeles.

But I must add a postscript that is something of a confession. I
have never taken the horseback ride or backpacked into the Tonquin
Valley in Jasper National Park, and those who have tell me it is the
most splendid vista in the park. Alpine meadows abound, and the
Amethyst Lakes, appropriately named, are set against the Ramparts,
the rock walls of the Continental Divide. It is scenery of a kind that
cannot be seen from the highway.

Nor have I ever taken the boat ride on Maligne Lake, and those
who have tell me that until you pass through the Narrows you haven't
seen Jasper, for the upper lake penetrates into a valley ringed with an
extravagance of snowy peaks. Mabel Williams, who writes so wisely
and so passionately of the mountains to which she has devoted a lifetime, has this to say in her book *Jasper National Park:*

> It is, perhaps, the splendid prodigality, the massing of effects that distin-
> guishes this region from all others. In the Rockies the folly of compar-
> isons where beauty is concerned is always obvious. There are a score of
> lakes, each different, which once seen hold their place in the heart for-
> ever. Yet this stands out among them all. Where many of the others are
> chamber music, Maligne is the great orchestra. In line, mass and colour
> the scene is unbelievably glorious, and in addition, it is completely
> unspoiled. . . . The lake lies like a sleeping beauty rapt in a dream of
> centuries from which one hopes it may never wake. It is good to
> remember that because this is a national park its beauty will be protect-
> ed from profanation and its virginal loveliness preserved for the inspira-
> tion and enrichment of human life.

John and I returned to Jasper, as a kind of personal centennial
project; but we did not hike into Tonquin. And while we got to the
shore of Maligne Lake, we turned away to make our own discovery of
what is most compelling about the ancient thrust of mountains.

RIDING HIGH: THE SKYLINE TRAIL

The Cree wrangler was a man of few words: he handed John the reins and said, "His name is Popcorn. He doesn't know his name. He bites."

We were about to begin a two-day ride, John Clendenning and my cousin Lorne, who spells his name Kroetch, and I: we were going to ride through Little Shovel Pass and out into the true high country – that alpine world of rock and meadow and flowers above the treeline. It was nine o'clock in the morning: we were standing now under a scattering of tall spruce on the shore of a lake so beautiful that we were tempted to spend our two days in front of the nearby chalet, watching the water and its ring of blue and snow-capped peaks.

The ride commences at Maligne Lake. The wrangler and the trail boss began to pack our little heap of gear into the canvas bags that went onto X-frames on the pack horses. I had already been introduced to the pinto I was to ride, a big horse called Pontiac; I put my camera and a flask of rye into the saddlebags and tied my raincoat on behind the cantle of the saddle. Lorne was pulling off his oxfords and putting on a pair of cowboy boots.

We were, the three of us, impatient; the horses held to the motionless stance of animals that had long ago learned to conserve their energy. Two horses were saddled but unassigned, and we wondered who would be going over the trail with us, when two men appeared, one of them introducing himself as a student from the University of Colorado, the other a dark neat man in his midthirties who said nothing, but who quickly excited our curiosity with his riding boots, his riding crop, his neat black gloves, and his polo jacket.

The Indian trail boss gave instructions in Cree to his wrangler, then mounted his own horse and signalled us to fall into line. The trail boss led the way, followed by three loaded pack-animals and a spare saddlehorse. We five trail-riders jockeyed our mounts into something resembling a column. The wrangler brought up the rear.

We crossed the saddlehorse bridge over the Maligne River and immediately began climbing into a dense forest of spruce and lodgepole pine. All of us were silent, getting the feel of our creaking saddles, settling our feet into the stirrups. Lorne, who was something of a veteran rider, repeated the Christian precept about the necessity of turning the other cheek.

The sky was overcast but clearing. The air was dead calm along the forest trail; a horse coughed behind me. Ahead somewhere, a hoof knocked a stone loose and it tumbled down the hillside. Already we were into a world of windfall, of lichens and yellow toadstools, of decaying stumps and rock outcrop. We turned to follow a rivulet, where the water seemed to have scattered an abundance of Fringed Grass-of-Parnassus, each white blossom filigreed and dainty against the solid banks of moss. Looking back, I saw that Joe Plante, the wrangler, was sizing us up, deciding how well we were going to stand up to the rigours of the trail.

Below us we could see a small pond: clear and pale, reflecting the green trees that were its setting, it showed also the dead straight trunks of trees that had fallen in. The necessity of death was all about us, the dying trees and moss that make new trees, new flowers, and new life.

The sun broke through the clouds for a moment as we caught our first glimpse of Mona Lake. The timber was big, including some black spruce, their bark scaly, their branches hung with a lichen that is appropriately called old man's beard; the needles of a spruce smelled fragrant when I crushed a few in my hand, light above the insistent but pleasant smell of the horse. Lorne identified a kettle, the hollow left when a buried chunk of a glacier finally melted. John called to me, and looking up I saw, across the lake, the naked high peaks of distant mountains: and I realized where we were heading.

We began to relax and talk. Now we were identifying the flowers of this subalpine forest: fields of purple asters, golden asters with their stems a muted silvery green, blatant fireweed, goldenrod, and the vivid red of Indian paintbrush, a red as shocking up in those mountains as tongues of flame. And fire had gone through here years before us; the old snags stood scattered, black and leaning, fire-carved totem poles.

The trail boss signalled us off the trail. We had to ride into the underbrush and fallen timber to get around a hornet's nest, for only recently two women had been thrown when their horses were stung. I began to appreciate the remarkable sure-footedness of the mountain horse who was to be my legs for the next two days. Pontiac, given rein, picked his way carefully but easily where a man could hardly walk.

We followed Evelyn Creek, a rush of clear water over water-rounded stones. Crossing an old timber bridge, we proceeded up the long shoulder of Bald Mountain. Now we were on switchbacks; the trail boss and pack horses were far ahead of us on the trail, yet only a few yards above us on the mountain. Kinnikinick, low on the ground, was high enough on the steep bank that I could pick red berries from my saddle. By 11:30 we were climbing fast, and the forest was thinning out, opening up; the blue-touched green of Engelmann spruce was soft against the yellow-green of pine. The meadows were more numerous, reaching upward from us and spreading out as the trees grew smaller. Here too dead trunks were rotting, the rotting wood silver, then, where it had been broken, an orange or yellow or brown inside. The timber-line was close above us as we angled along the hillside, then made a hairpin turn and angled back, always climbing. The brown shale tin-kled on the stillness.

We were breaking into high country. Making a hairpin turn, we faced into a cool breeze. Across the valley lay a patch of snow, ahead of us but no longer above. A stream glinted far below. At the horses' feet the juniper berries were blue and ripe. The shortened trees, spruce and alpine fir, were sometimes twisted now. A cedar waxwing treated us to a flash of yellow. A boreal chickadee sang, a wintry song indeed, for it sounded like a black-capped chickadee with a bad cold. It sang from a clump of miniature trees.

At 12:45 we broke out free of the last dwarfed trees into Little Shovel Pass. The sun at the same time blazed through a hole in the clouds, onto a spectacular choice of mountains. "Ahoy up there," Lorne shouted, from where he was riding at the end of the string of horses with the wrangler. "Crack out that snakebite oil. The trick is to drink it before you get bit."

Above the treeline we no longer had to ride single file. We stopped, all of us, around a watering hole, and the sweating horses drank deeply, began to graze. We were in a bowl of rock surrounded by mountains. Only a few yards above the watering hole a spring issued out of the rocks; here a river began. It hardly ran ten feet before its banks were a riot of mountain forget-me-nots, a flower so intensely blue it blurs the perceiving eye into doubt. The blue creates a haze of blue; the mind is fixed out of thought.

We drank straight from the mickey, John and Lorne and I, our confidence and pleasure apparent and unconcealed. The student refused a drink. The mysterious man in black still had not spoken, and now Lorne offered him the bottle. "Ah," he said. "Oui. Merci. Thank you."

Lorne and John and I pooled our college French and ventured a remark about the weather. The stranger responded. We began to converse – in French.

Albert, it turned out, was a Parisian. He spoke two words of English, and those he had already spent when he said thank you. We passed the bottle around again, and now Lorne and John and I found our French improving. Albert responded by telling us what had happened.

The previous day in Jasper he had approached a desk in the Jasper Park Lodge and inquired about riding the Skyline Trail. The girl at the desk, in her limited French, had explained the ride, casually mentioning that on the previous trip the trail boss led a group made up of five women and one man. Albert got the impression that he was to

be one man with five women, and immediately signed on. His aston-
ished silence at our point of departure had been more than a reluctance
to attempt communication.

I rode off to pretend I was helping the wrangler bring in two
straying pack horses. Then we went up over the pass to a view across
the four miles of alp-land we would have to cross before beginning the
last climb to eight thousand feet and the summit of Big Shovel Pass.
The climb began with a short, sharp, descent: and we got our first jarring introduction to the thigh-straining downhill ride.

The Parisian proved to be a delightful companion and a man of
infinite patience with our inadequate knowledge of French. He told a
joke three times. He translated our pointing and gesturing and mum-
bling into beautiful French prose. The sun was out now. Lorne, in turn,
looking more like a wrangler than did the wrangler in his old cowboy
hat and boots, quoted Chaucer to us:

> And smale fowles maken melodye,
> That slepen al the night with open yë,
> (So priketh hem nature in hir corages):
> Than longen folk to goon on pilgrimages . . . .

It was, unfortunately, not April but late August. We dropped
down into the beginnings of the forest to have lunch, and by the time
we stopped at 1:30 I was getting weak-kneed. The Fringed Grass-of-
Parnassus bloomed about us, and everywhere the western anemone had
gone to seed, the solitary blossom that has won it the name chalice cup
giving way to the green beard that leads some to call it the towhead
baby. We tied our horses to spruce, but they needed little encouragement to rest; and we riders threw ourselves down in the grass to watch
while the trail boss built a fire.

Before the coffee was hot in the two pails suspended from sticks
over the flames, another string of horses trotted into camp. Tom
Vinson, owner of the three-step brand, the brand we were riding, had

overtaken us with his nine-year-old son and two extra pack horses. They were coming in to close the overnight cabin for the season. In fact Tom, the outfitter, had closed the trail the day before, 20 August, and only against his better judgment had we been allowed to make this trip with the men who were to pack out some supplies and equipment.

But even Tom, his cowboy hat low over his eyes, mellowed a little as he consumed a second cup of the trail boss's coffee and some sandwiches out of one of the packs. We began to joke and talk. The trail is supposed to open 1 July, but this year five men digging through the snow in Big Shovel Pass didn't get it open until 12 July. The trail boss, Alfred Norris, assured us that an open winter was on the way: the hornets were busy, and the beavers were holding back the water in their dams. But Tom wanted to get his string of ninety horses out of the park and ready for the big-game hunting-season; he had already booked some American hunters. He went on to lament that the new hunting laws were so lax that in five years you would have to hold a draw each fall in Alberta to see who got permission to hunt a moose. And to make matters worse, he added, wolves were on the increase again.

While Tom and the wrangler got busy readjusting the load on one of the pack horses, we had a last cup of coffee and began to commiserate with the Parisian. Lorne and John and I each confessed now that we, too, had expected to find a few attractive women on the ride.

"There usually are," Tom said. "This ride is too tough for men who work all year in offices. It's a trail for women and children."

Alfred was muttering to himself. "You get women on one of these rides, and all the men start showing off." He put out his fire with water from a nearby stream. Now, carefully, he took the two sticks he'd used to make coffee and placed them against a tree as a preparation for winter, lamenting as he did so that for sure he'd have to get new ones next year. Then he mounted his horse and took the halter rope of a pack animal, for that one was what he called a "kangaroo jumper" and was likely to cause trouble on the trail ahead.

The moment when all the horses start into motion is one of the finest on a ride; their stillness and random groupings flow alive to become a moving line. We were nine riders now, with an extra saddle-horse and five pack horses.

We rode up onto an alpine meadow, a broad, humpy, soggy beflowered meadow inside a rim of bare, grey, snow-spotted mountains. "You got here a little late for the flowers," Tom Vinson said: and everywhere around us the green meadow was a melody of colour. We had already seen the purple asters and the first snow buttercups. Now the puffed white heads of the cotton grass were whiter than the nearby snow. The Indian paintbrush was white and orange and yellow and pink, as well as red. Tom, square-bodied and solid, got down off his horse to show us an elephant head that had lingered on into August, its leaves like a rubbery fern, its little purple flowers each like an upturned elephant's head. The western anemone was here, also gone to seed. The white heath carpeted acres of ground, a few white flowers remaining, the blossoms tiny against the violence of rock and torrent. Here and there were patches of shintangle, the low-growing evergreen that makes a fine shelter for little birds and animals. The mountain heather, red and white and unlike the heather of Scotland, stood less than a foot off the ground, a green carpet for the myriad of flowers. But in all those blossoms there was one that most caught our attention: deep blue, bell-shaped, and erect, it proved to be the large gentian.

We forded a stream to ride toward a herd of twenty Rocky Mountain caribou. An old bull was nearest us; he raised his antlers, swept back and slightly flattened; he must have given a warning, for the herd ran a short distance, then stopped again. Lorne, swinging his binoculars, spotted another six that were lying on a snowbank to get away from the flies. Here there was no trail to follow and we spread out, reluctant to move away from the now fleeing herd, watching also for bighorn sheep and white mountain goats.

A rust-mottled bird ran out of a patch of shintangle: the white-tailed ptarmigan. Finding it tame, though perfectly coloured to blend with the rocks and heather, Lorne and I followed until it came to more shintangle and disappeared. Lorne rode on to examine the white antlers of a long-dead caribou; I set to work persuading Pontiac to interrupt what had become for him a leisurely opportunity to graze.

Tom Vinson pointed out a waterfall and an unlikely green lake behind a rock wall. His son, small under a huge black cowboy hat that was an imitation of his father's, was making his first trip over this trail, and now that he had no trail to stick to, he set his horse to running across a purple field; his father rode off to stop him.

Alfred Norris, the trail boss, let both men and horses loaf across the wide meadow. We did not know we were saving our strength for the ride up over a ridge and down to our night's lodgings. As we grouped again and began to string out onto a trail and a steep ascent, a sudden heavy driving rain overtook us. I untied my raincoat, risked scaring my horse in the process of getting it on, pulled up the hood; as we rode on and up I heard the cold rain turn to pellets of ice.

Riding, I trusted to my horse and to his place in the column of horses. I could see nothing beyond me, and beneath me only a few short yards of tilted earth and rock. And as I rode, hardly watching, holding the reins with one hand, sliding the other under the rear of the saddle to warm it against the horse, I noticed suddenly, beneath the horse's hoofs, an alpine harebell. Two lines went through my mind from Earle Birney's poem "Ellesmereland":

> No man is settled on that coast
> The harebells are alone . . . .

That solitary blossom was a bright blue and, for this harsh world, an extravagant size; the horse's hoof missed it, and it was gone. But nature was shortly to outdo herself. As we were whipped by the frozen rain, as we hunched against it and the mountain up which we rode, I was to see another flower I might well have missed on a sunnier ride, for close beside the trail and nearly hidden by a rock I saw a monkshood. Hooded as a monk might be, royal blue, it stood extravagantly lush against the harshness of the land.

At 3:45 we pulled our horses to a stop at the top of the climb. The frozen rain passed over as suddenly as it had come. The ground was white at the horses' feet. We rested, hunched still in our saddles against the wind; then Alfred signalled, and we started down a steep and jolt-ing trail, down past the foot of a large patch of ice and rockfall, toward the promised camp.

We glimpsed a fleck of red roof below us. The camp was set in a mountain amphitheatre. Three walls of nearly vertical rock enclosed it, and we rode down the sloping rim of the third wall; on the fourth side a narrow valley dropped steeply downward, against a backdrop of more distant mountains. But we could only see those mountain walls sur-rounding us; we were in a cirque made by the grinding, cutting action of a glacier. The camp was set at sixty-six hundred feet. As we rode down we realized the trail we had yet to ride was far above us.

The student from Colorado sat unmoving when his horse stopped. "Don't talk to me; if I talk my face will crack with the cold." But he had to grin.

Joe Plante, the wrangler, unsaddled the horses and fed and belled them. Tom Vinson had disappeared to prepare our bunks. And Alfred, the trail boss, set to work splitting wood; an apron had transformed him into a cook. Like a true cook, he wouldn't let us trail riders into the cook-shack, for he was busy. Cold and stiff, we crowded into the shelter on the lee side of the little shack and spread ourselves to dry on the woodpile. Lorne treated us to a few of his favourite lines from *The Rubáiyát of Omar Khayyám*:

> Yon rising Moon that looks for us again –
> How oft hereafter will she wax and wane;
> How oft hereafter rising look for us
> Through this same Garden – and for *one* in vain!

"Because once is enough on that horse I'm riding," he added.

The cook responded by calling from his warm stove. "Don't feel bad, boys. You've covered fourteen miles. Only twenty-one to go."

Only Albert didn't groan. His form on the horse had always been perfect, even when the rain was knocking at his head and he had no raincoat. He sat now on a large block of wood, watching the stream that separated us from the scree, or fallen rock, at the base of the mountain slope. And he answered our groans by telling of his wonder at this ride: in Paris he had known only open fields and neatly kept paths. Here – he gestured, wordless, up at the clouds and the nearby mountain peaks.

"Come and get it," the cook hollered; and while we sat over a glass of orange juice he began to talk of his own life. Now in his seventies, Alfred Norris came up into this pass in 1902 with his Indian mother, when her tribe still hunted caribou and sheep to make dried meat and pemmican. "Pemmi-can," Alfred said, with the accent on the last syllable, and he added pointedly that Cree was spoken in Canada before either English or French.

With the establishing of Jasper Park the Indians were forced to move out, to the trading post at Grande Cache, where they were to have land and peace – except that the provincial government then made that area a provincial forest. Each year since 1924, Alfred has come back here to ride trail and cook. A small, quick, wiry man who on the trail wears a hat, chaps, and jacket that must have been the height of fashion in 1924, he is transformed by an apron into the best cook of steak and onions on the continent. When he decided we'd sniffed the aromas from his old wood-stove long enough, he filled the serving dishes and set them on the table. After the justice we did to his mashed potatoes and gravy, and steak and onions, I finally understood why they'd brought three pack horses to feed eight men and a boy for two days. To top it all off, our impossible Parisian excused himself for a few minutes after we'd eaten, then returned to the table with a box of

cigars that were made in Holland of Havana tobacco. We sat in a delicious cloud of smoke, talking and laughing, and Alfred went on to
prove that his ability as a cook was challenged only by his talent as a
raconteur: his best was the story of the time he brought four actresses
over this trail, and had to blindfold all four – he indicated the red
handkerchief around his neck – to get them down off the mountains.

Our spirits were so high that John, who'd promised at the beginning of our ride to be the party's malcontent, now suggested a climb up
the mountains. We had a choice of two: Curator Mountain at 8,604
feet, and Antler at 8,400. While we were close to the top of both of
them, they still towered above us. After a learned discussion and a
close look at a map, we settled on the low ridge between them and
started out. Albert, however, first cleaned and polished his already
shining riding-boots, then quickly overtook us.

Halfway up the scree, or talus, slope we were startled by a squeak-
ing sound. It proved to be a rock rabbit; more precisely, a pika, a little
animal that looks to be half rat and half rabbit. The mountain men
have a high regard for his industry; the pika cuts grass and lays it out to
dry; then, at the approach of bad weather (and he seems to know
exactly when winter is coming) he stores it away for winter use. The
nine-year-old Tommy scrambled up to the top of the ridge, while we
five hardy trail riders watched the rock rabbit and puffed. Perched on
what had looked like grey rocks from below, we found them to be mul-
ticoloured: green, yellow, red, brown. There were a number of kinds of
rock, with lichens growing on them and with moss growing in the
crevices. Not to be completely outdone by young Tommy, we
adjourned to a nearby glacier for a rousing snowball fight.

Below us our camp seemed to huddle for comfort against a stand
of spruce that must have been escaping fires for at least 150 years. The
hobbled horses had begun to straggle down the valley, eating the flowers we were forbidden to pick, their bells tinkling. A wild stream
foamed white from a hanging valley down the rock face of the moun-

tain we were to ride across in the morning, then joined the slightly quieter stream at the foot of our camp.

As we crossed that stream, Tommy and I lay down to drink, our faces touching the cold, swift water. Tom Vinson met us and told young Tommy not to climb up so high alone – he might run into a grizzly. One winter a grizzly broke down the front wall of the little cook-shack and raised her cubs on the two bunks where the wrangler and the trail boss sleep. We were all told that breakfast came early; if we didn't want to "jungle out," or sleep under the stars, our beds were ready.

Our quarters for the night were tents set up over pole frames. Lorne and John and I were assigned to one tent and found three cots set up in a row, with an eiderdown sleeping bag and two grey blankets on each. And indeed, the night promised to be cold; the old outhouse, propped up with a log, looked out on an amphitheatre of arched and soaring and protecting rock: but a chill wind blew off those mountains. Tom Vinson had set a wood fire to roaring in the small tin stove in a corner of our tent. John happened to discover a mickey of snakebite oil in his kit-bag: we set about proving that a mickey of prevention is worth a twenty-six of cure.

But just as we were about to turn in, the student and Albert came knocking at our tent flap. They'd started a chess game – Albert had brought along a chess set – and had no light by which to finish it. None of the tents had lights of any sort, but not to be outdone, Lorne found a flashlight in his packsack. While darkness came quickly upon us, while the wind outside rose and began to tear at our tent, we gathered around the foot of one bed and the flashlight's little beam. The student and Albert played chess. Lorne and John contributed their total knowledge of the game to the student's store. I was kept busy feeding dry wood to the fire. And meanwhile Albert quietly muttered "Ah... oui... oui... oui..." and won the game hands down.

Dawn was a soft and palomino light coming through our canvas roof. It was a quality of light fit for a Renaissance cathedral. Lorne informed us that three times during the night it had rained, and the wind had continued strong; but John and I did not sympathize with his restlessness.

Tom Vinson came in to wake us but found us awake; and while we learned that Joe had gone out walking at 5:30 to find the horses, he lit a fire in our stove. The stovepipe, making a loop before it vanished through the roof of the tent, began to radiate enough heat that I ventured out of my cocoon; taking an empty pitcher I went for water from the stream so that we could wash in the basin on the little log table between two cots.

Breakfast was three cups of scalding coffee ("Good," I said; "It's the water," Alfred said), fried eggs, and lots of bacon and toast. Alfred broke our greedy silence with more stories; he'd once been an interpreter for the Royal North-West Mounted Police. His white father, a man from proper Ontario, proved to be a bigamist and shortly thereafter went to the hoosegow. Alfred's mother then married an American who started a ranch in what is now Jasper Park – a ranch that became the Palisades school for park employees. While he talked and served coffee and fried more eggs, his bright blue eyes merry this morning, the student from Colorado showed up.

We four trail riders, unshaven and hardly combed, no longer regarded ourselves as rank amateurs. We talked knowingly of this horse's gait and that one's disposition: our very griminess was testimony to our having been initiated.

The door opened once more.

As I say, we had arrived in the cook-shack looking mangy, dressed in clothes we might have slept in: that impossible Frenchman walked in, ten minutes late, granted, but he was shaved, manicured, combed, and polished. He glowed. The dirtier we got, the cleaner he got. His riding breeches had surely been pressed by some invisible valet during the night; his gloves must have been new. We stank of horses.

He smelled of nothing but cologne. He was immaculate. And to make it all worse, he looked at our slovenliness and forgave us. "Bonjour, mes amis. Il fait beau."

We went to our tents to take our coats off the nails on which we'd hung them to dry. Joe was back with the horses; they were eating oats off the ground, their bells tinkling. While he went to have some breakfast, we attempted to help Tom Vinson take down the tents.

In half an hour the tents were folded and their pole frames stood naked against the wind. The horses were saddled, the pack horses loaded; then we all went to help Alfred.

The barren little cook-shack was now full of paraphernalia. Albert interrupted his own haste to tell how it took three pack horses to bring in the huge old wood-stove. Then we went on hanging the rafters full, with pails, dippers, a plastic bag of detergent, a sack of flour, a washtub, two traps. Joe meanwhile was piling folded cots and tents and mattresses and stoves and pillows into the little room. Alfred set to work polishing the stove, in preparation for next July; then we were all busy nailing heavy wire over the doors and windows, to try to keep out the bears. As Alfred picked up a washbasin he'd left outside on a block of wood, John remarked once more that he was a damned fine cook. "I should be," he said proudly. "I used to cook for the Mounties' dogs."

The student's horse, Pearl, had a lump in the middle of her back, and he was given the spare horse to ride. Lorne, on Sawbones, only by inches escaped a sore or broken leg, for my horse turned crankily on his and kicked. John expressed some concern as to why his horse had not once tried to bite him. Alfred had taken off his apron; in his old Mountie-style hat, the red handkerchief around his neck, wearing moc-casins and moccasin rubbers, he now checked the pack horses and their loads.

"Lead the way, *neistow*," Tom told him, using the Cree word for brother-in-law – a lovely word that is extended in meaning to include anyone regarded as a close friend.

Alfred untied his chaps from his saddle, pulled them on, and put his axe in the scabbard where it rode by his knee. He tied the halter of the "kangaroo jumper" to the tail of a second pack horse; then, leading that pack horse by its halter rope, he started out of camp. He had climbed well above us even by the time the last of the fifteen horses entered onto the trail.

The top of Curator was invisible in a halo of clouds. It was 9:00 A.M. when we left the camp to its nine months of winter; in a few minutes we had filed out of the protecting clump of spruce toward the open rock above us. The five pack horses were now heavily loaded with the food and sleeping bags and gear that might be of use on a hunting expedition. The switchbacks were steep and our muscles slow to begin to respond to the motion of horse and saddle. "Twenty-one miles," the student said. "All of it up or down."

We rode up onto rock, and were cheered at the sight of a tiny lake below us, blue-green as a tropical ocean. Above the lake and across from us were patches of snow; rocks rolling down across the snow had left straight lines, and a record of the rapidity with which even a mountain erodes. Just off the trail a rock rabbit, busy making hay, squeaked his alarm at our approach. But we were surely in greater danger than he, for we had entered now into a field of great broken rocks, and our reliance on our horses was total as their thin legs delicately found a path.

We were climbing so steeply we had to breathe the horses whenever we found a place where they might rest with four feet comfortably settled. Stopped, we could look around. Behind us were the snow-covered mountains surrounding Maligne Lake, those magnificent peaks named by Mrs. Schaeffer in her explorations of 1911: Sampson, after her Stoney Indian guide; Leah, after his wife. And across the lake were mounts Charlton and Unwin and Mary Vaux, all of them well over 10,500 feet.

And right at our feet, in the shelter of naked rocks, grew moss campion, its bunched flowers still pink to purple against the dark-green cushion of its leaves. Hugging the rock, surviving both snowslides and the grinding wind, this is the summit flower, the flower that blooms above all others.

"This is the toughest part right here," Tom Vinson assured us. We were zigzagging steeply upward through a waste of smashed rock. Above us now was the top of the pass; the trouble was, a field of snow clung to the mountain's side beneath the top. "We were crossing that snow," Tom went on, "when a pack horse slipped. He tobogganed on the snow, halfway to that lake down there."

The student was listening from some distance ahead. "Did he get hurt?"

Tom, patient at an infinity of questions, allowed himself a squint of surprise. "Dead as a maggot."

Alfred, at the head of our column and directly above us as he rode the switchback, brought us to a halt. His horse was stopped where the trail led out over the snow and ice. We let the horses breathe again. The snow before us, from the summer's melting, had a surface like that of a chiselled woodcarving. Now we could hear the trickle of water from beneath the icy surface, could see the small rocks that had melted their way into the ice.

Tom Vinson looked at the trail and told us to dismount. The horses, resisting at first, were driven across by themselves: Pontiac, Sawbones, Popcorn, Seven Up, Pearl. Albert was riding a horse named Moonshine and we had struggled in vain to explain to him the pun. I watched my pinto leap like a goat when a hind foot slipped; then he was safe on the other side. Alfred did not have to come back and blind-fold us, but we crossed cautiously, slowly, yet all the time filled with awe, perhaps a little at ourselves.

Once across the ice we could not find room on the face of broken rock to walk up beside our mounts and get on; Alfred led them the short distance to the top of the pass while we followed.

We broke through the pass at eight thousand feet. Our horses awaited us, bunched and silent; and we were silent too. We had for so long been pushing ourselves against the rock and snow that the sudden sweep of space before us was dumbfounding; miles to the west stood Mount Fryatt, at 11,026 feet; then Hooker Icefield, distant and a dazzling white, where the Whirlpool River begins its wild descent; then Mount Edith Cavell, looming cold and ribbed with ice; then Angel Glacier; then the valley of the Athabasca, its long river gathering the streams we had forded at their source, the Banff-Jasper Highway not more than a scratch in the forest. The giant cloud-shadows played below us on the valley floor. We stood wondering against the brisk wind, then separated out our bunched horses and rode across the slope of brown shale.

The ridge we were to ride was two miles long, all of it above eight thousand feet. From the summit of the ridge we could see in all directions. To the east the mountains, bare of snow, came at us, it seemed, in waves of rock – row and then row and then row of mountains, rising up out of the distant overcast, crashing like breakers toward us. To the west the mountains were higher, their peaks snow-dazzled, cloud-carrying; and they were such a multitude that the mind went dizzy and humble at the revelation.

Ahead of us: only a narrow path along the ridge. A pack horse just then began to buck wildly, its load flying loose; it plunged and jackknifed toward a precipice. Joe Plante, the silent wrangler, touched his heels to his own horse, and at the cliff's edge he caught the pack horse, a three-year-old; we learned that it, too, was making its first trip.

The slope on either side was brown shale, combed out by gravity to look like fields of growing stone. Far below us the rock turned green with creeping life; below the pale hint of green the dark forest began, and thickened down into the distant valley.

We rode without speaking, only the wind in our ears. Relaxing, finding ourselves in a world alien beyond all our imagining, we began to look for familiar landmarks; Jasper townsite was distant and small below us in the valley. And as we rode those two miles, tightrope-walking the top of the world, we knew the descent must begin.

We turned down off the ridge, away from the Athabasca side, away from the shale and into a field of grey and brown rock that might have been blasted by dynamite. I decided to walk for a while; I got off Pontiac, and quickly found the perspective awkward and wrong. I had become used to riding my tall horse, to watching the horizon. Now I had to watch my every step, and saw only my immediate world. I was reduced to being human. But I stuck with it until we came to a stream, and to ford it I remounted my horse.

Two marmots were watching in the rocks beside the stream; the Rocky Mountain hoary marmot likes the scree slopes and the alpine meadows. These two grey and plump youngsters tussled and played, then went off with a galloping humping gait and stopped and played again. And they whistled for us, the shrill sound that gave a name to the mountain called The Whistlers.

We were in a treeless alpine valley. Now our total view was dominated not by a miracle of mountains, but by one mountain. Mount Tekarra loomed up before us, layered rock, chimneys of sandstone, with snow and rockfall at its base: Tekarra, named after an Iroquois hunter. From the far side it can be climbed by a horse; on our side it was a kaleidoscope of cliffs. We were to ride toward and around it for the next two hours.

John, in front of me, turned in his saddle. "Maybe one mountain is enough," he said.

Lorne, magicianlike, produced a mickey of snakebite oil. Out of the wind now, we found the sun hot on our shoulders. We stopped our horses, the three of us, while the others rode on. "I don't know if it was a snake that did it," I had to admit, "but I'm beginning to hurt a little." We passed the bottle a second time, opening our jackets and coats to the warmth of whisky and sun, watching the marmots as they now ignored us, letting our horses browse a little, then drink from a stream.

The other riders had disappeared over a low ridge. When we overtook them, they had dropped into a basin under Tekarra's peak, where spruce had found enough heat and protection and moisture to become a small stand. Alfred was already setting two tin cans of water to heat beside a camp fire. It was 12:30 when I got off my horse: my calves ached, I discovered; my knees ached, my thighs ached, my ass ached.

Everyone but the student took a drink of rye, and the impossible Parisian, at our insistence, finished it off. Now we learned that even he was subject to mortal woe. He had broken his wrist watch somehow along the trail; his girlfriend in Paris had given him the watch when he left, as if to confront him hourly with the thought of her. To impress on us the gravity of the situation, he brought out of his wallet a picture of the girl.

Standing bareheaded and long-legged on the steps of the Louvre was a girl so beautiful that Lorne gave vent to an audible groan. Even Joe, the wrangler, a taciturn man if God ever made one, came back for a second look, then for a third. He shook his head. He scratched him-self. The smile faded from his dark face. It was too much. He went to tighten the cinch on a pack horse.

Tom, checking the horses' feet, found that Seven Up and Moonshine had each thrown a shoe. "The longest skyline ride in the world," he told me. "And a lot of people from everywhere say it's the most impressive." He emptied his coffee mug. "But I'll soon have it paved with horseshoes."

The trail we took after lunch cut upward out of the forest along a steep hillside. No sooner had we started than we again ran into hor-nets, and Alfred ordered us off the trail. He might have been inviting us to fly. To get off the ribbon of rock and clay, we had to force our horses over what looked like a cliff, down into a windfall so dense it seemed impassable. Now no one could think of the French word for hornet; Albert, unable to understand our most recent preposterous undertaking, finally gave a shrug and blindly followed along.

Again the horses saw us through. Back on the narrow track and out of the trees, we saw below us a moose, feeding at the edge of a meadow. Soon after, we saw two white-tailed deer, just on the timberline. I thought I could take a picture; again, with his unfailing instinct, just as I snapped, Pontiac moved. The three times he didn't move, I might add, I had left the cap on the lens.

The descent into the first timber and then down into the valley was slow and gentle. The trouble was my exhaustion. I was pulling leather; I was hanging on to the big saddle horn with both hands, pretending I was holding the reins. We had foolishly drunk our last drop of snakebite cure one hour before my torture began. Now we were past Tekarra, onto Signal Mountain, and ahead of us stood Roche Bonhomme, with its human face looking up at the sky, its green chin and brown forehead. Somehow Egyptian, the old face that I had earlier judged to be sleeping now seemed surely dead.

We returned to the forest world. The mountains were high above us again. Lorne stopped to pick some ripe gooseberries. Elk had scarred the aspen with their winter foraging for bark. I began to feel I had done nothing for hours but look at my horse's ears.

Riding in single column – and now they were all strung out ahead of me – those seven men began to sing. I damned them roundly for their enthusiasm, for even my stomach muscles hurt; and then I joined in.

Lorne had found a pole, a dead lodgepole pine, and had tied a handkerchief to it. It was our pennant as he held it aloft; victorious we rode down and still farther down, jarring our way over windfall and along dusty trails, down into the forest and the valley. "Roll me over," we went on singing for some improbable reason, "roll me over, lay me down, and do it again."

The forest trail was soft and muffled the fall of hoofs. The squeak of leather was louder now; my horse started to trot and I reined him back. My face burned from sun and wind. Even my ankles and toes ached.

We came, of all things, to a golf course. We were back in the known world. The course was fenced to keep the elk from eating the watered greens, and outside the fence a herd of fat elk were lazily at rest in the shade of the beautiful pine forest.

Now the horses knew they were home, and all together they struck out trotting. Unable to choose between the new agony of the shift of gait and the old agony of extending the time of my endurance, I simply let the horse decide.

Dust-covered, weary, spent, we fairly galloped through that last stretch of forest to an opening beside a corral. When I got there, the Frenchman was casually offering around a blue package of the famous Gitanes cigarettes. Lorne and John, slumped in their saddles, accepted the offer. I too accepted, though I don't smoke, for I needed time to figure out just how the hell I was going to get off that horse without falling flat on my face.

At that moment — and all of us saw it happen, so it was no hallucination — a girl rode up on a handsome bay stallion. She was hardly eighteen; she was dressed in a spotless and very expensive habit; she was, like Lorne's horse, a strawberry blonde, and her face might have been an ad for Palmolive or Modess. Young and fresh and innocent, she stopped to watch us. Only Joe stirred, for he was taking the load off a pack horse; fifteen horses stood unmoving; seven men sat silently on their mounts; even the boy under his big black hat was, if not tired, at least resting. Our dust caught up with us and slowly drifted past. "It's beautiful," the girl said. And then she rode away.

I got off old Pontiac as if I was a cavalry officer. I saw that Lorne with a vague smirk was now awaiting my collapse; I made a great show of helping him out of his saddle.

John must have been aching as much as I. He was motionless, sitting on his horse that didn't know its name was Popcorn. He gave a rub at his whiskers. He carefully gripped the saddle horn with both hands and took one foot out of a stirrup. "You know," he said, as he let himself down, "goddamn, it was beautiful."

The Undiscovered Trunk Road

The Trunk Road runs from Grande Prairie in the Peace River country through the forests, mountains, and foothills of the Rocky Mountains Forest Preserve, past uncounted fishing streams, to the Crowsnest Pass in southern Alberta. Begun in 1948 as a joint federal-provincial undertaking, it was not finished until 1963. Intended first of all to enable a handful of men to administer five forests and fight fires in a watershed of 15,000 square miles, today it is 620 miles of twisting gravel road, with steep inclines and few services; the special preserve of the adventurous, it enables a fisherman or hunter or camper to get away even from the people who are getting away from it all.

When I set out to make this journey, a number of forests were closed to the public; the extreme fire-hazard made this necessary for the first time in six years. I have only been fortunate enough to cover something like two hundred miles of the road and its numerous side trails; they varied from excellent gravel to hardly discernible tracks where, on one occasion, I had to repair a small bridge with nothing but an axe. I have seen only a few of the 114 campgrounds, the 55 camp shelters, and the 46 stopover cabins maintained by the Alberta Forest Service.

The forests through which this road winds are only five of eleven provincial forests; they are supplemented by the Willmore Wilderness Park and the three wilderness areas into which no wheeled vehicles are allowed: Whitegoat, Ghost River, and Siffleur. I especially wanted to see Alberta's forest world, for few of us Albertans have explored it.

I started out by attempting to visit the immense Willmore Wilderness Park that begins on the northern boundary of Jasper. Because of road construction, I got only as far as the shelters at Rock Lake, outside the park's entrance. It was at Rock Lake that I met an old trapper, Gilbert Hopkins.

Gilbert was in a happy frame of mind: he'd just been granted permission to build a permanent cabin on his registered trapline, an area in the mountains around Rock Lake covering two and a half townships. And his new rifle – he showed me a picture in the catalogue he carried in his old pickup truck – would be waiting in the post office when he drove south to his home.

A ruddy and somewhat roly-poly man who hardly looks like a mountain trapper, Gilbert Hopkins, leaning against a fender of his truck in the hot afternoon sunshine, explained that he'd sort of chanced into that occupation: "When I was a young fellow just roaming around, I took in the harvesting and the lumbering and the spring cropping. One of my sisters is still on the old farm back in Tobermory, Ontario."

As happened with so many of his generation, his roaming around did not take him back home. He owned and operated a sawmill for twenty years, moving west from Edmonton as the forest disappeared. He recalled a morning near Edson when he went to the cook-shack and found a bear and her three cubs had preceded the lumberjacks to their breakfast. If a bear bothered you those days, you went for a gun and shot it.

Gilbert feels that the little operators can't compete today with the big lumbering outfits and the regulations that insist you select trees for cutting and make use of most of the wood. The little companies had simply cut down everything to get at the big white spruce and had sawed out what was easiest to saw, burning much of each tree, or leaving it to rot. When he was in his late fifties, his family already grown up and gone, Gilbert turned from lumbering to trapping. "I'd like to have one man with me," he added, further destroying my image of the trapping man. "Just in case I get hurt, you know. But most of the time I'm alone."

Now in his early sixties, Gilbert goes out to his trapline in October. In the past he slept in a tent or lean-to, and simply went home to his wife and furnace when the weather got too bad. He complained that the previous spring he'd got only thirty-seven beavers; the gun he was using wouldn't kill a beaver when the beaver was swimming away from him. Now, with a new gun and a cabin, he'd be looking for fox, wolf, marten, fisher, mink, otter, wolverine, lynx, cougar – "You name it," he said. "Everything and anything." Gilbert likes tourists and dislikes big-game hunters. The hunters, as he vividly recalls, "used to knock down a critter just to get the head" – of bighorn sheep or mountain goat or elk or moose. This waste of food bothered the old trapper. He did add that now the outfitters are required to see that the meat comes out of the bush with the trophy.

The fishing is excellent around Rock Lake: Rocky Mountain whitefish, lake trout, rainbows, and grayling. And since the lake is only fifteen miles off the Trunk Road, summer visitors go out to camp and fish. This gentle, shy, round-faced man who kills for a living gave me a little smile. "Tourists don't hurt the fishing – oh, they catch the odd fish." He glanced out across the water. "When the snow blows, I'm here alone."

As I left him to explore an old logging road I met a pack train: American big-game hunters who were moving out into the bush to set up camp so they could spot some game before the season opened. They were after moose, elk, and mountain goat. But one man in the group already had all three of those trophies hanging in his living room; he wanted a grizzly or a mountain caribou. "Next year I'm going to India," he told me. "Want me a tiger."

Driving south on the Trunk Road, on the rebuilt stretch between Grande Cache and Highway 16, I noticed that the vain search for an abandoned logging camp had run me short of gas. After crossing the Athabasca River just above an immense gorge that I'd never heard of, I stopped at the Entrance General Store, and made another delightful discovery.

First of all, the two gas pumps each had a glass tank on top.

While I remembered such tanks from my youth, I also assumed I was not about to get any gasoline. But a kindly gentleman came out and promptly set to work pumping one of the glass tanks full. Then, as gasoline was gravity-fed into my car, he watched the calibrations on the side of the glass; then he went into the store for paper and pencil to figure out how much I owed him.

This general store caters especially to ranchers who raise pack horses and saddlehorses and to the outfitters who use them. It was stacked full of saddles, extra stirrups, lanterns, belly-bands for pack horses, pails, lariats, and fascinating items that I couldn't identify. For the cowboy himself it had cowboy hats and boots, not to mention the usual fancy shirts and work gloves and denims. Three kegs of horseshoes blocked the approach to the old coal-stove. A cardboard box full of Indian beadwork moccasins and gloves gave to the old store the necessary odour of tanned moosehide.

A gang of railway workers came into the store while I was resisting the temptation to buy a pair of moccasins; they'd quit their jobs and were going home to Montreal. But first they wanted to outfit themselves with cowboy boots; and while they tried on boots their talk was of physical strength, of how much earth they had moved, of the explosives they'd spent. Two men argued at length as to whether a certain Big Red could "hang a lickin' " on a certain foreman.

Near Entrance, at Solomon Creek, the new Alberta Resources Railway begins its tortuous journey northward into the wilderness. If railways have gone out of style, it's certainly news in Alberta. Not only will these 235 miles of new track bring the Peace River country closer to the Pacific ports; more to the point, they will mean that coke from the Smoky River coal deposits can be exported to Japan. The trading post of Grande Cache is slated to become a modern mining community of five thousand people. And since the southern portion of this railway touches on the Rockies, engineers had to plan for an easy grade up to an elevation approaching five thousand feet.

Earth-moving, somehow, is often a topic of conversation in Alberta; the new railway gave men a chance to move forty-two million cubic yards, to build new bridges, and to drain a small sea of water out of the muskeg. And even as they fought the summer mosquitoes and the winter blizzards, they were talking of exporting sulphur and gypsum, pulp from a new mill at Grande Prairie, and gas and oil from unexplored reaches of the Big Smoky and Sheep Creek.

The section of the Trunk Road that I know best runs from the town of Hinton on Highway 16 south to Robb, then through what was once coal-mining country to the David Thompson Highway and Nordegg, a ghost town that has been turned into an exemplary prison.

I waited nearly one week for the road to open; then, after a local rain, the fire-rangers allowed traffic to go south from Hinton into the Coal Branch, a nearly deserted area where at one time twelve thousand people lived in a dozen thriving towns.

Those towns, early in their history, were served only by trains; there was no access road, and entrance into the towns meant riding a coal train. The economy of the area was based entirely on the mining of coal. As the coal mines closed after the Second World War, and Canada's railways switched to diesel engines, the Coal Branch became not only a group of ghost towns, but a little ghost country.

Twelve thousand people had lived passionately in that secluded region of valleys and mountains and forest for thirty-five years; their departure to them was a form of exile. Even now, when two Coal Branchers meet, it is a reunion of people who cannot quite believe they won't shortly be called back. I know this for I travelled into that lost land with Peter Pavich and his two sons. Peter's wife simply turned away when we asked her to come with us; she refuses to visit her old home. His daughter, that sunny day, had gone picking berries.

Our excuse was that we were going fishing, and as we drove south from Hinton, Peter and his sons, my cousin Lorne and I, we indulged in fishing talk. Mike Pavich had picked up some maggots to use as bait for Rocky Mountain whitefish. Someone remarked that a good fisherman puts one on his hook, then keeps an extra one warm in his lower lip.

The change took place at Mile Thirty-two. The town of Robb (formerly Minehead) is made up of retired miners who fish, talk, and drink beer in the local beer parlour: the few men who were too old or too stubborn to go to other jobs when the mines closed. As we drove up to the hotel Peter remarked, "This is where we go through customs."

And this is where the Coal Branch really begins. Outside in the sun three Indians were talking in sign language to each other; I watched for a moment, wondering how one might write a poem in that graceful but silent language. The three Pavich men, big, dark, and handsome, crawled out of the car. Then we were inside the Bryan Hotel, and Peter Pavich was shaking hands, laughing, being slapped on the back, suddenly talking Serbo-Croatian again.

In the beer parlours in this country forty years ago a man could hear every language that is spoken in Europe. They say that in one of the towns at one time there was not a single adult who was Canadian-born. Peter Pavich himself came from Yugoslavia in 1925, four months after he got married; he worked hard, saved his money, and three years later he was able to bring his wife to join him, and to see the daughter he had not yet seen.

But in that land of promise he was already one of the fortunate. The depression and war followed the arrival of those solitary men; some didn't see their wives for twenty years. And after twenty years, others didn't bother to send the necessary boat fare. Even today when asking if a man is married, you specify, here or the Old Country? It was said of one man that he was married in Bulgaria but single here. Another was married here, but not in Scotland. Of more than one it was said, Oh yes, he's married here in the Branch and also back home – but not to the same woman.

With the personal gossip caught up on, we talked of the famous

Coal Branch hockey teams that could whip any outside town twice their size; meanwhile glasses of beer flowed in from all directions and we in turn bought beer, but never for our own table.

The talk turned inevitably to the mystery of Black Frank Knezevich, the hero of this violent land, and not a coal miner but a famous loner: a trapper and a socialist. Peter Pavich had his moment now, for he had once killed a bottle of rye with Black Frank when the tough old man had come out of the hills with his pack horse to get supplies. The mystery was that one day his cabin was found open, with potatoes sliced in the frying pan. But Black Frank had disappeared and was never seen again. One faction argued that the Indians killed him. They'd never dare, it was countered. Another faction argued that a grizzly got him. He knew the bush inside out, it was said.

We finally got through customs. "There used to be a mining-camp here at Mile Thirty-two, another at Mile Thirty-three," Peter explained when we stepped again into the sunshine. "Anthracite. Not as dangerous as the bituminous we were digging."

Driving away from the Bryan Hotel, we saw what remained of the old townsite of Robb. Tucked away in a deep valley hardly visible from the winding gravel road, a few old houses, some of them boarded up, only one painted, straggled along a lovely little creek. Here dwelt the few who refused to surrender.

Next we came to Coalspur, where the railway had divided into two branches. Young Mike Pavich, a schoolteacher now, worked underground for two summers before 1948 and the day when his father came home with the news that the trains using steam coal had switched to diesel. Mike and his brother had gone to dances in each of the Coal Branch towns. Long before they were twenty-one they had learned to walk into a beer parlour and order a round; and now they looked in wonder at the weathered and deserted building that had once been the splendid Coalspur Hotel.

The train came into the Coal Branch one day and went out the next; going either way it stopped at the Coalspur station so the noisy crowd of passengers could race to the hotel for a glass of beer or a bite to eat. The railway schedule was at best only a theoretical proposition: the engineer himself appreciated a quick nip.

We left the weed-grown streets and drove along the dusty road to the next ghost town. One thousand people lived in Mercoal; now, according to rumour at least, it has a population of only two: a postmaster and the man who gets the mail. A few houses remain where once a town throve in its unlikely way, for the railway ran straight down the middle of Mercoal's main street, and young boys preferred crawling between dirty boxcars loaded with coal to waiting for a train to move. Peter Pavich indicated a clean and grassy spot. "The grandest hotel in town stood right there." Mike remembered the Cookhouse Café, where teenagers gathered to talk and eat ice cream. Now two Métis girls came out of the silent woods and watched us darkly.

For the outsider, these ruins are more beautiful than sad. It is only the heaps of coal slack that speak of the back-breaking labour that made the region thrive. The forested hills hide the sawdust heaps where timber was turned into mine props. The call of a moose, the beaver ponds, or the rocky ledges in a trout stream make a visitor wonder if men were ever here at all.

Cadomin, the town eleven miles beyond Mercoal, has experienced something of a revival, for now a local mountain is being cut down and hauled away to a cement plant. But machines do most of the work, and most of the handsome log houses are empty; the new workers have moved into the frame houses that once belonged to the bosses. And here a school worth $150,000 was completed just before the mines closed. Two years after completion a scrap dealer bought it for fifteen hundred dollars. "Here in Cadomin," Mike Pavich said, "the wind blows 360 days a year through that gap in the mountains. It blew boxcars off the track, the roofs off houses. And coal slack; into everybody's eyes." We were driving across what had been a slack pile; the road simply went over it. "There," Mike went on, "is where the skating rink caved in from a heavy spring snowfall. It was May the twenty-fourth."

Peter Pavich indicated the nearly dry river bed. "The bridge washed out one day. All of a sudden. Three men were drowned. . . ."

We had been climbing uphill along a winding road through forest, passing the occasional hunter and many excellent fishing spots. Now, at Cadomin, we drove out onto the Grave Flats Road, a narrow, rough, crooked track directly up into the mountains. Along here the railway tracks are rusted, the bridges gone. Now the older son, Joe, a pharmacist out from Edmonton for a holiday, was unable to keep quiet. He pointed up to the fabled Cadomin caves high on a mountainside; caves into which for an entire boyhood he had planned to venture without quite making it. He remembered, as Cadomin disappeared, a sports day he attended in that bustling town. "The crowd – you'd have thought it was Expo."

"Yuh," Mike said. "Right back there is where John Gerlitz hit his home runs."

A few people had hung on for awhile, insisting the mines would open again. Even in Mountain Park a few had lingered, high in the mountains at the end of the rail line. Mountain Park had been the Pavich home. It was, at that time, the highest inhabited town in Canada, standing at sixty-two hundred feet. The summers were so short and cold the miners' wives could grow only lettuce, onions, and radishes. There, in the winter, water came frozen in a barrel to your door. Men fought on a Saturday night for the pleasure and release of fighting. There an emergency whistle sent women and children streaming into the long street that led to the tipple. And up there the scenery is right off a postcard, with open alpine meadows, a mountain stream, a classic hogback, and, precise above its surroundings, the flat top of Cheviot Mountain.

We edged across a decayed wooden bridge. It was nearly twenty years since Peter Pavich had moved his family to Edson. Yet his son

Mike recognized the Mile Three swimming hole. We were following the McLeod River; Mike, at fifteen, had worked on a section gang along the river, driving spikes, shovelling cinders: proud to be knocking down fifty-one cents an hour.

He recognized also the Mile One Draw, where he went so often to attend school picnics. Mount Everest, the kids called the low peak beyond the empty meadow.

We would not have known where to find the town, had not the graveyard been left unmoved. Where nearly one thousand people lived, one house is left standing. The spirit of Black Frank Knezevich has not entirely disappeared; maybe it was he who really understood the future, for that one house is now a trapper's shack. Mike studied it, looked at the bare hillside where it stands; his aunt lived in that house for many years. He went often to her for an aunt's affection, and cookies.

Someone found a market for the lumber and tore down the town. The coal company, as a last gesture, bulldozed flat the area where the houses had stood, then buried the refuse. Only a few heaps of coal slack enabled Peter to guess the location of main street. "Then that," Joe added, pointing across the barren earth, "must have been the old lovers' lane."

Peter Pavich got out of the car; he walked a few steps and then turned and walked again, uncertain. Rain had gullied the naked clay. He picked up a shiny chunk of coal and came back toward us. "This is what it was all about."

One man, they told me, owned Mountain Park, the mine, the houses, very nearly the people. So that his occasional visits might be pleasant, he kept a manor house with servants; it stood across the tracks from the nearby town of Luscar, up on a hillside. Then he closed his mines, the towns began to disappear, and one day, so the story goes, a bulldozer rumbled out of nowhere and drove straight through the manor house, before so much as a cup or saucer or a stick of furniture could be removed.

Peter was beginning to feel on familiar ground. "That hill over there was called Miners' Roof. At four in the afternoon, up we came, one hundred men in black clothes; over a wooden bridge we walked, and up that hill to our homes."

"Company houses," Mike said to the old man. "Nobody worried about the quack grass in those lawns."

"Where was our house?" Peter asked suddenly.

"Right there." Mike pointed.

"Where?"

"By that rock. Where that big rock is."

We had brought along bread and homemade sausage (*kobasa*) and a bucket of ice and beer, intending to have lunch. It was now well into the afternoon, and we went to open the trunk of the car.

"No," the old man said. And he was boss again. "Let's drive out over that trail." He indicated a trail that went winding up over a hill. "There's a pond back in there where they tried strip mining – "

We drove out past a new beaver dam, out over what passed for a bridge, and came to an ugly gash in the earth. It was partly filled with water. We jumped across the creek that fed the pond and found a sheltered spot against a cutbank, out of the raw wind. Lorne produced a hunting knife and with it opened the beers and sliced the bread and the *kobasa*.

Three hunters were camped beside the pond. They had shot an elk, and only recently two of them had packed it out two miles from up in the mountains. They'd cut it up to put it in cold water so it wouldn't spoil while they went on hunting, and their thighs and for some reason the windshield of their camper-truck were smeared with fresh blood. One of them noticed we had no guns and asked what we were up to.

One of us, casually, answered that we'd come out to look at the old town.

The three hunters looked at each other. "Old town?"

Mr. Pavich pointed. "Mountain Park."

There was a moment of silence.

"We thought," Lorne interrupted, "we might try our luck at fishing."

Now the hunters nodded. "ll tell you," one of them said. 'I got twenty trout in that pond this morning."

We finished our meal and started back. And we did plan to try our luck at fishing. We talked about the bull trout in Flapjack Lake. But we passed up stream after stream, finally stopping at a good-sized river. I believe it was the Embarras; an old man was cleaning a dozen rainbows while his wife, in their little camper-truck, set a frying pan to heating.

We found a cliff and a pool below it, and Lorne and Mike, balanced on slippery rocks, were able to cast neatly into the dark pool. But Mike wasn't thinking of fishing. "You know," he was still remembering, "when we saw a column of dust above the road below town, we knew a car was coming up to Mountain Park. That week was made for us."

Peter Pavich had found one last bottle of beer. "They say," he told us for the third time, "the Japs are short of coal. They're thinking of opening up the mines at Luscar again."

We had been unable to visit the promising town of Luscar because the road was completely washed out.

In an Alberta that boasts of its sixteen species of fighting game fish, Lorne hooked onto one small trout, and only by his deft skill did he manage to give the impression that it put up any kind of resistance. Mike hooked a willow.

We gave the maggots to a man who planned on getting up at five the next morning; we put our one fish on the ice that had cooled our beer and all climbed into the car, and we drove back to the Pavich home. We joked about Lorne's trout. "Have you got a cat?" someone asked. "How many like that would it take to fill a sardine can?"

Mrs. Pavich did not ask any questions about our trip. Mike's wife, the daughter of a Welsh coalminer-preacher who had carried damnation and salvation deep under the earth to tough men who, in turn, gave him their respect, made us a pot of coffee. Mary Pavich was back from her berry-picking party.

Mary, from growing up in the Branch and travelling, has learned six languages, and we got into a discussion of a major novel which (I suspect) only she had read. Everyone joined in, arguing stoutly, meanwhile doing justice to a plate of cold chicken that Mrs. Pavich had prepared, for she had witnessed the departure of other fishing expeditions. While Lorne argued for the triumph of love over the evils of the world, Mary cleaned some berries; and then we continued our debate over heaping bowls of huckleberries and sugar and fresh cream.

"Where," I happened to ask Mary in the middle of the discussion, "did you find berries the size of these?"

Mary glanced toward her mother, then lowered her voice. "Mike's wife and I – a bunch of us drove down to the Coal Branch for the day."

As I say, I have not travelled the Trunk Road all the way down to the Crowsnest Pass. People who have tell me that, going south from the Coal Branch, you must be sure to see the falls on the South Ram River. You must experience the drive over Corkscrew Mountain, both for its switchbacks and for its view of the valley of the Clearwater River. You must go over Highwood Pass at a height of 7,234 feet, to a startling view of Kananaskis Lake. The driver who rates himself as excellent can drive to the top of Plateau Mountain, at a height of eight-two hundred feet, an alpine plateau from which he can view five prairie towns. And he can use any film he may still have at either the Livingstone Falls or the famous gap in the Livingstone Mountains where the Oldman River drops through a gorge on its way from the mountains to the foothills.

I have driven north quite a few miles from Coleman in the Crowsnest Pass toward Highway One, and the Trunk Road there is a ride into a silence made more intense by the sudden chatter of a squirrel, the song of a bird; it is a memorable ride into a world of Lodgepole pine, of distant snow, and of vanished loggers, where new growth springs rank and green against the age-old insistence of rock.

3. BLACKFOOT COUNTRY: TO MEET THE CHINOOK

Characteristically, the chinook occurs as a westerly or southwesterly wind and is brought about by subsidence east of the western mountain ranges of maritime polar air from the Pacific. This air is cooled adiabatically at the saturated lapse-rate in its ascent over the mountains but in its descent to the plains it is warmed again adiabatically at the dry lapse-rate which is twice the cooling rate of the ascent. Consequently this air reaches the foothills at a much higher temperature than it had at a corresponding level on the western slopes. The chinook is most striking when it occurs following a cold wave that has been accompanied by snow. The sky clears abruptly and temperatures may rise as much as 60°F. in a relatively short time.

– *The Climate of Canada* (The Queen's Printer, Ottawa)

The wind gets fairly strong out here. For instance, you can always recognize an old fence: the barbs on the barbed wire all point one way. I
remember the time I stopped at a little service station out in the
Hanna district. "Man," I said, to make conversation, "the wind is blowing." An old gent sitting on an up-ended apple box looked me over,
though he could hardly see me for blowing dust. "You call this a wind?"
he said. "which road did you come in on?" "Just came down from
Edmonton," I explained. He nodded: "You notice that water tower out
there by the school corner?" "I did," I said. He nodded again. "That
used to be our well."

A stranger has to make certain adjustments. A greenhorn visiting
in Brocket wasn't watching, and his hat blew away. An Indian saw him
chasing it and told him not to bother. "Don't worry," the Indian said.
"In a couple of days the wind will shift. You can catch one your size
coming up from Montana."

But it's the chinook wind especially that leads even the local
people to make the occasional comment. In fact, twice each winter in
Alberta you hear about this fellow: "He was in town with a team of
horses and a sleigh, see, when he noticed the chinook arch in the west.
He left his groceries on the storekeeper's counter, ran for his team, and
struck out at a full gallop for home. Well sir, you'll hardly believe it, but
that chinook was so hot on his heels and blowing so hard that for
eleven and a quarter miles of correction line road he drove with his
front runners in heavy snow and his back runners kicking up dust."

When the chinook blows in southern Alberta, winter turns to
spring; the mere truth starts to grow and blossom a little. But it does
break a cold wave in a matter of hours, melting the January snow, lifting a freezing temperature up to 65 degrees Fahrenheit and droopy spirits a little higher. It means the cattle can graze again in the fields, a
man can turn off the heater in his car. It means that Calgary and
Lethbridge and Medicine Hat are oases for retired couples and wintering construction men.

Sometimes, however, the wind is only warm enough to melt the surface of the snow; it freezes again, forming a crust, and the cattle can't break through to the grass beneath. Sometimes it comes too late. After the blizzard of '51 the temperature in the Cypress Hills plunged to 42 degrees below. When the chinook finally blew, a hand on the Black Eagle Ranch rode out to check the stock. He came upon nineteen deer and antelope humped dead in a coulee. In April and May of '67, three late snowstorms hit the land while cattlemen watched in vain for the telltale arch of open sky beneath the clouds on the western horizon; thirty thousand head of cattle perished, mostly spring calves. And sometimes the chinook wind blows dry and hot in the summertime. Ask a farmer why he's ploughing his crop under in the middle of July. "That damn wind cooked her."

THE DINOSAUR ROUTE TO MEDICINE HAT

The Calgary Stampede is a ritual release from middle-class bondage for all the prospering region that is southern Alberta. Sociologists have found that city folk, and the well-to-do especially, put on high-heeled boots, tall hats, tight denims, western shirts that cost enough to outfit a genuine cowboy – and with a friendly "Howdy, pardner" they begin to unbend. Banks become stockades, flapjack breakfast is free at the tail end of a chuckwagon, square-dancers jostle in the streets of the financial district, and bars just plain bust loose.

Harley Youngberg and I decided the Stampede would be a fine place to begin a tour of the dry short-grass country. We were, to begin with, a little blasé; after all, any Alberta boy grows up attending local stampedes, where the best of the circuit riders drive or fly in to compete for top money – roping calves, decorating steers, milking wild cows, riding broncos and Brahma bulls. We had sung Wilf Carter's song about Pete Knight, the king of all cowboys: "He was born in Crossfield, Alberta, just a little cowtown in the west. . . ." We had seen pictures of Pete Knight under his big black hat, had heard the details of his heroic ride on Midnight. And we knew the story of his death under the hoofs of an outlaw horse named Sundown. But I had never seen the chutes and corrals where he won his first fame.

We arrived in Calgary in the early evening. Chuckwagon racing is a sport that originated in Calgary, and since the first race in 1923 it has been dominated by Alberta rigs. I went to see my first race; and twenty minutes after we found our seats in the huge grandstand I was beginning to understand why Romans liked chariots. Or to put it another way, mere horse races will never be quite what they were, pari-mutuel or no pari-mutuel.

Each outfit is made up of a wagon, a driver, a matched four-horse team of thoroughbreds, and four outriders on equally handsome horses.

The race begins in the infield of a racetrack. At the crack of a gun, the outriders load a stove and tent poles into the wagon, then mount their own horses while each driver swings his team in a figure eight around two barrels: and in a dramatic moment that lifts twenty-five thousand people out of their seats, four teams with their wagons converge, galloping, on a single point inside the rail of the racetrack. Then, death and destruction somehow averted (only one man to my knowledge has been killed in these races), thirty-two magnificent horses streak out of the apparent chaos and take the first turn.

As the teams go around the far side of the track, the drivers, envied and admired, become studies in concentration; each is hunched, tense at his reins, leaning forward to his four galloping horses, driving hard for position and the stakes that go with victory. And then in a dramatic finish, thirty-two horses break into the home stretch, outriders fighting for position near their wagons, the crowd roaring its partisanship, the lead teams coming neck and neck in one last fury to win.

In southern Alberta these races are broadcast the way hockey games are broadcast elsewhere. Teams and drivers are the subject of intense discussion. And a winning driver has to be able to avoid knocking over a barrel, keep a cook-stove on his rig, and have his outriders with him when he comes out ahead at the finish line – one minute and something under a dozen seconds after he let slack into his reins.

Meanwhile, inside the track, ten to fifteen waiting teams either circle at a slow trot or stand motionless in a thin cloud of dust, suggesting, by perfect contrast, the open prairie and the roundup and Indian raids. And near the bucking chutes, which won't be used until next afternoon, the cowboys sit on the fences, smoking and talking. The Blackfoot and Blood and Sarcee from miles around note the good and bad points of a passing horse or victorious driver.

After the races you can do what we did – listen to the barkers on the midway, eat pie in a Mormon tent, bet a dollar at crown and anchor, or simply watch the thousands of people intent on being happy-go-lucky cowpunchers. Or dudes.

But we had gone to Calgary to begin a drive east on the Trans-Canada Highway. Next morning the road was crowded with cars and trailers streaming into Calgary's already thronged streets.

We drove out past Lake Chestermere, where a few people were finding time to sail, and when we got to the intersection with Highway 9, deciding on an impulse to escape into the prehistoric past, we swung north and then east to go to Drumheller.

Drumheller is an old coal-mining city of thirty-five hundred people on the Red Deer River. We drove many miles through flat rich farmland, until suddenly we saw on our left Horse Shoe Canyon: our first glimpse of the Alberta Badlands.

The approach – I should say, descent – into Drumheller is an appropriate one for dinosaur country. The road leads down from the green wheatfields into an eroded sun-baked valley that is out of another epoch: that epoch lasting 130 million years during which those extinct reptiles, the dinosaurs, ruled the earth.

Fortunately, one of the best museums in Alberta is to be found in the centre of the city: the Drumheller Dinosaur and Fossil Museum. As many as two thousand visitors a day come to see among the rich variety of displays the thirty-foot skeleton of *Edmontosaurus*, the duck-billed dinosaur. Or the unique eight hundred pound skull of *Pachyrhinosaurus*. Or the fossilized seeds of prehistoric ginkgo trees (they grow today in China). Or the skeleton of an Ice Age bison that died eleven thousand years ago near what is now the town of Taber, and was found with a chipped stone embedded in its brain case – put there by a hunter as the last ice sheet retreated.

One of the most impressive displays is a recently discovered footprint of a dinosaur that did its walking seventy-five million years ago. It was my pleasure to meet the young Albertan who, with his father, made the discovery.

Allan Jensen, who grew up on a nearby farm, at twenty-five has already had a brilliant career as a schoolteacher. Now he has returned to the University of Calgary to do further work in the fine arts. As an artist he works in oils, plastics, ceramics, and graphics, all the while acknowledging that Alberta audiences are not only indifferent, but hostile, to modern art. "Do you argue with people?" I asked him. "I paint," he replied. And he paints so well that his was the first student work ever purchased by the University of Calgary.

But Allan is also a student of paleozoology, and his work has been much influenced by the connection he finds between the fine arts and the natural sciences: the overriding and persistent themes of life and death.

Allan had gone into the Badlands the previous day to meet a group of visiting students. Somehow missing them in the craterlike landscape, he was left by himself with only a camera and his curiosity about the past.

He rubbed his reddish-blond beard in an attempt at modest indifference as he brought out the boxful of specimens he had found in a few hours. Among the thirty pieces were fossilized sequoia cones, an ironstone cast of a snail, a seed, a gizzard stone (dinosaurs had gizzards), vertebrae from a hadrosaur, a tooth from a gorgosaurus, a leg joint from a birdlike dinosaur, and a toe bone which he had yet to identify.

For the rank amateur like myself, I can recommend a tour of the air-conditioned museum under the informed guidance of Mrs. Jessie Robertson. Years ago, when the Badlands were regarded simply as a mistake in the plans for creation, her husband, a mining engineer, insisted on going for drives and showing her various geological formations. "Watch your driving," was her usual response on the steep grades and hairpin curves. But today, having finally caught the bug herself, she is at eighty a student of this strange region that runs for 150 miles along the Red Deer River.

Finding our way out of the museum through a forest of petrified sequoia stumps, Harley and I drove along "The Dinosaur Trail."

A drive along this road on a hot day with a dry wind blowing is a lesson in human survival. But the rewards are many indeed: a coal mine, oil wells pumping, a homestead museum built by twelve local farmers, a church that seats six people, fields of rape and wheat, and a startling sequence of views of the Badlands. The drive includes a ferry ride across the Red Deer River, which proved unnerving in an unlikely way. One of Alberta's ferry-ride collectors was talking to the ferryman, who in turn nodded to me when he saw I was attempting to eavesdrop. "Keeping you busy?" I said. "Busier than hell," he replied. And I got the impression we were crossing the river Styx.

A short distance off the drive is Horse Thief Canyon, the site of Alberta's oyster beds; all the oysters are fossilized, but still worth picking up. And a short drive east will take you to Munson, a small town that is in the sad process of joining the dinosaurs in oblivion.

Harley and I passed up the swinging bridge and the hoodoos south of Drumheller; back on Highway One, we quickly found ourselves driving into Blackfoot country.

Today the tribes of the once proud Blackfoot Confederacy live on three principal reservations: the Blackfoot at Gleichen, the Peigan at Brocket, and the Blood at Cardston. Highway One, east from Gleichen, drops slowly but insistently, the plateau a pattern of wheat and summer fallow and pasture for miles, the sky conspicuously empty of clouds. At Cluny we turned south to see Blackfoot Crossing on the Bow River.

Here we found green but drying hills, which overlooked a wooded river bottom. Half a dozen little Indian houses were scattered about the prairies in the river flats. Far across the valley, grain elevators reminded us that here the white settlers replaced one of North America's greatest hunting societies.

The plains Indians of Alberta obtained horses by the year 1730, or shortly thereafter. The Blackfoot already had an elaborate culture;

the introduction of the "big dog" led to the flowering of that culture. They could move larger teepees on the horse travois. They could cover larger areas. And following the herds of millions of buffalo the skilled horsemen could easily provide a generous living in less than a forty-hour week, leaving much leisure time for crafts and ceremonies and war. The Blood and Sarcee and Peigan joined the Blackfoot Confederacy and for 150 years a plains civilization flourished in what is now Alberta, a civilization based on the buffalo herds, on horse-raiding parties, and especially on the Sun-Dance. This last, a complicated rite that required a number of days for its performance, was essentially a ceremony of rebirth. Profoundly religious in its meaning, the dance involved fasting and prayer, sacrifice and feast, and the services of priests who were in possession of special knowledge. It was part of the religion of a warrior society, however, and received unfortunate publicity because the dancers sometimes vowed to undergo self-inflicted torture. The priest, or medicine man, using a knife or awl, inserted two wooden skewers in the breasts of the warrior, just above the nipples. The skewers were then attached to the free end of a lariat that was, in turn, attached to the tall centre-pole in the Sun-Dance lodge. The dancer thus fastened could either dance until he tore free or attempt to jerk himself free at once. Endurance and purity and self-control were the characteristics of a good hunter and raider.

But with the horse had come the rifle, and the rifle spelled near extinction for the buffalo that was the basis of this flourishing society. White traders, seeking meat and then hides, hastened the process: Anthony Henday of the Hudson's Bay Company, entering the future province of Alberta in September of 1754, had smoked the peace pipe with a band of Blackfoot whose settlement numbered 322 teepees.

In September of 1877 the Blackfoot nation, under their great leader Crowfoot, assembled at Blackfoot Crossing on the Bow River. The Indians numbered 4,392; their horses and ponies numbered 15,000. A handful of white men led by the "Queen's Chief" presented a document called Treaty No. 7. "The plains are large and wide," Crowfoot replied. "We are the children of the plains, it is our home, and the buffalo have been our food always." But after the rhetoric, the chiefs began to make X's by their names: Crowfoot, Old Sun, Bull Head, Red Crow, Medicine Calf, Many Spotted Horses, Sitting on an Eagle Tail....

The plains Indians surrendered fifty thousand square miles to the invading white men on the understanding that a better future awaited them. In the months that followed the signing, more than six hundred Blackfoot died of starvation. In the year 1967, a child died of malnutrition on an Indian reserve in southern Alberta.

Harley and I walked the mile from a government cairn to Chief Crowfoot's grave, and that walk is an intimate introduction to the short-grass country: to the prairie wool, to the gentle odour of pasture sage and the leathery wolf willow with its sweet-tasting underbark. Wild flowers were everywhere in blossom. Inside the graveyard the artificial flowers were heaped gaudily on a row of new graves, while around them the prairie flowers, small and hugging the wind-swept earth, bloomed in abundance: wild roses, milk vetch, lupine, showy sunflower, the orange-red blossoms of scarlet mallow, the beautiful great-flowered gaillardia with its purple-brown bull's-eye – and a confusion of yellow blossoms that to me remain nameless.

The process of naming is hardly begun in Alberta. We who live here so often cannot name the flowers, the stones, the places, the events, the emotions of our landscape; they await the kind of naming that is the poetic act. One cannot help but admire a novelist like W.O. Mitchell who set out heroically to record prairie life, its sadness and its comedy.

Beyond the new graves, too many of them, are older graves with such evocative names upon them as Ruth White Pup, Annie Yellowoldwomen, Haughton Running Rabbit, Jim Big Eye, John Yellow Sun, Benedict Prairie Chicken, and Noella Bearhat (ASLEEP IN JESUS).

And there at the valley's edge stands an iron fence with buck-brush near by, and inside the black fence a grave and the inscription:

CHIEF CROWFOOT
Died Apr 25 1890
Aged 69 yrs (sic)

With Chief Crowfoot died the old West. Near his grave is a marker showing the site of Crowfoot's last camping place and the provocative inscription: "Where he pitched off for the last time in sight of the Blackfoot Crossing."

Chief Crowfoot was born around 1826, his father a Blackfoot chief, his mother a Blood Indian named Writing Woman. Destined to survive nineteen battles and six wounds, he nevertheless was to become renowned for preaching peace. In 1866 he rescued Father Lacombe from a band of scalp-seeking Cree. When Sitting Bull came into Canada after annihilating General Custer's troops, Crowfoot refused to join him in further battles. And it was Crowfoot who would not let his tribe join in the Riel Rebellion of 1885, even when his adopted son, the brilliant Cree chief Poundmaker, tried to persuade him to do so. The sixth Legislative Assembly of the Northwest Territories voted Crowfoot a gift of fifty dollars in recognition of his commendable loyalty.

The past, near and distant, had captured us. Harley and I, approaching the town of Brooks, decided once again to depart from Highway 1. Driving east and north over a gravelled road, through prosperous irrigation areas where the ditches flowed with water and the hay stood so thick it seemed we could walk on it, out onto bald prairie that was not irrigated, we came to Dinosaur Provincial Park.

The view here is better than in the Drumheller Badlands. Approaching the valley, the visitor is suddenly able to look out a distance of eight miles from rimrock to rimrock. Before him is a work of op art: the grey and brown and green of the eroded Badlands create an optical illusion that is dizzying.

The pinnacles and hoodoos make vertical lines, along with the infinite rills – depressions made in the steep hillsides by running rainwater. The horizontal lines are made by cemented sandstones, unconsolidated sandstones, bentonite shales, and ironstone concretions. The mushroom shape of a hoodoo combines both, for its startling height results when softer rock weathers away from beneath a layer of cemented sandstone. Erosion occurs so rapidly here that little vegetation can become established on the hillsides; because there is little vegetation, the hillsides erode rapidly. Mute testimony to this is the alluvial fan at the foot of each hill.

The Badlands began to form as the Wisconsin Glacier retreated, for the meltwater cut coulees into the earth.

Today the forces of erosion have cut down to strata that were laid down some seventy million years ago. One hundred and twenty dinosaur skeletons for the museums of the world have been excavated from these Badlands; or, to put it more scientifically, from the "Old Man beds of the Belly River formation, Cretaceous Period, in the Mesozoic Era."

At one time here, eleven species of duck-billed dinosaurs were at home in the high swamp-grass, the lagoons and the bayous; the tide came and went from the nearby ocean; the higher lands were lush with palms, sycamores, redwoods, fig trees, and magnolias. Dinosaurs, horned, armoured, and carnivorous, dwelt secure in the permanence of their kingdom. "My name is Ozymandias, king of kings. . . ."

Now sixteen kinds of wild animals including pronghorn antelope, deer, badgers, beavers, coyotes, and lynx live in this dry valley of bones. A glimpse of antelope is especially worthwhile; but these creatures have telescopic eyesight and will probably see you first; and having seen you they can run at speeds up to forty-five miles per hour.

We did see a horned lark, and hear it singing; birds of the plains, unlike birds of the forest, often sing while in flight. There is a heronry on the river here; I had hoped to see a great blue heron perched in its unlikely fashion on one of the twisted poplars that grow along the river. And I am told that the really fortunate might see a rare turkey vulture circling high above this land, riding an air current on outspread wings, watching for carrion.

The valley and its hills are a study in juniper, in sagebrush and prickly-pear cactus. The campground in a grove of cottonwoods by Little Sandhill Creek is lovely and exotic; an invitation to stay in this bizarre world for a while.

Here also are four of the most fascinating museum displays in Alberta: buildings have been erected over dinosaur skeletons where they were uncovered in cold rock. Dr. C. H. Sternberg, an internationally famous paleontologist, did most of the recovery work; three duck-billed dinosaurs and the scattered skeleton of a horned dinosaur are on display in a wilderness of hills and coulees.

Before tourists heard of this mysterious valley, the famous Negro cowboy John Ware had established a ranch here. A freed slave from a cotton plantation in South Carolina, he could neither read nor write, for he began working in the fields at the age of eight. Yet he came to run a thousand head of cattle on the Red Deer River.

He was a man of astonishing strength, and a man of legendary honesty, friendliness, and loyalty in a land where those virtues are almost taken for granted. Mr. Grant MacEwan, in his delightful book *John Ware's Cow Country*, tells us that when in 1905 a horse stumbled and fell on Ware, killing him instantly, the news set hundreds of people to weeping.

It was late when Harley and I left the park. We decided to take a short cut to Medicine Hat, driving west and then south from Patricia. We were low on gas; after an hour of driving during which we saw nothing but herds of cattle that looked like specks on the huge fields, we came to a texas gate. We crossed it, perplexed, and drove on, only to come to a barbed-wire gate that we very nearly hit, because darkness had fallen and the gate was almost impossible to see.

We decided we were lost. The sandwich we'd picked up somewhere for lunch was not proving to be very fortifying. Fortunately, we had noticed a small ranch a few miles back, so we turned around and drove toward the solitary speck of light in a darkness that was unearthly in its absoluteness. A gruff old man came to the door when we knocked. He wore no shirt, but had wide suspenders over the tops of his long-sleeved underwear. Behind us a windmill was creaking in the silence. "Where are we?" Harley asked. "On my damned ranch," the rancher replied. Harley squirmed out of that one by explaining our predicament; the rancher broke into a hearty laugh and ducked his head back into the kitchen, to make sure his wife was in on the joke. We were damned fools, he assured us, for not knowing that the spring snowstorms had created such floods that the roads were washed out. The only way to Medicine Hat was via the roads through a number of ranches. "For God's sake," he told us, "when you come to a gate, open it."

We did – again and again. And by the time our gasoline tank read empty we were driving into Medicine Hat.

The name itself is enough to make a visitor stop. The Chamber of Commerce, in the interests of order and simplicity, explains that during a great battle between the Cree and the Blackfoot a Cree medicine man lost his headdress while fleeing across the river to safety. The Cree were consequently massacred; the site of the tragedy was then called *saamis* or "medicine man's hat."

But another version connects the origin of the name with an attack on a party of white settlers: the Indian medicine man appropriated a fancy hat worn by one of the victims. Still another insists that the name derives from a hill east of the city that resembles the hat of a medicine man – assuming you know what that's like. A fourth theory insists that an Indian brave heroically rescued a squaw from the South Saskatchewan; the medicine man, in admiration, placed his own hat on the brave brave's head. Or – and I like this one – the locality got its name when a chief saw, in a vision, an Indian rise out of the river wearing the plumed hat of a medicine man.

I met two men who, for me, typify this region. Each of them, as we began talking, used the expression "This is big country." Gareth Jones and Claude Hassard are close friends, for both dearly love this dry, open ranching country where a rancher has to have from fifty to sixty acres per head of cattle. The Ross Ranch, incidentally, has 270,000 acres.

Gareth came from Wales, first to do graduate work at the University of Toronto, then to travel west. Discovering the big country and his liking for it, he earned his Ph.D. at the University of Alberta: today he is a geophysicist with the Defence Research Board.

A handsome bachelor, he lives in Medicine Hat in a big house surrounded by gardens and overlooking the South Saskatchewan River. Recently he brought his parents from Wales to live with him, and in the process he brought along three tons of antique furniture from his ancestral home. In the tradition of the British amateurs who first travelled in the West, he loves objects and distance. A passionate collector, he has a gun collection that includes a King's Improvement Winchester .45-75 that was probably used in the Riel Rebellion of 1885. His gun room is decorated with Indian artifacts and such prairie items as the skins of a bullsnake and a rattlesnake – indeed, he will pay five dollars a foot for any local rattler that is over six feet long. He collects Chinese jades, and his spacious library is full of old books and old furniture.

When not at home with his collections, Gareth is out exploring or hunting. He has driven as many as thirty-five thousand miles in one year, going as far west as the Kananaskis to look for elk and bear. But mostly he travels around on the local ranches, and he is proud of the fact that one day he drove 140 miles on one ranch without crossing a road. "There's good country down here: a hundred miles without a gas station." He is a man who openly dislikes big cities. In spite of his hard-headed financial awareness, in spite of recognizing that the safest way to start ranching is to inherit a ranch, he has a hankering for that way of life that overrules his statistics, and as a beginning has bought into a small herd of Columbia sheep. He is already enough of a rancher to be worried that Canadians won't take on the hard life of sheep-herding; you have to import a Basque herder from France.

It was Gareth who drove me out to, and around, the Cypress Hills, covering 150 miles in the course of our peek at the country. We took the Eagle Butte road rather than the paved highway, for it is more picturesque, going up past the busy United Brethren Church, over Bullshead Creek, and out past a lovely old deserted Anglican church with its tiny graveyard. In a distance of twenty miles the car climbed two thousand feet.

During the ride we saw partridge, marsh hawks, and antelope – but most important for me, we met the rancher, Claude Hassard. He put his hand on the hood of the car: in the old days, he explained, when a man in Medicine Hat bought a car he drove it up into the Cypress Hills. "If it didn't boil you had a dandy."

Old Claude Hassard came into this country from Saskatchewan well ahead of automobiles, at a time when a cowhand was lucky if he slept three months of the year in a genuine bed. Claude lived on the bald-headed prairie: the delicacy of the week was a cow's head wrapped in its own hide and baked for hours in a pit full of hot stones and glowing coals. Out riding, a man carried a pocketful of jerky, which served to keep your belly full, but "You could get awful damned thirsty." Water was sometimes thirty miles away. Claude and the other hands slept on the open prairie where they worked; he said he put down a hair rope each night around his blankets to keep away the rattlesnakes. "Did it work?" I asked him. "They never got into bed with me," he answered.

We were sitting in the small, plain, comfortable kitchen of his ranch house; Claude is now a widower. He poured us more coffee. "Good coffee," someone said. "It'll be good," he answered, "until I start adding water to make it go around." Then he commented, "Coffee's got to sit awhile."

One spring, on a ranch south of the Hills, he and one of the Mitchell boys from High River were assigned the task of riding five hundred saddlehorses to get them ready for the season's work. Some had never been ridden. Some simply hadn't been ridden since the previous fall. Not only did the boys do their work, but they took to riding broncos as a sport. On Christmas afternoon in 1911, Claude Hassard, in Medicine Hat, rode Scarhead – the horse that Tom Three Persons was to ride the next year in Calgary to become the first world's-champion bronc-rider. "Did you fellows organize your own rodeo?" I asked. "No," I was told, "some bastard with a few dollars got the competition going. And those days," Claude went on to explain, "there was no ten-second limit to a ride. There were no pickup riders. You rode out on a bronc – and you had to come back on that son of a bitch."

Claude refused a tailor-made cigarette; he rolled his own. With his gentle voice and colourful language he talked of trails and landmarks and water holes. He remembered a Mexican who roped elk with an eighty-foot rawhide lariat. He remembered selling butter to Tommy Tweed's old man in Medicine Hat – interrupting himself to explain that this is now Hereford country, because Herefords winter better. He told of roping two hundred wild horses with the hope of selling them to the Italian government during the First World War. "We never got them sold, but we had a lot of fun." He told of a friend of his getting a letter from a new museum, asking for a famous bridle and set of spurs. The old man wrote back saying he might still need them himself. History is that way in Alberta. He remembered men who ran whisky overland across the border during American Prohibition – and like most of the old-timers, he was pretty sure a lot of whisky is still cached in these hills.

And inevitably the talk turned to brands. "I know every iron in this country," Claude said. His own is the Ten Half Diamond.

In this country you don't ask of a man, "How big is his ranch?" You ask, "How many calves does he brand?" That's what matters.

It was early in July and branding time when we were there. A group of ranchers take turns meeting on one another's ranches. They start riding at three in the morning, branding at six. When all goes perfectly they expect to have a calf a minute on the branding table. The trick is to "heel" a calf – to throw a lariat in front of a calf so that the rope hits the calf's belly causing the calf to jump and catch its hind legs in the loop. One minute later it will be branded, vaccinated, and, if necessary, dehorned and castrated.

But the talk of branding made Claude remember the last big round-up. In 1908, as he recalled, seven or eight wagons went out, each wagon with 100 to 125 horses and 7 or 8 men. "Baldy Buck, a breed, was the big boss. . . ."

Other sources say that the bad winter of 1906-07 made 1907 the year of the last big round-up. Cattle were scattered by blizzards from the Cypress Hills to the Kootenay foothills, from Montana to the Big Bow. Something like 130,000 head of range cattle had to be accounted for, and Baldy Buck began the job with eight outfits and over a hundred riders. Beginning from Lethbridge, his riders had to sweep as far east as the Saskatchewan border.

Today around the Cypress Hills the talk is as much of tourists as it is of round-up. For now a conflict is developing over water rights and leased grazing lands. The ranchers want to run cattle on the bench in the park. The city folk want more open space in which to escape from the cities they have created. And surely Cypress Hills Provincial Park, that low hump of blue hills to the south of the Trans-Canada, is something unique and beautiful.

The countryside around Medicine Hat is, for me, lacking in definition. To appreciate the stern beauty of this ranching country, you should drive into the park and even south of it a few miles on Highway 48. In that wide open land of long coulees and bare rounded hills you might try to find the town of Thelma that looks so obvious on your map. The only movable town in Canada, I suppose, Thelma is actually in the living room or kitchen of whichever rancher is taking his turn at being postmaster.

We were driving across the prairies. I looked down at the map on my lap. I looked up and we were in a forest.

The Cypress Hills, that suddenly, transform the short-grass plains. No wonder the first whites to get there looked at the lodgepole pine and thought they were seeing cypress trees.

The town of Elkwater on Elkwater Lake is 4,050 feet above sea level. This area of high hills (240 square miles, on the Alberta-Saskatchewan border) is an erosion remnant – once the bottom of a lake, a thick layer of conglomerate rock protected it while the surrounding area was worn away by water and wind and ice.

A great fire burned through the entire Cypress Hills in 1874. Destroyed in the fire was the climax forest of white spruce; only slowly is it recovering its territory from the poplar and lodgepole pine. Also in the nineteenth century, white hunters came through, killing over fifteen hundred elk in one year. By the turn of the century the Cypress Hills elk were extinct.

Fortunately for us, seventy-eight square miles of these hills have become a provincial park, elk have been reintroduced, and it is once again possible to hear an elk (wapiti) bugling from beside a stream. Red squirrels have been introduced; their midden heaps – heaps of pine-cone scales – are easy to find. The wild, or Merriam's, turkey has also been brought into the area, from South Dakota. A hiker can quickly get to a beaver pond: if you played Indian as a child, on this hike you'll have a chance to attempt to identify moose, elk, and deer droppings. And if you enter the forest, trusting to your instincts instead of the trail, you can watch for skunks, porcupines, and the great horned owl, where he sits, silent and motionless, on a branch near the trunk of a tree. I stayed on the trail and settled for a glimpse of a yellow warbler; what we Albertans call the wild canary.

But I was curious to know more about that part of the Hills that escaped the last Ice Age.

"The fossil beds," a ranger explained apologetically, "date back only thirty million years. The dinosaurs were already long extinct." I nodded and waited. "However," he went on, "if you're interested in the fossils of crocodiles, turtles, giant hogs, sabre-tooth tigers, camels, three-toed horses –"

Two little girls came running and squealing up to the ranger. One of them held cupped in her hands a tiny frog. I thanked him for his time and information. He waved me into silence and patiently began to explain that the leopard frog eats only. . . .

Harley and I and our host, all of us disapproving of the commercialization of the resort, went and joined a long queue waiting to get hamburgers, chips, and milk shakes.

The Garden Route to the Crowsnest Pass

Medicine Hat is a small city of tree-lined streets, of sunshine that brings in many retired people from the prairies of both Alberta and Saskatchewan. It has a reputation for producing local characters; it was the birthplace of the internationally known artist-photographer Roloff Beny. Twenty-seven of Alberta's fifty-odd religious groups flourish in the area. The mysteries of Petrified Coulee invite investigation. But late one evening Harley and I persuaded ourselves to leave that valley oasis; we drove up onto the arid plain to turn west on Highway 3, the alternate Trans-Canada route. The Southern Route. Or, as it quickly and unexpectedly became for us, the Garden Route.

The Sweetgrass Mountains in Montana were starkly visible to the south and west of the Cypress Hills. Daylight lingered on, as if reluctant to yield that haunting landscape to darkness. When we came to Seven Persons, it seemed we were entered into the Arctic summer, for the little town, with its few small scattered buildings and its absence of trees, looked like a tundra settlement at midnight in July.

All this changed at the larger town of Bow Island. From Bow Island west to Lethbridge, the parched land had been made rich and luxuriant by the long pipes of the irrigation system and the sprinklers spinning water onto the fields. At Grassy Lake we stopped to look at a field of sugar beets; the old dry-landers would hardly know the scenes of their suffering and defeat. Ideal irrigation country is flat, and this surely is, but in Taber we found the horizon broken by tall trees. Taber also has on its horizon a sugar factory with its huge bins, and everywhere we saw the machinery necessary to the handling of the beets.

Coaldale is a big Mennonite settlement that has thriven on hard work and the assured flow of irrigation waters. From there a four-lane highway took us into Lethbridge, a city of over thirty-seven thousand, which in its size, atmosphere, and location has the makings of the most attractive university town in Alberta. And recently the University of Lethbridge enrolled its first classes.

Reflecting the irrigated countryside for which it is centre, Lethbridge is a city of gardens and parks. Sick's Landscape Garden is a beautiful rock garden surrounded by enough empty (presumably) wooden beer-kegs to give even an Alberta teetotaller a tickle of thirst. Galt Gardens is gracious, a word which can seldom be applied to Alberta's parks, which are more usually impeccable or overwhelming or neglected.

Indian Battle Park, on the Oldman River, marks the site of the last Indian battle fought on the North American continent and, according to tradition, the site of the last taking of a scalp. Inside the park is the reconstructed whisky fort, Fort Whoop-Up.

Lethbridge also has a federal agricultural research station that is second only to the one in Ottawa. But for me, and for thousands of visitors to come, the new garden, the Nikka Yuko Centennial Garden, is the rarest experience in the city.

When the Canadians of Japanese descent were forcibly relocated from the Pacific Coast during the Second World War, many of them came to the irrigation district of Lethbridge. Today they and their descendants number four thousand. Under the guidance of the Japanese architect Dr. Tadashi Kubo, the people of Lethbridge have turned both a disgraceful fact in Canadian history and four acres of flat prairie into a Japanese-Canadian Friendship Garden.

The central pavilion was built in Japan and assembled here by five Japanese carpenters. The basic wood is cypress wood from Taiwan, hand-planed and left natural: a lesson in beauty to Albertans, who love stucco with an uncontrollable passion. On entering the pavilion the visitor takes off his shoes, and the effect is immediate. I watched a big man in a Hawaiian shirt and jeans pull off his cowboy boots: he was transformed into a quietly thoughtful guest. He was then ready to experience the dry garden, also called the garden of meditation.

Appropriately, the dry garden represents the sea. White chipped stones are the ocean, larger stones represent fifteen islands. Odd numbers are lucky, so there must be an odd number of islands. The harsh prairie sun sends sharply etched shadows moving across this abstract creation, and the person who gives himself up to meditating on the sea of stone will see the rock-islands take other shapes and forms.

Each element in the garden is conducive to serenity and peace. The turtle-shaped island represents long life and old age. The five-tiered pagoda represents fire, water, land, wind, and space. This is truly a place where you can expect to find "books in running brooks, sermons in stones. . . ."

But it was finally the human element itself that caught my attention, for my hostess was a tall, gracious, and lovely girl in a *yukata* with a bow at the back; on her feet were a fascinating pair of one-toed white socks.

Miss Mae Senda was born in Raymond, Alberta; her father is now a painter and decorator in Lethbridge. Mae is a student at the Lethbridge Collegiate Institute, and when she graduates she wants to go to university and become an elementary-school teacher. I wanted to talk about Japanese culture; Mae wanted to talk about her school. She and her fellow students want to switch to the semester system, so they can take fewer subjects at a time and concentrate more on a subject. And like so many good students today, she and her classmates have social as well as academic protests to make. They aren't concerned only to wear miniskirts in school. Rather, they are disturbed about the prejudice shown by a few teachers toward a number of Canadian Indian students who have recently enrolled.

Mae teaches gymnastics and swimming in the local Y. Her motivation is social, not religious, for Mae is a Buddhist. The Buddhists in Lethbridge, like their Christian neighbours almost anywhere, have had a disagreement and have broken into two sects. Mae's group is busy building a new church.

Watching her as she moved gently and gracefully about the pavilion, I asked finally about the gymnastics she teaches.

"It's easy," she replied. "Dad is a judo teacher, a fifth dan. My two brothers and my sister and I – the whole family except grandmother and the dog – study judo."

By this time Harley had escaped his absorption in the beautiful tearoom. He came up to us and asked Mae, "Where can we get a cup of tea?"

"You'll have to go downtown I'm afraid," Mae explained.

And after one more moment of rest in the *azumaya*, after one more illegal tap at the huge bronze Friendship Bell, we went downtown to a cool old restaurant for a cup of hot water and a tea bag.

Outside Lethbridge the mountains were blue against the green of the prairie. Along the road to Fort Macleod we saw excellent examples of strip farming, the technique that conserves moisture and keeps soil from drifting on a dry land farm. And then we were driving down the pleasant main street of Fort Macleod.

The North-West Mounted Police under Assistant Commissioner James F. Macleod began building their outpost here in October 1874. Macleod is now the local hero; frankly, I find Jerry Potts, the bowlegged little guide and interpreter, half Scot and half Peigan, more interesting. He picked the site on the Oldman River, knowing the 150 redcoats would need the nearby cottonwoods as building materials and fuel. Winter was near, but so were good winter pastures for the men's horses. And all around them were the deer, elk, buffalo, and antelope that would weigh welcome on a December table. The police, come west to help the Indians survive, needed the buckskin-clad little figure of Jerry Potts for their survival.

West from the Fort museum the rising foothills were quilted blue and pink with great patches of wild lupine and three-flower avens, for in July the vast open prairies are themselves a garden. Brocket, on the Peigan reserve, offers a beautiful view of a deep wooded river valley with the grass-covered foothills beyond. At Lundbreck the strip farms are no more; trees begin to clump the prairie, and the mountains loom directly ahead.

Two miles west of Lundbreck we stopped at the Lundbreck Falls on the Crowsnest River, a river that from here on is somehow gently bucolic as it races down from the mountains. But here it tumbles white and roaring to cut a gorge through solid rock. Someone has crawled out on a ledge to print GOD IS LOVE on the face of a cliff. Beside the falls is a pretty campsite of the kind that dots Alberta, giving campers an intimate experience of every kind of landscape. In the guest book the campers are invited to comment, and some of them have: "Darn cold." "No chipmunks!" "Boss!" "Looks like miniature Niagara Falls." "Gronk." "Never seen it yet." "Très belle." "No pen, no axe." "Marvalus falls." "No toilet paper, you finks."

Driving on, we noticed, just off the road, the fine stonework of abandoned buildings and coking ovens. Farther up, we stopped at a Bible museum and a little church in which at the press of a button we heard a sermon; once a settlement flourished in the open field around the two old wooden buildings. We had entered the coal-mining country of the Crowsnest Pass. Ahead of us a string of old towns sprawled up the narrow valley floor: Bellevue, Hillcrest, Frank, Blairmore, Coleman. On the British Columbia side of the Divide lie Michel and Fernie.

Two mountains dominate the lives in the valley. Near the British Columbia border towers Crowsnest Mountain itself, a great dome or castle of living rock that is always visible and present, as if holding up the sky. Nearer at hand stands Turtle Mountain, a dumb monument to the force of nature.

Today that mountain is simply a "Historical Point of Interest": tourists pull off the road in the rock-filled valley to have their pictures taken by a big sign that gives the details of the Frank Slide. At 4:10 P.M. on 29 April 1903, ninety million tons of limestone, in a hundred seconds, roared down onto the prosperous mining town of Frank. Three thousand two hundred acres were buried to a depth of one hundred feet.

Seventy people died and a legend was born. The names of the dead are hard to find. But many people have heard of the baby girl who was found unhurt on a pile of boulders. Nineteen miners on a night shift were rescued from a flooding mine shaft. And now those tragic hundred seconds seem so distant they've become a joke: "I haven't been so busy – ," or "I haven't seen old so-and-so – ," or "I haven't been up this early – since the Frank Slide."

The Pass, while it contains the odd ranch, the occasional sawmill, is to this day coal-mining country. Harley and I arrived in the evening and tried immediately to find something to eat. The first hotel we went to in Coleman was closed and gone out of business. In the second, an old hotel that hadn't been painted in at least ten years, we met and talked with Walter Biela. And from that old miner with an injured back we heard the kind of stories that characterize this town: stories of strength and stories of fights. There was the fellow who single-handed carried a telephone pole up a mountain to plant a flag and surprise his friends. And one night many years ago, a young Walter Biela and four other miners walked into the Grand Union Hotel and whipped twenty-five loggers. Walter was born here and feels at home on a shabby street that ends with a tipple. We heard stories of train robberies and of an immigrant Italian bootlegger who became the local Robin Hood. But finally old Walter leaned toward us, lowered his voice, and told us he had a secret.

The legend of the Lost Lemon Mine is part of the dream life of this region. Walter himself was once trapped underground for two days and one night with thirty other miners. Men who live this dangerously like to think the stakes are immense.

Two men named Blackjack and Lemon travelled north from Montana in 1870 to prospect for gold. Somewhere north of Coleman and west of what is now the Trunk Road, they found not only placer gold but the mother lode. That night in camp, Lemon stayed awake while their fire died down, seized an axe, and killed his partner where he lay asleep in his blankets.

Unbeknownst to Lemon, two Stoney braves had witnessed both the discovery of gold and the murder. Lemon, half out of his mind at the realization of what he had done, fled south to Montana to confess to a priest whom he knew. The priest, in turn, sent a man named John McDougall to bury the murdered man.

Word of the discovery soon leaked out. And a search was set in motion which to this day has not ended.

It seems that the two Stoney braves went back to their tribe near Morley and told Chief Bearspaw what they'd seen. To keep gold seekers from destroying his people's hunting ground, Bearspaw swore the two young braves to secrecy and sent them back to erase all signs of both the discovery and the grave.

Lemon himself, attempting to lead a party to the mine, simply went raving out of his mind as he approached the vicinity of his crime. John McDougall, on hearing there was gold where he'd buried the corpse, set out to return north; he drank himself to death in the whisky fort called Fort Kipp. Whites next began to offer the Stoney Indians every conceivable bribe to break their silence; to this day not one Stoney, offered cattle or land or money, has yielded up a word of the secret.

Men in the Crowsnest Pass have spent their lives and a lifetime's earnings on the search. Walter Biela, for the price of a beer, was willing to share the knowledge and leads that failure had brought to him. He hinted that the southwest branch of the Castle River might be a good place to begin the quest. He took a long pull on a glass of beer. "Now, listen," he continued. "Do you know where Grizzly Gulch is? . . ."

Harley and I, sworn to secrecy ourselves, next went to a beer parlour in Blairmore where I was supposed to meet two of the best miners in the Pass. They were on holiday and had been fishing all day, but were supposed to come in for a beer that night.

Nick Schlosser and Kenneth Rees are partners: they are contract miners who work together as a team. Nick, Canadian-born, has been underground for twenty-eight of his forty-seven years. At one time five Schlosser brothers worked here; now only Nick remains in the mines. Kenneth Rees, Welsh-born, came to the Pass in 1929 and has spent thirty-eight years as an underground miner. At one time ten Rees brothers, famous as fighters and miners, went underground together. One was killed by a fall of top rock. Only Kenneth now makes his living in a mine.

These men ride two miles underground to work together in a mine where there's so much water that seldom are they able to stay for a whole shift. I asked if they'd ever had an accident. "No," Nick said. "We call a fatality an accident. Close calls are everyday occurrences."

I asked about working conditions and Rees laughed. A neatly dressed man in a suit and tie, square-shouldered, intense, he told me, "Look. I was a Social Crediter under Aberhart. He was progressive. But when the Social Credit began to support the big guy while pretending to help the little man, I had to fall back on the politics of that hero of the Welsh, Aneurin Bevan. Any miner who isn't N.D.P. must be bloody stupid." And then he went on, "I belong to an international union. But I do not believe in an international union where I am dominated by Washington. We need a situation where a Canadian union can be allied to, but not dominated by, the American unions."

Schlosser, a huge man with a soft, gentle voice, had been listening gravely. "Politics, unions," he said. "Communications is what beats us every time. Radio. TV. Every newspaper in Alberta. You goddamned writers." He pushed me another beer.

Next morning Harley and I explored a valley to which economic depression has brought back the sun. In prosperous times, when the coke ovens were working, the clouds of black smoke turned day into night. Greenish-yellow fumes came billowing down the streets to peel the paint off anything a man was foolish enough to put paint on. Back in those days a man, by working a double shift, could make good money. Police and mine operators came in to break up strikes. And for every one hundred thousand tons of coal mined in Alberta, one human life was lost.

In 1910 an explosion of gas, called fire-damp by the Old Country miners, killed thirty-one men in a Bellevue mine. But the greatest disaster in Canada's mining history was shortly to occur only half a mile away.

No. 1 Mine of Hillcrest Collieries, a firm run from Montreal, had been idle for two days for lack of orders. On the day before payday a shift was called to work; happy and joking, groups of miners began riding down the slope to the workings at 7:00 on the morning of 19 June 1914. By 7:30, 236 men were laying new tracks, moving cars with the horses that lived underground, and digging coal.

Barely two hours later an explosion rocked the mountain. The men working above ground first heard a muffled roar, then felt a rumbling of the earth. Both the north and south entrances of the mine, two miles from the occurrence, were shattered. The roof was blown from a cement building at the north entrance. Then a thick black smoke began to pour up from underground.

Charles Ironmonger was thrown from the mine by the force of the explosion; the first man out, he was to die quickly of his injuries. The new north workings were not hit so hard as those in the south; but at best only fifty men were in that new area. In the town of Hillcrest, near by, the blast rocked the little miners' houses and rattled windows. As the womenfolk went to their doors, thirty-some men were staggering up from the north entrance, dazed and blackened and gasping, but alive. One man vaguely remembered leaping over a dead horse. W. Guthro, nearly safe, had his heavy mining boot catch in the frog of a track; he cut the boot from his foot with a pocketknife and stumbled to the entrance before the gas overcame him.

In ten minutes the men outside the south shaft had organized themselves and had ventured a short way down; nearly suffocating, they located a dozen men who were still alive and rushed them to the surface. And they came up from their short descent knowing that at twelve hundred feet below the surface the gas-laden air was surely unbreathable.

The first rescue train, carrying a government team from Blairmore, was on the scene in forty-five minutes – this in a time when engines had to get up steam. And word had gone out to all the coal-mining towns in the province and into British Columbia: rescue trains were starting from Lethbridge and Cranbrook, from Canmore and Fernie. All available doctors and nurses were rushing toward Hillcrest from Pincher Creek, from Passburg and Burmis and Bellevue.

The wives and children from the town gathered quietly on the hillside facing the mine. They did not have long to wait. The experts guessed that fires were burning in the interior of the mine, they knew a second explosion might occur, but masked and determined they went down the slope. And shortly, the coal cars began to come up with a grim regularity, each loaded with bodies wrapped in blankets.

The mine wash house became a morgue. The first fifty-two bodies were not too hard to reach. Forty-two were easily cleaned and laid out; the other ten were badly mangled. Now the womenfolk came into the wash house to walk down the long rows, trying to identify husbands and sons.

Meanwhile, in Montreal, the mining company made an announcement: "We have hopes." The rescue teams worked on toward midnight, and past. One man was found propped against the rib of the mine with his pick in his hands as if ready to begin work: they had to break his arms in order to fold them. By Saturday afternoon, rescue parties reached the point where the explosion was most severe: some bodies were burned crisp, others decapitated. The clothes had been torn

from some. Some men were so cramped and twisted by their death ago-
nies their limbs had to be smashed so they might be properly arranged.
A few quite simply couldn't be assembled.

An old drayman and his team were kept busy all day hauling up
stacks of pine boxes from the railway station. By the Sunday after payday, some 150 bodies had been found and prepared; they were buried
on 21 June in a common grave as sleet and rain and snow fell gustily on
the flowers and the mourning families. The names of the dead were too
many to read aloud. David Murray was killed with his two sons, leaving
a wife and nine children. Thomas Brown left a family of six children,
the oldest aged ten. Mrs. Petrie lost three sons, aged thirty, twenty-four,
and seventeen. . . . On one street in Hillcrest, a short street called
Peaceful Valley, there were thirteen widows.

A second funeral was held in the days that followed, but some of
the bodies were never recovered. At least 189 of the men of Hillcrest
had died. Inadequate ventilation meant that most of the miners were
killed not by the force of the explosion, but by suffocation after. Coal-
mining companies are regarded as being careless of their employees,
and the tradition survived yet another disaster. An inquiry came to the
conclusion that no one was responsible.

I spent two hours wandering through streets that were eerily quiet. I
came to a rock on which children had once smashed empty bottles;
now no children played anywhere. The sheets of plastic nailed over the
windows that faced up the valley and into the wind were faded and
torn. Growing braver, I found in the inevitable coal bins only discarded
tires, a broken toboggan, tin cans. Posters on the boarded-up windows
of an old store said "Vote for Garth Turcott," a quiet young lawyer who
has become the new hero of the Pass. Birds sang undisturbed. Flowers
bloomed around the heaps of ashes: buttercups, delicate bluebells, the
shooting star. A Crowsnester in Edson, Al Catonio, had told me that I
couldn't know the joys of living in the Pass until I'd found one rare

lady's-slipper, or seen a mountain meadow yellow with glacier lilies. In the course of a vain search I hit upon quite another lesson.

The bleak little town of Coleman, rich in history, sprawls shabbily down the Crowsnest Valley. To the south, old mining refuse heaps overlook the town. And to the north, up on a hillside, a vast graveyard overlooks the scene.

When the Pass was prospering, miners came here from almost everywhere that coal is dug. The graveyard now is shockingly huge, the gravestones somehow extravagant, the spruce in the graveyard overwhelmingly large. Inside the gate I found fresh tiger lilies in an empty tin of Ogden's cigarette tobacco. Then I began to walk aimlessly in the pleasant morning, reading at random the names: Smith, Siska, Lardinois, Glendenning, Nimcan, Nahorniak, Fraser, Sudworth, Ewing, Soroff, Peterson, Anderson, D'Appolonia, Cecchini, Nicholas, Aristone, Sullivan, Catonio. . . . Men died young here. The grass grows extravagantly on that mountain hillside. Here were the men from the empty rooming houses, the boarded-up restaurants, the closed hotels. The old stones had weathered, had already become a part of the mountain.

And then, as I was leaving, as I was about to hurry down into the town and find Harley so that we might continue our journey, I hit upon a bright new stone: and the new stone reads simply:

> John Grabowski
> Apr. 24, 1924
> Feb. 28, 1965
> KILLED IN THE MINE

WATERTON LAKES TO THE DINGMAN WELL

The road from Pincher Creek on Highway 3 south through Twin Butte to Waterton Lakes National Park is possibly the most pleasant short drive in Alberta, combining as it does high ranching country, farmland, and mountains with a pioneer town and a resort centre. Harley and I started out simply to get to the southern border of Alberta and turn north; we ended up loafing along, trying to guess how good the upland game-bird hunting might be in the fall. We saw one grouse from a distance and debated as to whether it was ruffed, sharp-tailed, blue, or spruce.

At the gate to the park we found the road crowded with trailers, with boats, with cars bearing licence plates from a dozen different states and provinces.

This park is unique in the national park system for its sudden transition from prairie to mountain; thus it offers, in one small area, the flora and fauna of both. Waterton, with its 105 miles of trails, is great hiking country; since I seem to be a little out of shape each time I arrive, I like to begin by driving out past Lost Horse Creek for a self-guided walking tour from Red Rock Canyon to Blakiston Falls.

Harley and I joined an old gentleman who, while he had no camera with him, was resolved to become a photographer of flowers. Together we quickly identified blue larkspur, Indian paintbrush, wild geranium, and blue-beard tongue. As we moved down the canyon, over Bauerman Brook and into the forest, we came upon western thimble-berry and bear-grass. The wind soughed in the trees. Somewhere near-by, the Clark's nutcracker was giving his loud call. A windfall tree rubbed dryly against a lodgepole pine. The path turned.

Although I had hiked the trail before, the Blakiston Falls came again as a surprise, the meltwater ripping through a magnificent gorge where shrubby cinquefoil grows yellow on the grey-green rock. And facing us stood Mount Blakiston, at 9,347 feet.

This park and Glacier National Park in Montana together con-stitute the Waterton-Glacier International Peace Park. At the time of its formation in 1932 it was the first of its kind in the world. Whether you are simply climbing the Bear's Hump Trail from beside the infor-mation centre or riding out to Hell Roaring Canyon and on up to Crypt Lake at sixty-five hundred feet, Waterton offers an exhausting variety of experiences within its 202.8 square miles. I have never trav-elled the Akamina Highway out to Cameron Lake. But I do know that, after a refreshing hike, it's a pleasure to recover on the boat ride south from the townsite to the head of the lakes.

Highway 5 leaves the park and joins Highway 2 at Cardston, the site of Canada's only Mormon temple. To enter the temple, you must be rec-ommended by your bishop as an L.D.S. (short for members of The Church of Jesus Christ of Latter-Day Saints) in good standing. This restriction is necessary because, inside the temple, members of the Church are engaged in two basic religious activities. They are "doing vicarious work for the dead" – that is, the living may be baptized on behalf of the deceased. One's ancestors who were not L.D.S. can become so, and Church members are encouraged to search the records of the world for the names of ancestors. Further, "marriages there are solem-nized for time and eternity"– the L.D.S. reject the belief that marriage will last only "until death doth thee part."

Visitors are permitted into the attractive nearby chapel and its attached combination auditorium and basketball court. But in my own experience the outside of the temple itself is well worth the stop.

It is square, angular, and earth-bound by comparison with a European cathedral, somehow very much of this continent, a little bit secretive in its use of windows, self-contained to the point of seeming partially a fortress. But these people experienced violent persecution in America in the early nineteenth century, after the angel Moroni first revealed to Joseph Smith, the prophet, on the Hill Cumorah in New York State, the ancient metal plates from which was to be translated the Book of Mormon.

In 1847 they made their heroic trek to Utah. In 1887 a small group of Mormon farmers' wagons crossed over from Montana into the Blackfoot country that was to become the province of Alberta. Brigham Young dreamed of a Mormon community stretching from Canada to Mexico. Charles Ora Card, married to one of Young's forty-seven children, was dispatched as the agent of that dream in Canada; his log home stands today in the town he founded.

These settlers had learned in Utah the importance of irrigation. In 1890 they dug their first ditch in Alberta. With the financial backing of the Galts of Lethbridge, they formed an irrigation company in 1893; in 1898 the church became the chief contractor on fifty miles of canal construction, encouraging its own members to take up land along the canal. In 1903 a Utah family opened a sugar beet factory in Raymond. In 1906 the Church was able to purchase the huge Cochrane Ranch. And it continued to prosper, for today local Church units maintain farms, livestock, canneries, and large thriving ranches in southern Alberta. Such towns as Stirling, Magrath, Hill Spring, Raymond, Picture Butte, and Taber are Mormon towns. Many of them are also irrigation towns, located in sugar beet country. From the impetus given by Mormon settlement, irrigation has gone on to turn many miles of arid land into fruitful farms.

Harley and I, driving along a reservoir that was something like seventeen miles in length, encountered another wedding between religion and irrigation – and the connection is somehow valid, in terms of the lost garden that is so basic to Christian belief.

We visited a Hutterite colony.

Like the Mormons, the Hutterites have known bitter persecution. The major movement of Hutterites into western Canada occurred in 1918 after they were severely persecuted in the United States for being conscientious objectors. Today, in Alberta, the forty-odd colonies are up against the Alberta Communal Property Act, which limits one colony to sixty-four hundred acres of land suitable for cultivation and states that any new colony must be at least forty miles from an established colony. The hostility on the part of other farmers seems to spring from the fact that the Hutterite sect doubles its population every 17.3 years.

Driving into the prosperous colony, we felt at first as though we were going back at least two centuries in time. The white wooden buildings and shade trees made an open square in which children played, the girls barefoot in long skirts and headscarves, the boys in dark baggy pants and shirts and puffed black caps that would be the envy of any hippie or mod. At first we saw no adults. The children and geese stopped in their activities. Then I noticed a bearded old man, dressed in a wide-brimmed black hat and an old black suit and vest, sitting on a bench on a veranda in the shade.

As I joined the old man he motioned me to sit down beside him, then he began busily to turn on his hearing-aid: the first crack in the illusion of the past.

Neither of us was ever to know the other's name, for I tried to exchange introductions before he was tuned in. I explained briefly my curiosity about Hutterite life. "The human being is created to work," the old man assured me; "Wait," he added. He arose and went in at a door at the end of the veranda. I waited, listening to a group of handsome boys who shyly approached me; they spoke alternately in English and in what I learned later is a High German dialect they have preserved since a group of Austrian peasants was first named after its leader, Jacob Hutter, who was executed for his teachings in 1535.

Harley Youngberg, who is a farmer himself, came back from a large garden he'd been looking into; now the old man motioned both of us to join him, and we entered into a large hallway onto which opened four large rooms.

The old man had a room of his own. Its spic-and-span neatness already reflected a society that has a substantial labour supply. A huge bed, a huge storage chest, and a huge chest of drawers were the only pieces of furniture in the usual room, we were to learn shortly. In this man's room there was also a large bookcase full of books beside the bed. He motioned us to chairs at a small table, went to select a handful of books, and sat down himself.

By this time two pretty little girls had followed us into the rooms; very shortly a girl of fifteen found an excuse to pop in, for a look at the strangers. This went on during our entire visit; children in their early teens came into our presence to pick up random objects or perform random tasks and inevitably we found ourselves under the scrutiny of curious blue eyes.

It was late afternoon; the old man had been working all day. His thin, ascetic, and gentle hands were covered with soil, I noticed, as he opened a book. "We have to have rules and regulations," he began to explain. Then he, too, noticed his hands and apologized; he took off his old black hat and placed it on the sill of an open window; he found a comb inside his plentiful clothing, combed his grey hair forward, parted it, and combed it back all without a mirror, for there were none to be seen anywhere in the colony. We returned to his philosophizing.

Community life and religious life are one to a Hutterite, he told us. He explained briefly in his precise English how the sect came to be divided into three factions. But in all the factions, he continued, property is held in common and work is carried out collectively under the direction of a boss. Social stratification and government are kept to a minimum. And he handed me a psychological study that found in this religious group an exceptionally low incidence of mental disorders or crime. "Work," he began to elaborate. . . . And he offered to show us the colony.

As I followed him I again banged my head on a door frame, for at least half the doors in the colony seemed to be under six feet. Across from his own room was that of his wife. She unlocked the room for us. Their children are grown. In the third room in that building slept another man, this time with his wife, and with a crib at the foot of the bed for a baby. In the fourth room slept my host's only unmarried child and the two older children of the second family.

The colony, the old man remarked, is composed of twenty families, or 118 souls.

The adults – all those from the age of fifteen up – have their own dining hall. Along one side sit the women, along the other sit the men. These people make up the working population of the colony. Four or five women were setting the two long tables when we peeked in.

The children aged seven to fourteen have a separate dining hall. They were eating when we looked in on them; a remarkable silence characterized the event. I thought immediately of offering them two young daughters for training. Distinctions of sex were not so important here as ties of friendship and age; but all were deeply interested in their stainless-steel bowls and their meal of whole milk, soft-boiled eggs, potatoes, and radishes. These are the schoolchildren; they are expected to go to a public school on the colony grounds until they are fifteen and complete grade eight.

"Now you see," the old man said again as we crossed the open yard or square toward another severe but gracefully proportioned white wooden building. "We have to have our rules and regulations."

The children from three to six attend a kindergarten; it was the Hutterites who invented this institution. Beginning at eight in the morning, the assembled children study the principles of their language and of their faith; a series of precepts was written in a neat hand in German on a small blackboard. From twelve to two they sleep on a long padded bench off the room in which they study and play and sing. From two to four they again work, returning to their parents at four o'clock. The children under three are left with their mothers.

Wherever we went, I was impressed by the authority of age. The old man, patting his long grey beard into place, received a remarkable deference, yet he was very gentle with the children, pointing out to us his grandchildren, especially one beautiful round-faced little girl who seemed as spoiled as any child – to use the old man's phrase – "out in the world."

The kitchens proved to be so modern they would be the envy of any housewife. Like all the other rooms in the colony, they were, first of all, big. The huge ovens turned out the biggest loaves of bread I have ever seen; it was approaching suppertime, and the smell of fresh home-made bread nearly drove me to theft. The old man proudly pushed us next into the refrigerator; it was of walk-in size, containing whole car-casses of mutton and beef.

We drove out to the spotless milking parlour where we watched milk on its way from the cows through an overhead glass tube to the electrically operated cream separator. Fortunately for me, there was one point in the ultramodern system where a bright-eyed young girl in a long dark skirt, spotless rubber boots, and a dark but flowered apron could insert a tin cup and come up with a pint of fresh warm milk. I drank it off and the old man had his pint; but Harley, the farmer, declined. Then we were off to see more of what modern farming is like.

The hog barn with its automatic feeders, the chicken coop with its thousands of chickens in their little wire pens laying eggs into racks, the feeder pens for the beef cattle, the row of tractors and self-propelled combines, the machine shop: everything was spotless and new. This colony farms five thousand acres. Harley, who employs one hired man to help him with 960 acres, very nearly gasped when we came upon at least eight men unloading bales of hay with the help of a conveyor belt. "They get their education right here," the old man said. "You don't go to school to learn this, any more than you go to school to learn to talk."

Finally he took us to the laundry. Here, in a long hall, two women managed a group of oversize washers and driers. And now the old man, triumphantly, led us to the end of the large hall.

We faced two doors. He opened one: inside was an oversize bathtub and, far above it, a shower nozzle. "You see," he said beaming. He tried the second door. It was locked. He was visibly disappointed. "Someone's using it," he said. "It's just like the first."

We were outside in the sunshine. A boy of about thirteen came by and took a long time to pick up a hammer that lay outside the door; the old man's granddaughter was waiting for us and she'd been joined by at least six of her little friends. We walked slowly to the car, the children following. Somewhere a bell rang. An older girl came up shyly and said something to the old man in German; he turned to me and said it was time for the evening service.

I thanked him for his attention. But still he did not leave. He leaned against a car door. "New York?" he repeated, for he had earlier asked me where I'd lived recently.

I said yes.

A look that I can only describe as one of longing came into his quick, alert eyes. "I've never seen a big ship," he said.

I was taken by surprise; I felt I was supposed to say something impressive and could only nod my head.

"You've been on one?" he asked.

I explained that I had, somehow feeling just a little ashamed at so gross an extravagance. Around us the geese ventured close again; the boy-men were moving toward the dining hall. The children had disappeared to pray.

"A big ship?" the old man went on, almost to himself now. "They say it's something awful to see."

The girl had come back and was speaking to him in his dialect that has been preserved through four centuries.

Maybe I was watching the girl; her dotted head-scarf could not quite contain a coil of curly brown hair. At any rate, I turned to shake the old man's hand and ask him his name; but he had disappeared.

The country north of Cardston toward Fort Macleod is flat prairie, the Blood Indian reservation; approximately 350,000 acres in size, it is the largest reservation in Canada. From Fort Macleod north, a handsome row of grain elevators marks each town: Granum, Claresholm, Stavely, Nanton, Cayley, High River. Generally the country to the east of these towns is rich farmland, to the west, ranchland. But the whole area is a fascinating mixture of Indians, cowboys, religion, oil, and scenery, with High River as its centre.

A group of old-timers in High River, organized by Mrs. Evelyn Leitch, wrote one of the best local histories ever to appear in Alberta. Mrs. Leitch in 1912 attended the first Calgary Stampede, yet she began to write only after hearing Senator Buchanan of Lethbridge remark that the past of Alberta was being lost through the death of the first settlers. Of a sudden she recognized that her childhood was history. She knew at first hand the story of the EP Ranch, once owned by the Prince of Wales. She was a friend of Billy Henry, the bronc-buster and wagon boss who worked for the Bar U when that ranch was running forty thousand head of cattle (Alberta has two cows per resident). W. O. Mitchell of High River, in his "Jake and the Kid" stories, had captured a prairie boyhood. Mrs. Leitch in 1955 organized a group of ranchers who would put their adult memories into a book. She herself recalled two cottonwoods on the Round T Ranch; they were joined together four feet from their base to make a rough letter *H*. Indians had long believed the two trees to possess magical properties, and had come from miles around to be healed. They proved to be an inspiration as well; the title chosen for the book was *Leaves from the Medicine Tree*.

In the "Appendix of Oldtimers" that concludes *Leaves from the Medicine Tree*, I found a portrait of an early prairie settlement that is so telling I can do no better than quote a few characterizations:

> BARRY, James – Drifter.
> BEECHAM, "Oregon" Frank – Worked on Bar U for several
>   years. . . . Good hand, but wouldn't ride a horse.
> BELL, George – Homesteaded opposite Joe Fisher on
>   Sheep Creek, and married Joe's sister.

> FEIRON, J. W. – Thrown from a buggy by runaway team
> and killed in 1902.
> FORD, Frank – Foreman for W.W. Fisher for two years.
> No ranching experience, put hired hands out in
> February to break sod, but broke all harness and
> equipment instead.
> MEXICAN JACK – Early Bar U rider. Stood six feet
> two inches and weighed two hundred pounds.
> MEYER, George – Good butcher and fast cutter.

Harley had to get home to work his summer fallow; I had to hurry into
Calgary to meet my wife and two little daughters. But when we came to
the turn-off that goes west a few miles to Turner Valley, we decided to
run out quickly for a glance at that historic town.

In Turner Valley in 1914 a group of pioneer oilmen put up a big
wooden derrick and began drilling the Dingman well. Natural gas had
been discovered as early as 1883 near Medicine Hat when a railway was
drilling for water. The gas was regarded as a great nuisance. In 1890 a
hole being drilled in a search for coal near Medicine Hat again yielded
gas; and this time it was recognized that the natural gas could be used
by industry. In the following year a group drilled for oil near Pincher
Creek, because farmers in that area had found oil seepages which they
used to lubricate their machinery; but the drilling only produced a dry
hole. Then, in 1902, a hole drilled in the vicinity of Waterton Lakes
National Park actually yielded oil for a short time. The search throughout the foothills became a serious one. And twelve years later, in
Turner Valley, the Dingman well suddenly blew in to give Alberta a
producing oil field.

Turner Valley is a synonym for success in Alberta. Harley and I
went to see the town. We were just a little bit sorry we did. In the last
fifteen years the population of Turner Valley has dropped to something
like six hundred people. Here is where the oil was found. But to find
the prosperity that followed, we had to drive on into the city of
Calgary.

FROM CALGARY TO CULTURE

There is a good opening for a grist mill here now and also for a first-class hotel.

> – *District of Alberta; information for intending settlers.*
> Compiled by the Calgary Agricultural Society,
> J. G. Fitzgerald, Secretary. Ottawa, 1884.

One hen is supposed to produce $1.50 a year. Any young woman starting a poultry farm in Alberta should possess a capital of from $2,500. to $3,000., ambition, a practical turn of mind, and a goodly amount of determination.

> – *Calgary, Sunny Alberta, the Industrial Prodigy of the Great West: Her Phenomenal Progress, Thriving Industries and Wonderful Resources. . . 1911.*

We have lost the decencies and judgments which made moral dirtiness repulsive, and a tide of slime and filth oozes into our homes and institutions. The fathers have discarded their faith and their children are eating LSD.

> – "Editorial Page," *The Albertan*, Calgary, 12 August 1967.

"What does it look like to you?"

"What's it *really* for?"

"What does it make *you* think of?"

They gather at its base and tilt their heads up and back, their mouths opening, their gaze following the slender bone-white curve to where its high point swells against the sky. They watch it from old verandas and new patios, and from the balconies of glittering high-rise apartments. They see it from far out on the prairie and marvel at what they behold.

Calgarians have invented for themselves a new Rorschach test. It is no ink spot on a folded page, but a smooth tower of concrete with a revolving restaurant on top.

To a child, it is a turret that makes his home a castle. To a preacher outside the gate of the Calgary zoo, it is a beacon that draws the innocent to this new Babylon. To a young man who soars six hundred feet above his high city to be served and pampered, it is proof to his date that he deserves her pampering too. To a student at the university, it is an embarrassing symbol of his city's materialism and raw taste. To the oilmen, it is higher than the Rockies on the horizon far to the west; it is the axle-tree of God's universe, and they, by God, built it.

And as the sun sets on the chatter and speculation, the Husky Tower burns splendid and tall in the warm soft night, in the caressing chinooks that blow down over the Rockies. This is the city's long, hard, and enduring dream.

Calgary is a masculine city. It dreams of cattle and oil, of money and women. Meat packers are the biggest employers here. Calgary is headquarters to some three hundred oil and gas companies. Calgary's money has long been a legend in Alberta; and Calgary's women are so at home with the bright sexuality that money breeds in the heart of their praying city that they, too, are a legend. Yet they, too, have changed as their city has grown: for to find the excitement of their presence, you must forsake the cocktail bars and the churches and go now to the art shows, to the theatres and the riding stables and the balls.

Calgary is a city of shrewd, rich, business families, and the wisest among them have begun to recognize what most city leaders in Canada have yet to see. In the affluent world of today, culture is essential to business.

In the past, when you went to a serious movie or a music concert in Alberta, half the people in the audience spoke with accents that indicated they were recently arrived from Britain or the Continent. Today the audience is dominated by young executives just in from Boston's graduate schools, by engineers from Texas and professors from Toronto and research scientists from Montreal's laboratories.

In today's marketplace, big salaries are available in lots of cities. The young man being courted by half a dozen prospective employers is quick to ask: What does your city have to offer?

The leaders in Calgary know that to dominate a region's economy you have to be a centre for home offices and banks, and, above all else, for education and research. To get the necessary professors and executives and research scientists, you have to beat southern California, the St. Lawrence Valley, and America's East Coast at their own game. Thus, today, while most of Alberta talks about resources, Calgary has begun to talk about *environment.*

All the national and provincial and city parks of southern Alberta, the chinooks and the sun, the dude ranches and ski resorts and fishing streams and community skating rinks, the universities and junior colleges and fine-arts schools, which now begin to outnumber the old Bible schools, the concerts and plays and art shows – all are part of the new image.

The new breed of young men on the make is asking new questions. A few years ago a friend of mine in Calgary bummed a ride with a blonde in a Jaguar. "How do you like Calgary?" he asked her, for she was obviously from out of town. "Honey," she answered, "I don't like it at all. But this is where the money is." Today a young man drives up in a station wagon with his educated wife, a dog, and two kids for whom he is very ambitious, and he asks the questions. How good are your schools? he wants to know. How good are your libraries? Who conducts your symphony orchestra? How many plays can I see in a year? When did your city last build a new park? Who is doing what research at your universities? Can I add to my art collection here? Can my wife pursue her interest in ceramics? Can my son study violin? Can my daughter take riding lessons? How much opera can we hear? How good are your bookstores? How big are your computers?

Calgarians are able, more and more, to answer: The best. Fine. Great. Excellent. Yes. . . .

These positive answers are made possible today by a few quiet people who yesterday opposed the vociferous group that wanted to be sure that Cowtown was not violated by so much as a single idea or a solitary tax-collector. That declining group, supported by a combination of incredible newspaper-editorials and "God-hates-the-poor" businessmen, argued against the spending of money on everything from public parks and child welfare to fluoridation. They applauded when a librarian found a picture of a fetus in *Time* and pasted two pages together so it couldn't be seen. They'd rather watch for flying saucers than see a play by Beckett. When they laud the Queen, one has an uneasy suspicion that the lady being praised is Queen Victoria.

In spite of all this, Calgary has a handsome new public library and experimental theatre workshops. It produces poets and painters; it boasts of parks that represent the history of the West and the history of the world. Its new University of Calgary, an actuality after some fifty years of fighting the provincial government, supports Environmental Sciences and Cosmic Ray laboratories. The university is opening a school of social work and a new medical school; it sends students to study archaeology and economics and history in Europe and South America. Mount Royal Junior College is now affiliated with the new university. The Southern Alberta Institute of Technology, on a modern campus, trains people in everything from aeronautical-engineering technology and advertising arts to the television arts and welding. The Calgary Philharmonic Orchestra has a growing reputation. The Allied Arts Centre, working in a small building with a small budget, is trying heroically to satisfy a community's growing cultural demands. And the city's wealthiest families have an enviable record for their support of a variety of educational and creative activities.

Appropriately, the pioneer in Calgary's coming of age was the richest oilman, and therefore the richest man, in the West.

Eric Lafferty Harvie is Mr. Calgary to many people, and surely a city's choice of heroes is indicative of its origins and aspirations. Mr.

Harvie was born in 1892 in Orillia, Ontario, and perhaps that town gave him some of the insights and ideals it gave to Stephen Leacock. At any rate, Eric came West early in his youth, and in 1915 he was called to the Ontario Bar, having studied at the University of Alberta and Toronto's Osgoode Hall. A year later he was wounded in a battle on the Somme front. Hit first in the elbow – in the funny bone, as he wrote home to Calgary – he put his useless hand in his pocket and pressed on in the attack until he was hit again, severely wounded this time and hardly able to crawl into a shell hole where he was almost buried alive. But even here he was aware that he was fortunate, for the battle was so murderous, the air so full of exploding shells, he could not quite imagine how anyone escaped alive. He was already, in an unlikely way, earning another of his names: Lucky Harvie.

After the war he returned to Alberta, married into the Southam publishing family of Montreal, and resumed his career as a lawyer.

It was in his capacity as a lawyer that his luck was to earn its greatest fame. Here the versions differ, as they should in a growing legend, but one thing is certain: he acquired the mineral rights to vast blocks of land in Alberta. Some say he accepted the mineral rights to 250,000 acres in payment of a legal fee of forty-eight thousand dollars during the thirties. Some say it was during the Second World War that a British land company found it could not pay its taxes and gave Harvie the mineral rights to nearly 500,000 acres when he paid the tax arrears, a total of five thousand dollars. In beer parlours and grocery stores the story has it that he gave help to penniless farmers and took mineral rights as payment for his services.

By 1944 he was able to organize two oil companies. When the Leduc well blew in, in 1947, he found he held the mineral rights to a block of land in the Leduc area. When the discovery well blew in in the Redwater field the next year, he held the rights on the three square miles of land surrounding that well.

Within a few years his growing fortune was estimated at $120

million. And it was in 1954, ten years after he started his first oil company, that he announced the formation of the Glenbow Foundation.

Mr. Harvie had long been interested in the history of the West.
He had earlier been active in the establishing of the Banff School of
Fine Arts. Now he gave special impetus to the preservation of items of
historical interest and to research into Alberta's disappearing early history. He proceeded to make Calgary a centre both for scholars and for
the people of Alberta, who in their concern for the future had failed to
notice they had a past.

Today the Glenbow Alberta Institute offers displays that indicate
an interest in the whole of human and natural history. A visitor can
study the lives of Australian aborigines in one room and the career of a
British army officer in the next. He can see renowned collections of
birds' eggs or coins or the carved argillite of the Haida Indians. He can
see how the Indians lived in Alberta before the disappearance of the
buffalo, or how a Hutterite colony organizes its routines and its beliefs.
He can feel the history of the West come alive when he looks on Louis
Riel's tobacco pouch or a lock of his hair, on the white hood used at his
hanging, on a beautifully decorated moccasin taken from the body of
that strange hypnotic father of the West, who was first in a long line of
God-obsessed rhetoricians who have striven to shape a Western
destiny.

The Glenbow Foundation has collected thirty-five thousand artifacts; it has collected paintings, glassware, jewellery, medieval armour,
farm implements, and rare minerals – the list is a long one. On the outskirts of Calgary, in Heritage Park, the Foundation has helped recreate
the West itself in a sixty-acre prairie settlement, by recovering from the
past a blacksmith shop that was operated in Airdrie, a furnished ranch
house, a North-West Mounted Police barracks, a paddle-steamer which
now carries passengers on the Glenmore reservoir, a windmill built by a
White Russian settler, a general store from Claresholm, a carriage-
house, a barber shop, a rectory, a church, a fort – again the list is a long
one.

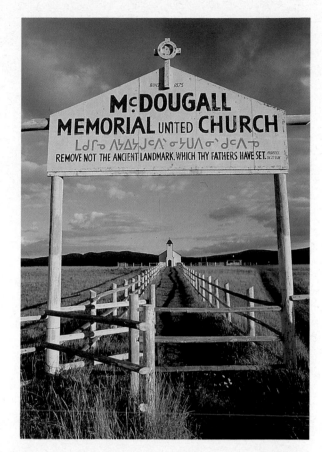

Less dramatic but equally important are the Foundation's library and archives. The library, specializing in Alberta, western Canada, and the Arctic, has an exceptional collection of Alberta Social Credit materials for the use of future historians. It has rare old brand books, in great demand now, and unique copies of Bob Edwards's satiric newspaper, *The Eye-Opener*. The archives have the excellent early photographs that make up the McDermid collection and the W. J. Oliver collection. They have numerous personal and business papers, such as diaries kept by a manager of the huge Cochrane Ranch and by the first mayor of Calgary.

The contribution that Eric Harvie has made to Calgary and Alberta is difficult to overestimate. One man gave every man a history. He is a city's hero, and perhaps our final curiosity is about the hero's hero. Mr. Harvie, in 1966, presented to Calgary a huge bronze statue of Robert the Bruce on a charger. From beneath it one can look out over the valley of the Bow River to the city's modern office towers and beyond to the delicate blue fringe that is the distant immensity of the Rocky Mountains. In the fourteenth century, Robert the Bruce helped to make of his home a nation.

Calgary has other heroes: men like Senator Pat Burns, a man of little education and great generosity, or Viscount Bennett, that cold figure who gave his name in the thirties to the Bennett buggy – a car without gasoline or a licence plate pulled by a team of horses. And there are men and women of heroic proportion who gave more genius than money to their city. Dr. Alexander Calhoun gave a great impetus to Calgary's intellectual life by establishing and developing its first public libraries. The visiting Rupert Brooke was able to observe in 1913 that:

> There are perceptible in the prairies, among all the corruption, irresponsibility, and disastrous individualism, some faint signs of the sense of the community. Take a very good test, the public libraries. As you traverse Canada from east to west they steadily improve. You begin in the city of Montreal, which is unable to support one, and pass through

the dingy rooms and inadequate intellectual provision of Toronto and Winnipeg. After that the libraries and reading rooms, small for the smaller cities, are cleaner and better kept, show signs of care and intelligence; until at last, in Calgary, you find a very neat and carefully kept building, stocked with an immense variety of periodicals, and an admirably chosen store of books, ranging from the classics to the most utterly modern literature.

Joyce Doolittle, actress and director, promotes children's theatre and has developed an audience that applauds *Krapp's Last Tape* or *Lysistrata*. Professor Victor Mitchell at the University of Calgary can now direct an experimental theatre that finds a considerable and appreciative audience.

I went to the university to see a showing of John Snow's lithographs. On this spanking new campus you get a sense of daring and excitement. The architecture is as youthful as the students, and hardly in keeping with the Alberta tradition, established at the University of Alberta, that insists that learning may be necessary but must never be enjoyed. John Snow's prints were appropriate and magnificent in the handsome new library; his light is the vivid, hammering light of the prairies, his forms are the strong dark forms of the prairie night. Out of this tension come still lifes and abstract designs and portraits that record the clash of dream and stark daylight that is so much the Alberta experience. In prints like "Picnic," "Cornelia," and especially "Masque," he confronts us with ourselves: by good fortune I was able to confront the artist.

John Snow is a successful banker and a serious artist; in this he represents the Calgary tradition at its best. A tall, gaunt, gentle man, he works in oils and does experimental work in sculpture, but it is his lithographs especially that are giving him a national reputation.

John was born in Vancouver in 1911; then his father on returning from the First World War took up land near Innisfail, Alberta, and John grew up in an elemental world. This was to be important later, for

John Snow the artist works from visual memory. "You notice a colour or light that is right. You remember an attitude in a person. You recall it years later."

In 1928 he entered his career in banking, with no intention as yet of becoming an artist. Then the Second World War began and he went overseas as a navigator with the R.C.A.F. In England he spent some time with two of his aunts who were painters, one on each side of his family. His mother's sister, Margaret Thompson, was well known for her water colours. Both aunts communicated their interest to their nephew; when he was transferred to North Africa he began to make a few sketches. By the time he returned to Canada in 1945 he was resolved to do some serious painting.

The next important step in his artistic career was his meeting with the Alberta artist Maxwell Bates. Bates had spent five years in a German prison camp after being captured at Dunkirk. He had returned to Calgary to teach at the Provincial Institute of Technology and Art. John Snow was his student for two years; they have been friends ever since.

It was not until 1957 that John acquired two lithography presses. I saw the machines in his basement, the great intriguing blocks of lime-stone that can be stirred to life by an artist, and the newest prints drying in a heap. John makes twenty-six prints of a new work, then erases the lines from the limestone block so that he can begin again. We went on talking about art. "Even my abstracts," he said, holding up a burst of strong colour, "relate to remembered landscape and cityscape."

We went upstairs to his studio, crowded with prints and sculpture and oils. I tried to ask about his work, but he insisted on talking about the genius of his old teacher, Maxwell Bates, a pioneer Canadian expressionist, who now, because of illness, can only work fifteen minutes at a time, yet who goes on producing great pictures and writing poems.

Sitting in John Snow's living room with his wife and the friend who had arranged our meeting, surrounded by paintings and prints and books and sculpture, I asked him if he ever feels the impulse to teach.

"I'd rather work in the bank than teach art," he said. "I thoroughly enjoy banking, and the complete change to art is like using a different part of myself. It's a great advantage."

The next afternoon I visited an engineer who considered a variety of positions and chose one in Calgary. Stan Hauck, on graduating from the University of Alberta, went east to what seemed a perfect career, a job with a big Montreal distiller. I once stayed for a few days in his cabin on the St. Lawrence. Now he was living near the Bow River, married to a sophisticated Irish-born teacher who was busy organizing libraries in new schools. Only a few hundred yards beyond their big new house, cattle grazed on a bare hillside that had never known a plough. Stan and his wife and two children, and I and my wife and two children packed ourselves into his car for a Sunday drive. I was shortly to know why he made his choice. We went first on that dry prairie landscape to an aquarium; but the Hauck children, Brian and Maeve, hurried us along to see the Horseman's Hall of Fame.

Here Calgary's history comes alive around a central exhibit of magnificent buffalo. Maps and photos, artifacts and life-size models capture the transition from a world of mounted Indians to one of creaking oxcarts and bull-trains; from a world of buffalo herds to herded cattle.

In the forefront of change comes Captain John Palliser, an Irishman who played a decisive role in Calgary's future. Today the Palliser is Calgary's first hotel, and Palliser Square is the centre of the city. Palliser was sent out in 1857 by the British government to explore the Canadian prairies and the Rockies. He had the wisdom to take with him a group of brilliant men, including the geologist Dr. James Hector and the botanist Eugène Bourgeau. Palliser worked in the field until 1861, recognizing for the first time that the prairies consist of three steppes. One of his greatest accomplishments was to travel through the plains country of the Blackfoot, the Sarcee, the Blood, and the Peigan without losing his scalp. And he became popular in the Calgary of a later day by recommending against the two things that made the city possible: the settlement of the prairies and the building of a Canadian transcontinental railway. Calgarians have a great affection for those who dare them to do the impossible.

In August of 1875, Troop F of the North-West Mounted Police, under Inspector E. A. Brisebois, established its post on the west bank of the Elbow River, where it joins the Bow. The new Fort Calgary began immediately to flourish.

The discovery of Kicking Horse Pass through the Rockies meant that the railway would be built across the prairies instead of through the parklands farther north. Until it arrived, in 1883, the fort was supplied by bull-trains out of Fort Benton at the head of navigation on the Missouri in Montana. Calgary had its first land-boom in 1883. By 1893 it was incorporated as a city.

The Horseman's Hall of Fame is concerned especially with the men connected with Calgary's rich ranching history. Another Irishman, Sam Livingstone, was the first farmer-rancher in the district. His dates tell how new this land is: born in 1831, he died in the West in 1897. Here also in the Hall of Fame is the Colt .44 Frontier Model and holster carried by John Ware, that huge, gentle Negro who dared to ranch in the Badlands.

It was 1 April 1912, when a vaudeville performer named Guy Weadick arrived from Cheyenne, Wyoming, with a scheme as big as the country. He announced that he was going to organize something called the "Stampede"; he promised it would be the greatest gathering of Indians and cowboys and bucking broncs the world had ever seen. He promised it would be a rodeo to end all rodeos, the show of shows. And the superlatives were more than Calgarians could resist.

Calgary's first Stampede was held that same year.

Weadick had to sign away most of his share of the theoretical profits to get things started; he and his wife survived for a while on a living allowance of twenty-five dollars a week. The great American rodeo star Tom Mix refused at the last minute to participate. But the Stampede came off as announced, and today it is still the greatest rodeo on earth.

The four wealthy ranchers who first supported the idea have gone down as Calgary's Big Four: George Lane, Patrick Burns, A. E. Cross, and A. J. McLean. George Lane's success story is typical of the group. Born in Iowa in 1856, he came up to Alberta from Montana in 1884 to work as a stockman on the Bar U Ranch, twenty-five miles west of the High River Crossing. Seven years later he went into business for himself. Shortly before Weadick arrived, he branded twenty-five hundred calves on his property in one spring. And he owned the largest and best herd of Percheron horses in North America.

The Horseman's Hall of Fame has other success stories. Here also is the story of Wilf Carter, the boy who came west for the harvest with some of his Cape Breton friends and stayed to become a famous balladeer. Stan and I sat down by an empty beer keg to remember old Wilf Carter songs, and while our children studied Calgary's past we wondered who the young men gambling on Calgary's future today are.

We thought first of a man who has become a millionaire by selling prefabricated houses around the world. We talked of Peter Lougheed, the young leader of the provincial Progressive Conservatives who seems to promise more than a little political excitement both in his city and in his province. But then we agreed that the most unlikely dreamers were those who recognized Calgary as a potential wine-making centre. Anjo Wines is now making fourteen varieties and 200,000 gallons a year, importing its grapes from California while waiting for the British Columbia vineyards to expand. Vintage Wines finds that European wines are weak competition. Chalet Wines makes eleven varieties ranging from aperitif cherry to burgundy, including the types that are put away to age and become expensive and rare. "This development is more startling to me," Stan said, "than the love-in they held in Riley Park."

We drove from the Hall of Fame to St. George's Island to visit the Calgary Zoo and Dinosaur Park. Indeed, St. George could have tilted here against the *Triceratops* or the huge *Tyrannosaurus*. But in fact only a black squirrel appeared to do battle; brazenly he defied all the giants of the earth from the branch of a cottonwood.

A combination of fossils, bears, apes, popcorn, swings, an eight-foot baby giraffe, and a tropical aviary finally exhausted the children so we drove for awhile, going at our leisure to see Calgary's more effective buildings: the big flour mill beside the railway track that divides the city, the old Burns Building, white and ornate and speaking of another and a lost concept of Calgary. I liked the corner of Seventh Avenue S.E. and the Macleod Trail, where the sandstone city hall with its red roof and clock tower (A.D. 1907) stands across the avenue from the marble and glass of the Calgary Public Library. Calgary's one-way streets are notorious, and even Stanley was perplexed for a moment. But we found the new planetarium, which may be the most powerfully conceived building in the city; it stands beside an old-fashioned statue of General Wolfe. On the university campus the Students' Union Building seems inspired, in combination with Calgary Hall and the new library.

We drove out past the university and onto the famous section of the Trans-Canada Highway that leaps up from Calgary to the Rockies and Banff. Stan insists that the alternate route, 1A, is even more scenic. But we were only going as far as something called Happy Valley.

The afternoon sun was hot on the road; ahead of us the mountains were blue and, as usual, inviting. As we swung onto the trail toward Happy Valley, Stan glanced once more at the mountains. "Come back in November," he said. "We'll all go skiing. We'll take the kids."

And this, too, is one of the reasons why people come to live in Calgary. The nearness of Banff National Park, of Waterton Lakes

National Park, and of the forestry roads means that close by the new towers and busy highways is the immense Alberta wilderness.

Monday morning. On Monday I went to talk to a man who left Calgary and returned, and that is surely the final test.

Normie Kwong is probably the best-known football player in Alberta; he played for both the Calgary Stampeders and the Edmonton Eskimos. His incredible speed as a small fullback led to the belief that he ran under the big men he opposed. Having met little Normie Kwong, I'd say he just hit them and kept going.

Normie was born in Calgary in 1929 on the day of the stockmarket crash. Today he is a stockbroker. His father came here from Canton, China, to work on the Canadian Pacific Railway. When the railway job folded, he opened a grocery business in Calgary, married a woman who'd come from Canton to Victoria, British Columbia, and began a family. During the depression years that were to follow Normie's birth, he raised a family of six children and somehow found the means to help others. "Bad weather and hardships," Normie said. "People tended to help each other. My dad supported people through the hard winters. They still come by to thank him. They get to thinking about it and just phone up to say hello."

We were talking in his spare, solid-looking office in one of Calgary's tall new office buildings. As we talked the telephone rang often, and Normie answered quickly: "Closed at one-ten. . . . New York is taking a clobbering today. . . . They're testing tomorrow in Turner Valley. . . ."

He is a wonderfully pleasant and relaxed man, who exudes the same easy efficiency in an office that made him a leader and a winner on the football field. He played in seven Grey Cup games, and as an old fan of the China Clipper I couldn't resist asking which game was the best.

"That game in 1954," he said, "when Edmonton was playing Montreal. We were the underdogs. Then Parker picked up a fumble and we were ahead. We were downgraded so badly in the newspapers before the game – coming back and winning gave us a great deal of satisfaction."

It was typical of his team spirit that the game he remembered most was the game in which someone else made the saving play. "Do you miss the game?" I asked.

"You miss football the way you would your youth. You know it's over with. It's nice to be young; it's nice to play ball. When you're playing you don't realize there's a lot of life after. But there is."

The telephone was ringing again. He owns two dry-cleaning establishments with his brothers and he spoke briefly, offering advice. Then I inquired about his three young sons. "Do you think they'll play?" I asked. He smiled. "I'll give them every opportunity to give it a whirl."

He began to talk about the past and the future. He had recently driven out to the coast and had taken his father along to visit Lytton, British Columbia, and the first railway camp in which he had worked in Canada. "All my experiences are Canadian," Normie added. "That's what I pass on to my children."

I knew that Calgary has Alberta's largest community of people of Chinese origin. I asked Normie if he encountered any prejudice. "I've never run across any situation anywhere in Canada," he said, "where I felt I was being slighted because of race. Maybe it helps to be a football player. But I do feel more comfortable in Alberta than anywhere."

That brought me to another question. Normie had started with the Calgary Stampeders in 1948. He was injured in 1950 and it appeared possible that he wouldn't recover from a bad ankle; Calgary traded him to the Edmonton Eskimos, where he went on to be an outstanding player for nine seasons.

"Why did you settle in Calgary rather than Edmonton?" I asked. He hesitated. "I was single when I was in Edmonton. To be on a winning team is like being part of another family. We took pride in representing Edmonton." He was reaching to answer the phone. "But I guess

– Calgary has better parks for the kids. And Calgary – well, it's friend-lier, you might say."

And then he was talking stocks. "Still around forty-two. . . . The weak sisters are out of that one. . . . It's got to be bullish for it. . . ."

"Naturally," he explained as he saw me to the door, "we favour oils here in Alberta."

4. THE KINGDOM OF OIL: LET US NOW PRAY

From the successful speculator, owner of whole blocks, to the waiter
bringing you a Martini, who has paid up a fraction of the cost of a quar-
ter-share in a town-lot – all are the richer, as well as the prouder, if
Newville grows. It is imperative to praise Edmonton in Edmonton. But
it is sudden death to praise it in Calgary. The partisans of each city pro-
claim its superiority to all the others in swiftness of growth, future population, size of buildings, price of land – by all recognized standards of
excellence.

– Rupert Brooke, *Letters from America*

Mrs. Nellie McClung stumped the Province and made many votes.
Great Temperance parades were held in Calgary and Edmonton and the
United Farmers of Alberta, with President James Speakman and his col-
leagues, did strong service. . . . On July 21 the Act was approved and
Prohibition carried by a large majority. . . .

– *The Canadian Annual Review*, 1915

Highway Two: In Praise of Digressions

"Calgary has millionaires; Edmonton has money."
My mouth was full of lobster Newburg. I nodded.
"I mean, Calgary has its Establishment. The McMahons, the Crosses, the Bells, Eric Harvie. When you want to do something in Calgary, you wait for them to nod – even if it only indicates they're asleep. Edmonton is different. It's *prosperous*, baby. I mean *everybody* has *some* money and a scheme for making *more*. Leaders, baby. We got leaders on every block in this city."

The waiter was filling our glasses again. We had resisted the offer of an Edmonton Eskimo Cooler, a Mustang, a Klondiker, or an Alberta Rose, insisting on a quiet white wine. We were dining, I had already been reminded twice, in the world's largest revolving restaurant. The second is in London; the third in Tokyo. And you guessed it, baby: we were dining in Edmonton.

Let me call my host Eddie. He has business connections in Calgary and wants to remain anonymous. He and I were once members of the same crew on a riverboat on the Mackenzie. We had met again the previous spring when, by one of those accidents that make living fun, we found ourselves together on a T-bar riding up a mountain in Marmot Basin in Jasper National Park. "Listen," he said then. "I'll give you a ring some day for lunch. Edmonton isn't the city you used to know." He hesitated. "You are from Edmonton?"

"No," I said.

"You take this hotel," he was saying now. "Edmonton is an old Canadian National town; Calgary is a Canadian Pacific town."

"We're in Edmonton," I said. I was being the straight man. "This is a Canadian Pacific hotel."

"Precisely," Eddie said. He levelled a finger at me. "Baby, even the Canadian Pacific Railway knows this old city is all systems go." At the table next to ours was a group of Midwestern businessmen who'd just flown back from a fishing trip to Great Bear Lake. They were talking steel mills and telling the fish stories that had cost them each a hundred dollars a day. Eddie raised his voice too. "This is where the action is. The provincial government goes on dreaming about its wealthy agrarian society. They're farm boys after all, small-town boys. But industry has *got* to come, and we city boys know it."

I watched out the window; I could see the Roman dome of the Parliament Building, with the heavy black lines of the High Level Bridge beyond spanning the valley of the North Saskatchewan. It grows on you; the heavy old bridge where the trains flash across, coming north from Calgary, the valley deep and green below, the river running free. Beyond an unmarked spot that was mile zero to the voyageurs and their fur-laden canoes stand the towers of the University of Alberta.

"Look at the specialty shops," Eddie told me. "We've got the second-highest automobile ratio in North America – after L.A. We've got culture: a new art gallery, a new library. Symphony. Opera. Theatre groups till you can't count them. A few millionaires with a bankful won't give you good restaurants. You need a lot of people with a fistful each."

The high-rise apartments marched along the riverbank, almost to the horizon. And then, behind them, the Canadian National railyards, and a yarding-engine pushing boxcars into neat long rows; a cement plant farther out; and the tall round bins of the federal grain elevators.

"Look," Eddie kept saying. "Look. Do you want a tycoon or a management team? It's like Chicago and Boston. Boston had its Beacon Hill. Chicago had its immigrants. Boston is politics and snobbery and a nice place for a tourist to see once in a lifetime. Chicago is *the heartbeat of a nation*, baby."

The eight-storey Tegler Building was for years the tallest building in Edmonton. Now it is dwarfed by banks and offices and the cranes that raise new buildings. The C.N. Tower is a truly impressive structure, slender and driven skyward by its black and white lines; beneath it the city hall and the city library give a grace and elegance to Sir Winston Churchill Square.

Eddie had found himself a good listener. "The first generation," he explained, "was too busy breaking land. My grandparents walked out here from Winnipeg. They weren't about to risk a nickel on anything. The second generation was a little ashamed of the first. This third generation – they're proud of their hard-working ancestors, and they're ambitious, and they like to swing. Bill Hawrelak: he was elected mayor by the second generation. But he was too cautious, say what you will. This guy Dantzer gets the young vote, baby. He sees the future, and the future is *big*."

"Calgary," I said, "is just about the same size as Edmonton."

"Baby," he said, "I'm talking about the future. The immediate future – like tomorrow morning. Did you ever hear of the Yellowhead Route?"

I said it had stayed within a year of completion ever since the day I was born. Eddie shook his head indignantly. The Canadian Pacific Railway, I explained, *almost* used that route to build the first Trans-Canada railway back in 18 –

"Trans-Canada!" Eddie interrupted. "Let me give you an example. When the Rogers Pass route opened, the old United States route – why! business in Spokane dropped forty percent. Overnight. Just like that, they were decimated. This Yellowhead Highway means there's another route across Canada. This road means we've got Calgary in our hip pocket. Now we're going after Winnipeg. Then Vancouver!"

He tried to pour me more wine but the bottle was empty. I wanted some coffee.

I listened. I sat watching: the Macdonald Hotel came around, with its uneasy wedding of continental and modern architecture; or, as the local joke has it, the Macdonald and the box it came in.

Immediately below us was the McDougall United Church, a little wooden church built in a clearing in the forest less than one hundred years ago; out beyond both the hotel and the church were the meat-packing plants. And out beyond them was the flat horizon and its trim of virgin bush. We kept on talking and turning. The North Saskatchewan flowed east below us again, a raft with a tent on it drift-ing slowly in the current. In the centre of the lovely valley, the city incinerator and a power plant smoked on, in a setting that might have rivalled New York's Central Park had someone thought to save the land. A ski jump tipped crazily down into the valley, over a paved road. To the east now the oil tanks of chemical row gleamed silver in the wheatfields. To the south the old Calgary Trail was a four-lane highway crowded with neon signs. Death Road they call the first fifteen miles.

We declined to have our coffee cups refilled. "Hey, look," Eddie said; he was picking up the bill. I was about to remind him of the time in Aklavik when four of us flipped to see who'd pay for eight cokes; I got stuck for $2.80. Eddie pointed his index finger again. "A couple of damned fools are drifting down the river on a raft. Now what can you see from down there, I ask you?"

I didn't tell him.

In Edmonton they call it the Calgary Trail; in Calgary they call it the Edmonton Trail. On a hot day in July it's 186 miles of four-lane high-way from the rip-roaring Calgary Stampede to the rip-roaring Klondike Days. It's the change from a soaring hawk above a dry prairie to a fami-ly of ducklings on a green slough; from the excitement of foothills country to the exciting presence of the North.

Highway 2 is Alberta's axis; when you make the trip you brag about how many minutes under three hours you spent on the road. But even at seventy miles per hour you can make distinctions.

On the southern half of the drive, the section from Crossfield to Innisfail offers an excellent picture of the short-grass country: coulees with cattle grazing or asleep in the sun, flat wheatlands above, farmsteads square and weathered. The elevators stand tall and dignified off to the west – Carstairs, Didsbury – and beyond them the mountains fade blue, then gather jagged and hard on the farthest horizon. The country is progressively less flat, less hot, less open; at Innisfail you top a rise and start to watch for Red Deer.

On the northern half of the drive, the section from Ponoka toward Wetaskiwin offers an excellent picture of the parklands: mixed-farming country and some of the richest soil in the world. Driving up a low hill, you see on the east side of the highway a shallow valley and rolling countryside, and, neatly at home in the valley, the town of Ponoka. Here the land is greener than it was farther south, the green accentuated by the glaring yellow of a field of rape. The rich loam is blacker. Thanks to the Hobbema Indians, a large block set in the distant fields is solidly wooded with poplar and spruce. You have left the Blindman River and crossed the Battle into the basin of the North Saskatchewan.

The throughway, very efficiently, avoids most of the towns, curling rinks, parks, gopher holes, prairie trails, barns, churches, beer parlours, ball diamonds, moonshine stills, colleges, jails, and people that make Alberta interesting. I recommend the ultimate heresy: somewhere, at random, turn off the main road.

Bentley is a lovely town set in a beautiful valley. Buffalo Lake is quiet and relatively unknown. The Red Deer River has unexplored coulees. But one morning I turned west on Highway 11 and drove out past Sylvan Lake toward the mountains.

The poplars began to give way to spruce; the farms seemed but precariously wrested from the forest. Loafing along, I noticed a fence made up of many old tractors. It turned out that there were one hundred of them, making a centennial fence, surely one of the most improbable projects in that year of extravagance. I was not the first curious person to drive into Ted von Holland's yard.

A huge, striking figure with twinkling blue eyes and a "biblical" beard, he greeted my curiosity with a shake of his head: "I've got to stay away from sales; got to avoid the junk at auction sales."

I admitted to sharing his weakness for a Saturday auction on an isolated farm. He'd been fixing fence: I no sooner spoke than the hammer was lying in the sunlit grass, we were both sitting on a spruce slab, and two boys were chasing a herd of beef cattle toward the far end of the pasture.

"Sure," Ted said. "People come in and ask, 'Why don't you sell those tractors?' I ask them in turn, 'What do you want me to buy?' "

Like those who preceded me, I didn't have an answer. Ted stood up, the better to expound. "They say a man can't make a living on a quarter-section. I'm living proof that if you work hard and live by the Good Book you can eat all you need to eat and –"

And he began to elaborate. I stood up, the better to listen. He keeps between one hundred and three hundred pigs, a herd of from fifty to one hundred feeder cattle. He and his wife and sons run a planing mill in his backyard, buying the unfinished lumber from a local sawmill. And now and then he lets himself be persuaded to sell some of the junk he has accumulated.

"All on 160 acres?" I asked.

"Right," he said. "Just recently I bought a swamp quarter for pasture. But I hardly needed it. It's the government; they're making laws that are meant to kill the small farmers."

Ted von Holland is wonderfully alive. "It's too bad we ain't got no seers in the government. Prophecy is the main thing. The people in Ottawa are blind."

Finding me in agreement he went on: "You see, the end of this kingdom is about at hand. This era of the devil is almost finished."

Encouraged, I nevertheless inquired as to the evidence.

"Look at the way de Gaulle made a fool of himself in Montreal," he said. "Look how the Israelites won by God's intervention – the tanks that wouldn't start for the Arabs started right off for the Israelites. Look how that space craft burned in the States. It ain't meant for a man to be on the moon. Look what happened when people tried to build the tower of Babel."

Ted and I further agreed on the primacy of God's command to love, and on the naturalness of nature. ("The closer we stay to animals, the more it accounts for our success.") When he first married, he took his young wife out to a homestead in the bush. But one day while he was out working to get a little cash, a bear walked in on his wife. She decided they ought to get a little closer to civilization – which they did, by squatting on muskeg land and buying two pigs. Twenty years ago his hog ranch was prosperous enough that he was able to buy the valuable farm he lives on now.

Ted was obviously enjoying the sunshine and our mutual wisdom, and I no less. When he wasn't quoting the Bible he was being quotable himself. A man came up to buy some lumber and was told to go pick out what he wanted. Meanwhile, Ted told me about his pastime: he likes to run rafts through the rapids on the North Saskatchewan River. "If you want a thrill you go through them rapids."

When he pointed to where a small raft was drying in the sun, I professed an interest in other sports. "I'll pitch horseshoes with anybody," he said. "I once grew a beard, myself," I countered.

But again I found my story topped. Ted was sick one winter, and one day met a friend who had been sick and got well. "How'd you do it?" Ted asked. "I ate garlic," the friend answered. Ted went to the store for garlic, and while buying it he decided if he was going to eat garlic he might as well grow a beard. "Never had a cold or sore throat since I let it grow," he explained. "And if you had one yourself, you know how the wife likes it."

We explored further the psychology of that phenomenon, both of us agreeing and chuckling.

"Look," Ted said. "Do you ever take a little stout, just for the tonic?"

I was supposed to be somewhere in a hurry, but talking to Ted I realized I had time at least for tonic. We walked together to his house, both of us dismissing the things of this world, both of us surrounded by his astonishing collection of cars, sofas, lumber, farm machinery, house plants, and centennial tractors. Geese got out of the way as we walked. His only daughter left her swing and came running to take his hand.

Silently I followed along behind, careful not to break a leg on a discarded wheel or engine block. "You see," Ted was explaining, "even in the worst plague, God intervenes so that all flesh isn't destroyed. . . ."

Refreshed, I drove on to Rocky Mountain House. Here the last grain elevator meets the forest. A sawmill stands next to the elevator. Men in rough clothes talk and joke in the clean new streets. This is frontier country, as it was when David Thompson made Rocky Mountain House his base back in 1810.

Thompson was fourteen when he landed in Churchill, an apprentice in the fur trade. Between 1784 and 1812 he travelled 50,000 miles on foot, on horseback, or in a canoe; he mapped 1,700,000 square miles of western Canada and the United States. Today we recognize this pious, secretive, determined man as the greatest land-surveyor the world was ever to know; in his own time he died neglected and in poverty.

I visited two stone chimneys set in a small grove of poplars. The log buildings long ago burned to the ground. But the North Saskatchewan still runs milky green and loud where the fur traders wintered; the ice and high waters of spring eat relentlessly into the bank. Nearby a farm prospers, and beyond it the mountains shine. And the drive west from here to the Banff-Jasper Highway, 108 miles distant, is an experience of the country that confronted the traders and explorers.

The David Thompson Highway is a dusty gravel road; for the faint of heart there is always a swim in beautiful Crimson Lake and a night in a motel. But among fishermen and campers it's no longer a secret that this road opens up some of the most fascinating wild country in Alberta.

Unlike the drive west from Calgary, this approach into the mountains is gradual. The section of road beyond Nordegg, through the Clearwater Forest and flanked by both the White Goat Wilderness and the Siffleur Wilderness, is the goal of an annual highway cavalcade. As many as five thousand campers journey out to the Kootenay Plains and camp in the mesalike terrain; in a natural amphitheatre set among the mountains they enjoy Indian dances, share the open meadows with a great herd of wild horses, and wind it all up with the traditional Albertan bang-up breakfast.

The Windy Point section of the highway overlooks the North Saskatchewan for miles, and threatens to become as much photographed as the poppies at Lake Louise. Fishermen gather to speak in their mysterious way of Ram River, Whirlpool Rapid, Swan Lake, Littlehorn Creek, Bighorn Falls; and they exchange statistics about Rocky Mountain whitefish and half a dozen kinds of trout, including cut-throat, Dolly Varden, and rainbow. Hunters, outfitted in Rocky, come riding down from Job Pass with trophies that set big-game records: Rocky Mountain House has seen a first for brown grizzly, a second for moose, and a third for wapiti, not to mention all kinds of records for bighorn sheep and mountain goats.

For me, the most informative encounter was with a forest ranger. He made me aware of the immense store of human knowledge that goes into keeping a forest green and the water resources secure. I learned not only of the persistent threat of fire, but of the less obvious danger from insects such as spruce budworm, ugly-nest caterpillar, and poplar serpentine miner (severe along the Ghost River between the mouth of Waiparous Creek and Devil's Gap), and from diseases such as shoestring root rot, pine-needle cast, dwarf mistletoe, red belt, and atropellis canker. Less glamorous than the men who bomb fires, these men go quietly into the field, return quietly to their laboratories.

But we were driving north along No. 2 from Calgary to the cities of the parkland. Red Deer, Wetaskiwin, Stettler, and Camrose in some ways represent what is most stable and inviting about Alberta: they make up an area where the land is rich and the crops seldom fail. The people have an attachment to locality that is reflected in their interests and accomplishments. Kerry Wood of Red Deer is a respected naturalist. Wetaskiwin, once the smallest city in the British Commonwealth, boasts a fine museum full of such things as antique steam-engines. Stettler won a terrible fame for the number of casualties that small city suffered on the beaches of Dieppe. Camrose, home of Sunny Boy Cereal to many a Westerner, is also home to past Olympic skiers like the Servold brothers and to the great diplomat Chester Ronning.

Seeking a key to this region, I visited the Lacombe Research Station of the Canadian Department of Agriculture.

The landscaping of the station shows what luxuriance can be produced in a land of long winters and intense summers. And the meteorological data gathered here is of singular importance in understanding the whole area: since 1907 the station has averaged eighty-seven frost-free days per year. The sixth of June is the average date for the last spring frost; 1 September is the average date for the first fall frost. Fortunately, a killing frost is one of twenty-eight degrees, and the area is free of killing frost for an average of 118 days per year.

The precipitation averages 17.74 inches annually, with 10.6 inches falling between 1 May and 31 August. The sun shines for 2,132.8 hours a year: May is the sunniest month, with 301 hours; next come July, June, and then August with 213.

Farmers in this area produce fifty percent of Alberta's wheat, eighty percent of its oats and barley and hogs, and sixty percent of its cattle.

The station is perhaps best known for its development of the

Lacombe breed of hog. Here, between the years 1947 and 1958, Mr. J. G. Stothart and Dr. H. T. Fredeen directed the development of a bacon hog that today is being exported to breeders in Britain, Germany, Italy, Japan, and Russia. But the scientists here have also developed new varieties of such cereal crops as barley, wheat, and oats; they have perfected garden varieties suitable to the local climate; they have done extensive studies in forage crops and plant pathology. And they are especially concerned nowadays with the problems involved in farming Alberta's several million acres of solonetzic soils – "gumbo" to a man trying to cultivate it when it's dry and hard, or trying to get it off his shoes when it's sticky and wet.

Driving north from Lacombe one sunny afternoon, I noticed a turn-off to the tiny hamlet of Morningside; and at that moment I recalled one of the rumours that brighten Canadian literary history. Any short biography of Canada's leading poet, Earle Birney, gives his home town as Calgary. The rumour has it, however, that he is in fact from Morningside. Speeding along, I decided on an impulse to play literary detective; it would be tantalizing to learn that so deliberately cosmopolitan and international a poet was, like Shakespeare, a country boy.

Morningside has not been corrupted by sidewalks; the general store and the post office face directly onto a sandy road. Across the road is the railway track; along the track stand the grain elevators. It was that time of year when Alberta's stores are piled high with wooden boxes of B. C. fruit. I went into the store and bought myself some pears, and I casually inquired about the Birney family. The lady behind the counter and another who was sitting on a sack of beans doing a mental-stability test in a pulp magazine had only been in town sixteen years; they suggested I go to the post office. I did; inside the door I found a bookcase full of frayed books that turned out to constitute the local library; I felt much encouraged. The lady on the other side of the

wicket put down an old book and stepped into her shoes – it was blis-
tering hot in the tiny wooden shack – and came graciously to me and
my questions. She thought hard, her hot face almost angelic in its concern and sincerity. No, the name Birney was a new one to her. Not
Blundell? Birney, I insisted. But she'd only been in the area thirty years.
I ought to check with a rancher out east of town who had come in here
when the country was opened up. You can't miss him. He's got a herd
of black cattle. It's easy. No, really, I explained, I'd better be getting
on. . . .

But as I retreated to my car a goldfinch flashed by, yellower than
the blaze of sunshine. As I looked up, I beheld on a nearby hill a lovely
sorrel horse. Dammit all, I couldn't resist. When the Muse herself
deigns to give you a sign –. Instead of turning back onto the paved
highway, I swung around and struck out down a narrow sandy side-
road.

The lady in the post office was right: I couldn't miss the black
cattle. I turned into a long and rutted lane. An old man met me, tall,
bent, walking slowly, his face craggy and stern beneath a very ancient
Stetson. He listened patiently to my question – which by now had
become more apology than question, for I felt an intruder. He did not
speak but signalled me toward a hayrack beside the windmill; we sat
down together, the old man and I, on the hayrack's side.

He raised a gnarled hand and pointed as if aiming across the low
valley that was his field, toward another.

"The Birneys left there in the fall of 1912. They was well-
thought-of people."

Even then I did not rejoice; I was certain he was referring to
another Birney family. Or maybe he'd thought I'd said Blundell.

"Little Earle," the old man went on, "was known hereabouts as
Tommy. I guess he's about the best-known person that ever came out of
this district. There's a breed woman here was a great friend of his
mother. . . ."

The old man talked and I listened. There's an old apple tree that's all that's left of the Birney place. Each fall it freezes before the apples are fit to eat; but each spring it bears more blossoms. The old man chuckled, shifting on the hayrack to ease the pressure under his knees. "I like history," he explained. The Morningside district makes a small patch of wild hill-country on this fertile plain; when the Riel Rebellion collapsed, the Indians and Métis came here for the water and grass and forest. "I'm a Protestant myself," the old man said, "but the Ontario people were wrong about Riel. The Orangemen's propaganda was wrong. I know the Indians around here." He pointed on his own land to where a chief had lived. "If you want the truth straight about the past, talk to an Indian or a half-breed."

The fine old gentleman is a close friend of the local Indians; he shares their tea and their table talk. And he spoke to me of the passing of the buffalo, of the coming of the railway, of the Rebellion. Gabriel Dumont is the hero here, he explained. He told of a nearby graveyard where the Reverend George McDougall buried six hundred Indians, victims of the smallpox. He told of the greatest trip of his life – to the site of the Frog Lake Massacre – and how the Indians came after to ask him what he'd seen and heard. He told me of Crowfoot's anguish when, with his people starving, he had to sign away his land to get food. And we talked of the break-away Crees who wouldn't go treaty.

The sun warmed memories out of my gentle host. An old dog gave up all hope of our company and ran off to bother a cow. A nephew arrived, listened impatiently to our history, then climbed up on a garage to replace some missing shingles.

I listened to stories and thought of a young boy listening, on his way to poet-hood. After I left the old man, I stopped at the Birney homestead. I crawled through a barbed-wire fence; the wild roses, the fireweed, and bluebells and daisies and sunflowers and wild bergamot were extravagantly in bloom against a background of spruce and balsam and birch. His father's land, I must say, was better suited to growing poets than wheat.

The pears I had bought proved insufficient to my hunger, so I stopped in Leduc for a bite to eat. Leduc is recent history. Here is where a wheatfield spouted oil. The town itself, after its brief hour, is once again a farm town; even the few farmers who got rich are not likely to betray their wealth. My one oilman story is not of a farmer but of a man who made a lot of money providing steel tool-bits and oilfield mud and supplies to the drilling rigs.

On his best day in the fields, at least so the story has it, he cleared sixty-four thousand dollars; I suppose for him to build a thirty-five thousand dollar cabin on Pigeon Lake was nothing exceptional. The parking-lot by itself, rimmed with silver-painted oil pipe, is larger than most lake lots. The four extra cabins around it are bedrooms for guests. However, it was not the cabin but the parties the owner gave in and around it that turned this place into a legend. They were, I am told, so lavish and long that the Great Gatsby himself might have felt a little envy. Gatsby's guests managed to wreck the occasional car; this man's sons wrecked three in one week.

Like the Nick Carraway of Fitzgerald's story, I rented a modest cabin nearby. Hoping to emulate him further, I awaited a mysterious invitation to a party that would fill the immense silence of a night on that lake. But no invitation came, for the oilfield action had moved north, and with it the cabin's fabled owner. His piers and docks and boats, in my time, were a great place for the gulls to sun themselves, and they were splendidly confident that they mustn't be disturbed. Of an evening, two grebes, a loon, my older daughter, and I might wander by. An invisible spirit mowed the lawns and trimmed the hedges; I never saw mortal do it. And sad to say, I never saw the owner, nor drank his Scotch and rye.

And the visitor is not likely to crash the party either, wherever it may be. I recommend a short, quick, middle-class drive west from Leduc on Highway 39. This is an area of rich farms with lovely big

barns and pleasant windbreaks. The houses, like so many houses in
Alberta, seem ill at ease in the landscape. Here and there a windmill
turns. And everywhere across this farmland, the oil pumps nod and
stagger, sucking up oil from Devonian depths. Drive as far as the lovely
Greek Orthodox church two miles west of Calmar, then turn back and
try once again to count the pumps.

Just north of this road, on a cold February day in 1947, the
province of Alberta found itself dizzily afloat on pools of oil. Derricks
sprouted on the long horizon. Seismograph crews decked the trees and
fence posts with bright red and yellow ribbons. A 2,023-mile pipeline
soon joined Leduc to Port Credit in Ontario, transporting a gallon of
crude oil for the same cost as sending a postcard. Then a pipeline went
over the Rockies, down to the Pacific coast. And pipelines were built
to move natural gas: to Quebec, to Vancouver and Seattle and on to
California. Quickly the world learned new names like Redwater,
Pembina, Wildcat Hills, Jumping Pound, Westerose South, Viking-
Kinsella. Toronto and New York and Chicago vied for control of the
new wealth. And meanwhile, in Alberta, Calgary and Edmonton each
confidently billed itself as "The Oil Capital of Canada."

EDMONTON: THE TOMORROW-SEEKERS

> The establishment at Edmonton is the most important one in the
> Saskatchewan district, and is the residence of a chief factor, who
> has charge of all the minor posts. It boasts of a windmill, a black-
> smith's forge, and carpenter's shop.
>
> — Viscount Milton and Dr. Cheadle,
> *The North-West Passage by Land* (1865)

> For the collecting and shipping of furs Edmonton existed. . . .
> Towards this goal men and dogs and horses and oxen pulled and
> strained and starved. For this purpose isolation and hardship
> almost inconceivable were undergone. For the securing of and
> bringing in to Edmonton of the pelts of buffalo and bear, beaver
> and badger, martin and musk-rat, fisher and fox, otter and lynx,
> the interest of everyone living in the country was enlisted.
> Thirteen different peoples, speaking eight distinct languages,
> made this post their periodic centre; and while at Edmonton was
> shown the wonderful tact and skill of the Hudson's Bay
> Company in managing contending tribes, yet nevertheless many
> a frightful massacre took place under the shadow of its walls.
>
> — John McDougall, *Saddle, Sled and Snowshoe:*
> *Pioneering on the Saskatchewan in the Sixties*

Edmonton during Klondike Days is the one place in Canada where a
full beard proves you're not a hippie. Wear one here and you get free
trims from competing barbers, photographers lure you in off the streets,
the unfortunate beardless stand you no end of drinks, and hundreds of
high-kicking housewives are just dying to kiss you. Here in Edmonton,
bank clerks wear goatees in the teller's cage, oil executives look like
Victorian villains, and floor-walkers look like stranded bush pilots.
Here young matrons wear jewelled black garters above their shapely
knees and very little above their shapely bosoms; old ladies don the

false rumps and hourglass corsets they rejected so violently in their teens.

Edmonton, like modern man, has experienced a long crisis of identity; the anguish was heightened by the annual success of Calgary's Stampede. Now Edmonton has emerged from its enduring catastrophe into nine glorious Klondike Days.

The success of this festival/wingding/ceremony, this nine-day wonder, does not reside in its carnival or its excellent livestock show or its parade or fireworks or visiting starlets, but in a single moment: that precious and ultimate moment when the Klondiker, in his high-rise apartment or suburban bungalow, in his West End mansion or rented basement-flat, *puts on his costume.*

A businessman told me proudly that Edmontonians, in one year, spend two million dollars on silk hats, vests, striped pants, long-tailed coats, spats, bow ties, and watch chains; on parasols, Gay Nineties feathers, and can-can shoes. And, he added, that's not allowing for the thousands of women who make their own costumes. But he was missing the point.

In putting on a costume we abandon our old identities. We cast off, slough off, an old self, like a snake getting rid of a skin that's too tight; we are freed, liberated – from shyness, from the inhibitions and neuroses of a fundamentalist society, from the rawness of our frontier backgrounds, from the bourgeois pressures toward conformity, from financial worries, from memos and deadlines, from the in-basket and the out-basket, from the suddenly unbearable monotony of our daily lot in life. And more important: we put on an identity which is surely closer to our true identity.

The Edmontonian, for nine days in the last half of July, while the heat hangs burning on the wheatfields and dust writes its name on every window sill in town, becomes a debonair fellow who carries a cane; he dances in the streets, squires his love to a melodrama, sings all night in a barroom, and goes to work in the morning, if he bothers at all, confident in the knowledge that most of the day will be spent in chatting with friends on a busy corner where they're sure to be seen, watching parades and judging marching bands, and nipping out for some hair of the dog. His money burns holes in his pockets; his way of saying hello comes out sounding like, time for a quick one? Women can't keep their eyes off him. And he doesn't pretend to ignore a pretty thigh or a low neckline, for the ladies are all decked out in tassels and frills and silk, and a wink of admiration is the least they expect.

Life is a poke full of gold dust, and a kindly fate has handed it to a lusty young swell from Edmonton who was cut out to spend it in nine short days. He's a born winner, a handsome good-natured cuss, a bit of a boozer, God forgive him, and something of a bounder with the ladies. But the ladies are more than willing to forgive, for as the poet says, "'tis better to have loved and lost. . . ." And all the world pines to be an Edmontonian.

The image succeeds because it has its kernel of truth. The father who gets a gold-embroidered vest and a stovepipe hat for Christmas, the teenage boy studying his young beard in the locker room in January, the ladies, after bridge on a bitter February afternoon, looking at patterns and buying warm-coloured cloth by the bolt: they are part of a past that goes back to the erection of Fort Augustus in 1794, to the erection of its rival, Fort Edmonton, in 1795 – and in Alberta that ain't history, it's archaeology.

Although the voyageurs who danced and sang on these same riverbanks before they paddled their fur-loaded canoes to Fort Garry were a hard-working bunch, they also knew how to get dressed up and have one hell of a good time. Their lamented failure to keep diaries was due to more than illiteracy; sometimes it's wise just to keep your mouth shut. Buffalo hunters such as Gabriel Dumont and Donald Whitford enjoyed a good cut of steak as well as do the executives sitting down to their expense accounts and a Klondike Dinner in one of Edmonton's

twenty better restaurants. And gold dust has been found where the ritual of discovery is now enacted. By the 1860s a number of men were
panning the Saskatchewan for gold, and coming up with enough pay
dirt to make Clover Bar a place to remember. Hope hung eternal in the
frosty air.

The first missionaries cut grand figures too: the Reverend George
McDougall sported a beard that would have won the vote of any
Klondike Queen. Father Lacombe is applauded for introducing the
ploughshare and peace to Alberta, but when five grizzlies became a nui-
sance in St. Albert, he preached a hellfire sermon against the offending
marauders. Soon after that, the voyageurs gave way to trains of Red
River oxcarts, then to the crews of the S.S. *Northcote* and the S.S.
Northwest. Any man who drove an ox across the prairies or fed wood to
the boilers of a sternwheeler was glad to see the palisades of Fort
Edmonton; and he was more than able to express his joy.

When the railway got to Calgary in 1883, someone started a
stagecoach service north to Edmonton. Any passenger who boarded
the stage Monday and got off Friday, if everything went according to
schedule, was certain to have abandoned all restraint by the time he
saw John Walter's ferry. And when the Calgary and Edmonton Railway
finally completed its track into South Edmonton in 1891, it brought
with it a bunch of young fellows who were bound for the Athabasca
and the Arctic. They felt under some obligation to terrorize the local
inhabitants in their own merry way before departing, a custom that
persists in Edmonton to this day.

The railway brought in homesteaders who, contrary to the image
encouraged by their social-climbing descendants, were given to dancing all night as well as working all day, a feat made possible by a combination of fiddle music and some of the finest moonshine that ever
dripped from a brass tube.

When George Washington Carmack struck gold on Bonanza
Creek, Yukon, on 17 August 1896, he sent something like two thou-

sand Klondikers racing to the end of the rail. Like the Klondikers of today, they outfitted in Edmonton, celebrated the historic occasion in a fitting manner, and failed to lay eyes on the Yukon. But some of those who survived the incredible ordeal of trying to get there helped open up the huge northern hinterland that assures Edmonton's growth and prosperity.

Bush pilots were to follow within twenty-five years – men who aren't much given to working an eight-hour day. They prefer to work until a job is done, then relax until the next one starts. Edmonton is synonymous with barn storming and bush flying, and men like Jimmy Bell, George Gorman, Punch Dickins, and Grant McConachie are as much a part of the city's history as the earlier voyageurs. Appropriately, one of the first flights north, in 1921, was made to take men into a booming oilfield, the newly discovered field at Norman Wells. The men flying out of Edmonton were soon to carry mail north, assist prospectors, drop fishermen on unknown lakes, take Eskimo children to school, bring out uranium ore, and fly the sick and injured from the wilderness to hospitals. But Wilfrid "Wop" May, more than any other pilot just back from the First World War, was to capture the imagination of his fellow Edmontonians. Young Wop was within seconds of coming into the sights of Baron von Richthofen, the Great Red Knight, when Roy Brown zeroed in on the German ace. Wop lived to shoot down thirteen enemy planes himself; he returned to Edmonton to live just as dangerously as a pioneer bush pilot and aviation business-man.

The development of bush flying out of Edmonton exemplifies the tie between the most northerly large city in North America and the wilderness to which it is gateway. The annual festivities acknowledge that tie and illustrate its complexity.

During a recent Klondike Days celebration I met a gold miner just back from Yellowknife who told me that Edmonton is the second-best place for a fist fight in Canada. Naturally, I couldn't resist; I asked him what beats it.

"Flin Flon," he said. "One night me and my brother got cornered by six hardrock miners. . . ."

And that's the thing to recognize about Edmonton. It's second to Flin Flon as a place to pick a fight because only one half of Edmonton's spirit is looking for a good brawl; the other half is looking for respectability. Once you've gone off to the wilderness and struck gold, the next job is to come back and buy yourself a place in society.

It's no wonder that Edmonton's men are the best-dressed males in Canada (the women can't quite compete with those of Montreal). Edmontonians love to get dolled up: in costumes for a Halloween dance, in formal wear for a ball, in the latest fashions for a play in the Citadel Theatre. But the Klondike celebrations best illustrate the conflict in the heart of the city. I saw a group of men who had pitched a tent outside a popular bar, waiting for a chance to get in and get seats: they were dressed in spats and silk hats and silk shirts.

Edmonton is a frontier town that only in the 1960s became a genuine city. Appropriately, Marshall McLuhan was born here: modern communications have enabled Edmonton to overcome the disadvantage of not being a seaport. In the 1960s it ceased being an isolated and overgrown small town to become a nerve centre in McLuhan's global village. And to complicate matters, it is now both a sophisticated international crossroads and the capital of a province that is desperately concerned to guard its own provinciality

Reflecting this contradiction in a painful manner is an aging man who was once the nation's youngest premier; the man who, from this city, rules the province. I am almost the only person I know who finds any warmth in the public personality of Premier Ernest Manning (one is tempted to believe he invented the name to serve his own political ends). Underneath his famous smugness and self-satisfaction, it seems to me, is a man who is profoundly aware that he is a one-shot affair, an anomaly; he belongs to no tradition. And he desperately wants to: listen to his pathetic overtures to the national Conservative Party, even to the provincial Conservatives who make up his Opposition.

My wife comes from North Carolina; the first time she saw Manning on TV she said, "Good grief. Don't tell me you have southern politicians this far north." And I suppose this is the key.

He has the voice and manner of a country preacher, and that's what he is: to understand Manning and the portion of Alberta that he represents you should listen to his Sunday-morning radio program, "Canada's National Back to the Bible Hour." And you might glance at *The Prophetic Voice*, the magazine that is the official organ of the radio program.

Manning is overwhelmed by a nostalgia for a lost pastoral world, as his hymns and preaching show: a nostalgia which easily finds its counterpart in rapidly changing rural Alberta. Further, he constantly insinuates a criticism of theology and ceremony, for he recognizes that he must draw new church members from the established churches. Third, he sees in Alberta and Canada a desperate need for the return of Christ to this earth; and he is not unwilling to have it supposed that God in His wisdom has already sent a pretty stout representative.

Manning takes these three rather commonplace teachings and transforms them into a seemingly unbeatable political formula.

He wants to recover and preserve a rural paradise in which the twin evils of industrialism and cities are unnecessary, for they have, in his eyes, bred atheism and socialism and appetites for dance and liquor and tobacco. The notion that rural virtues are superior to urban virtues is taken for granted in Alberta. Almost no one has challenged the Social Credit Party's right to keep the electoral divisions heavily weighted in favour of rural areas. It is agreed that farmers have steadier judgement and sounder principles.

The criticism of the intellectual activity called theology is based on the supposition that right and wrong are easily determined by a look into the Bible. This translates politically as an assurance to Alberta's newly well-to-do (and the vast majority are well-to-do, not rich) that the self-reliant individual shouldn't be hampered by manmade regulations and the necessity of sharing his bounty with the less fortunate. Man's lot in life is not a cause for social unrest but a manifestation of God's will. The poor, then, as well as the prospering, should recognize that they are a part of God's mysterious plan.

W. E. Mann, in his fascinating study *Sect, Cult and Church in Alberta*, reports that "In 1937 Manning forecast the coming of the Lord within a year, and asserted that the present era preceding 'the last days' was fulfilling Biblical prophecy. . . ." This messianic concern translates into politics as an authoritarian attitude. Manning has professed on television his impatience with the notion that a government needs an Opposition. His is a God-given mission, and he appears to carry the burden with marvellous ease. He is, for instance, his own attorney general.

In his version of paradise, even death is done away with; or if not death, at least two thirds of the inheritance tax. What the federal government collects, he returns. If it so turns out that you can take it with you, at least it will be yours to take.

The trouble is, Mr. Manning sees that if Alberta is genuinely to prosper and to grow in fulfillment of God's plan, it must become industrial. And he knows that the industrial, urban society is a secular one. The predicament, the tension, becomes immensely subtle in this brilliant and complicated man. His religious teachings make him the hope of the uprooted and the underprivileged. Yet his social philosophy has made him the darling of the wealthy oilmen. To date he has found no middle ground such as the Conservative Party seems to have found, at least in some parts of western Canada.

In this climate of unease, good minds have seldom entered into provincial politics. The members of the cabinet are expected to stay discreetly in the shadows; backbenchers become an inarticulate blur. It is to the civil service and to city government that the best minds have turned; as a result, today the cities are experiencing what I am tempted to describe as a little renaissance.

I don't mean to suggest that the past doesn't have its victories in the cities as well. To take an extreme example – and people from outside Alberta sometimes refuse to believe it – at one time the reaction against civilization was so severe in Edmonton and Calgary that men and women weren't allowed to drink *together*. Beer had to be sold; the provincial government, after a try at prohibition, saw that the revenue from beer parlours and liquor stores was very respectable indeed. But you could at least stop people from *enjoying* their vices; so each sex was allowed to drink, but each went to a separate beer parlour.

The waiter was allowed to enter both (by what qualification, I hesitate to inquire), so after saying farewell to your wife or date at her door, you hurried in at your own and asked the waiter to take two beers to the lady in the yellow hat. Assuming you had remembered the hat correctly, and assuming that only she in that vast hall of cast-off women wore a yellow one, she got two beers. The male then sat in meditation on his fair lady's distant virtues. There was no means of communication, so the problem of the lady's wanting a refill or to go home or to a dance or to eat was a matter for considerable speculation. When you reached a decision you told the waiter to tell the lady in the yellow hat to meet you out on the street. With a little luck you were joined by your spouse or date, or someone else's, and could exchange opinions and decisions and inquire as to the nature of each other's speculations and reveries.

Fortunately, Albertans are as adept at getting around these laws as they are at making them. In those good old virtuous days, small towns near Edmonton passed laws inviting the sexes to drink together and built huge beer parlours for their accommodation. On a Friday or Saturday night, the traffic jams in St. Albert and Stony Plain and Fort

Saskatchewan were measured by the mile. And Edmonton was a deserted city.

Today the weekend traffic flows the other way: from the small towns to Edmonton. But the visitors are coming to see plays, museums, and art galleries, to hear concerts and attend meetings on everything from slum clearance to astrophysics. Edmonton has become a city of culture and leisure, exploiting its isolation from other large cities to insist that all facilities be available right here.

I attended the opening of Edmonton's centennial library building, an impressive structure with richly textured walls, strong planes, and fortresslike windows. Perhaps the most modern building of its kind in Canada, it has a special children's library, a 250-seat theatre, and an imposing collection of mechanical and electronic devices for the control and amplification of the five senses. The artist Norman Yates contributed a mural on the theme of Alberta; Jordi Bonet of Montreal created a sculptured wall that stirs the most indifferent visitor to awareness. But for the opening the library hung a showing of Charles M. Russell's paintings of the old West.

Appropriately, thousands of Edmontonians entered the air-conditioned, carpeted, and softly lit library to relive a more rugged past. Russell, a Montana artist, worked often in Alberta, and lived, in 1888, with Alberta's Blood Indians. Today's sophisticates, newly and proudly aware of their past, crowded to see his record of an Indian war-council, of hunting parties, of stolen horses, of the first white intruders on a prairie and mountain landscape. He captures the Indians' uneasiness and confusion at the sight of an orderly wagon-train, he gives a sense of the noise and the dust and the smell of herds of buffalo. His pictures are often pictures of action and violence: cowboys roping a grizzly, Mounties and trappers and ranchers coming to grips with a harsh and beautiful land.

Only recently has Edmonton become aware of its architecture

and history; now it is launching on a dramatic plan to recreate its own rich heritage. Fort Edmonton Park will slowly be developed under the guidance of Mr. J. C. Finlay to give, on its 150 acres, a vivid portrayal of the geological history of the site, and then the course of human activities from the early prewhite Indian village, through the great change that came to Indian culture with the introduction of the horse, to the first white traders. The fort of the midnineteenth century will be reconstructed, for we have excellent descriptions of the life in that fort from such early travellers as Dr. Hector of Palliser's party and the artist Paul Kane. Kane, visiting in the fall of 1847, decided to winter in Edmonton. The fort was the source of buffalo meat for the traders to the north and west, and Kane found that seven hundred to eight hundred horses were kept nearby, along with two hundred to three hundred dogs. He went out to shoot one buffalo in a herd of three thousand; in order to get to a bull he had shot for its head, he had to shoot three others that stood in the way. No one bothered to eat the meat.

The later eras of homesteading and bush flying and oil exploration will also be represented by realistic and authentic reconstructions. Even now a visit is worthwhile for the guided nature-walks.

Whitemud Park preserves the only major Edmonton ravine that hasn't become a highway; its forest and prairie cover is still home to such rare birds as the barred owl, the red-tailed hawk and the pileated woodpecker. Here the visitor finds deer tracks at the edge of a large city. And here, too, is made evident the dire need to preserve the beautiful river valley that makes Edmonton one of the three most beautiful cities in Canada.

For the visitor interested in animal life, the Alberta Game Farm offers an experience that is not to be equalled in the West. Al Oeming, on one thousand acres of woodland fourteen miles from the city, has collected animals from around the world. Yaks and porcupines and gazelles and llamas and dromedaries live in harmony near each other. Here is a rare opportunity to see the woodland caribou or a herd of musk-oxen. Here is the fascinating kit fox, now extinct on the open prairies where once it lived. A giraffe is shockingly beautiful as it nibbles at the uppermost branches of an Alberta poplar. And the huge Siberian tigers, unforgettable in their power, suggest to me the beauty and violence of a western winter.

But for the visitor interested in both the natural world and the people of Alberta, the Provincial Museum and Archives is the supreme experience. Driving north across the Groat Bridge, one sees the old Government House and the new museum become an abstract and contemporary fort against the city's skyline. The architecture is somehow equal to the immensity of earth and sky that meet here on the bank of the North Saskatchewan.

I saw the museum in its process of growth; one wintry fall day I stood in the snow beside the waterless fountain, watching the ice that ran in the river below the edge of the hill. The noise of distant traffic came throbbing up from the valley. Downstream two bridges patterned the view, separating or joining, I knew not which, the university to the south, the dome of Parliament to the north. I thought of the river's seasons: an urgent brown in the spring, when it forces life into the white and shadowed stillness of the long winter, a cool green in the summer. Steel-grey at that moment, it smoked against a lowering sky.

I joined a man who was staring gravely into the empty fountain. We were alone out there and small, he and I, the unfinished building quiet, the snow hardly tracked. Someone was constructing a huge and handsome sculpture in the fountain's centre. "I wonder whose work this is?" I said.

"Mine," the man answered.

I was talking to Olle Holmsten, the Calgary sculptor; tall and intense and friendly, he began to tell me of the skill with which Edmonton workmen had cast his bronze figures. As we talked, a truck drove up and five men began lifting a bronze man up against the curved surface of concrete that dominates the pool.

I asked Olle about the figure. He pointed to a tiny model of the huge unfinished sculpture. "There are four groups."

"Four is symbolic of the earth," I said. "Four winds. Four seasons. The four corners –"

"No," Olle said. "I'm not a symbolist. This one is . . . well, it's the creation of the universe. That second one is man and woman dreaming: about the universe and the limitless things beyond themselves. Next is Icarus. Icarus and a woman; it means . . . accidents, failure. . . . And yet in the fourth, in spite of all, man tries to lift the curtain." He stepped into the empty pool to pull at a rope. "That's it, isn't it; man's urge to discover, to go beyond the known?" We both helped a workman lift a heavy bronze woman upright. "I'm no poet," Olle added. "Don't ask me. I work in bronze, in concrete."

"Grab that leg," a workman yelled.

I watched: there were six men working together at the delicate and rough task of creating something that might endure. Appropriately, they spoke with four different accents.

Oil has made Edmonton's cosmopolitan dimensions possible; the University of Alberta has been central in making them a fact. Today, the university recruits faculty from all over the world to teach its student body of well over thirteen thousand students. Planners talk of twenty thousand and twenty-five thousand, and the need for more junior colleges to handle all the freshmen. Graduate programs burgeon and flourish. It was here that Alberta's first premier, A. C. Rutherford, flew in the face of his whole province and turned 258 acres of brush on the banks of the Saskatchewan River into a university. Today that same university must buy up blocks of houses to give itself more space.

Appropriately, and perhaps inevitably, the handsomest building on the campus is SUB – the new Students' Union Building. It represents the culmination of an old University of Alberta tradition by which professors, administration, and parents assume that students are responsible and creative.

The tall black-and-white building, framing a courtyard where
varieties of steel and concrete and wood are reflected in great sheets of
glass, is set beside the old brick walls and ornate landscaping of
Pembina Hall: the juxtaposition is one of the architectural highlights
of Alberta.

Thousands of students voted to increase their own fees to build
SUB; at least three hundred worked directly at the task of planning the
building, finding and talking with an architect whose design philosophy appealed to them, and taking their plans to the bargaining-table
with administrators and treasurers.

Girl watching is uniformly ideal in a complex that skillfully
blends a bank and a bowling alley, a ceramics club and a chapel, a barber shop and a theatre. The construction budget included a generous
allowance for the best nonfigurative art being done in Canada. The
curling rink, walled in glass, facing onto a huge bookstore, is itself a
work of art: a happening where students become actors and audience
and critics at once.

This university helped establish a Boreal Institute devoted to
northern studies and research. It has a centre for the study of mental
retardation in children, an archaeological centre in Rome, and an
institute for the study of theoretical physics. Its chemistry department,
under Professor H. E. Gunning, sends graduates to all parts of the
world. But at the moment, its Health Sciences Centre is the biggest
single development in the field of teaching and research.

I had borrowed a book on the history of medicine in Alberta
from Dr. D. F. Cameron, associate dean of Medicine; when I went to
return it, I found him preparing to fly to New York to read a paper. But,
unlike most travellers, he was ahead of schedule; we sat and talked for a
while. I asked him about the proposed Health Sciences Centre I'd
heard mentioned so often.

"What did you hear?" he asked.

"That it'll cost eighty million."

"Exactly," he said. "But bricks and mortar don't make a great health centre."

"Well," I said, "I heard about heart surgery and kidney transplants."

"They're dramatic subjects," he said. "But how many people have heart surgery and kidney transplants?"

And then he began to talk about the medical future of the province.

Alberta's new centre is well under way, with the Clinical Sciences Building already a fact, and enough buildings planned to keep construction cranes swinging over the campus for seven more years. But behind these concrete towers is a radical change in the way medical service is to be provided for Albertans.

The truth is, the day of the solo practitioner who does everything to all people is over. We can't train enough doctors for the task, for there simply aren't enough candidates applying to medical school. The answer lies in team medicine, with doctors, nurses, dentists, pharmacists, physiotherapists, and others pooling their resources. And if they're going to work together as a health team, they should train as a team.

The University of Alberta Medical School is one of the small group of excellent schools making the change to this plan. Involved in the change is a recognition of a basic error in the medical training of the past.

Of a cross-section of one thousand people in Alberta, two hundred and fifty will go to see a doctor in one month, eight will be sent to the hospital, and one of those eight will enter a specialized university hospital. "In the past we've been teaching students on the basis of that one exceptional patient," Dr. Cameron explained. "He's an extreme case, often an incurable case. It's like teaching forestry in a lumberyard."

The new health centre will concentrate on the ambulatory

patient, the man who walks in off the street to consult someone about an ailment. The new medical school wants to acquaint its students with a cross-section of the population, with the two hundred and fifty rather than the one – with the one thousand ideally. In this way medical students will have an ideal environment in which to study. And further, this cross-section will provide an excellent research environment.

Dr. Cameron remarked that he, like the famous Indian weather-forecaster Chief Walking Eagle, was one of the few local "medicine men" who were actually born in the province. But today a group of young people in Edmonton – film-makers, painters, musicians, journalists, poets, politicians – are speaking out, not with the visitor's sense of wonder, but with the native son's passionate concern.

Mel Hurtig is a young Edmonton bookseller and publisher, who has done impressive service to his province by reprinting early accounts of western travel such as Paul Kane's *Wanderings of an Artist*. He has published political studies and collections of folk tales. And he has commissioned such valuable books as J. G. MacGregor's *Edmonton: A History*. I asked him about the popular, or, perhaps, the Easterner's, view of Alberta.

"Our outside image is terrible," he explained. "You mention Alberta outside the province and people think it's a place where screwballs live, a place full of nuts and reactionaries. We get lumped together with right-wing hotbeds like Texas and Southern California."

Mel had recently published Eli Mandel's *An Idiot Joy*, one of the most sophisticated collections of poetry to appear in Canada. He himself has been on Edmonton's grants committee for aid to cultural institutions such as the symphony and the local theatre. He is past president of the Edmonton Art Gallery. He is vice-president of the Canadian Booksellers Association. And he has bought the early work of such excellent young painters as Sylvain Voyer.

"Have provincial politics hurt the province's image?" I wondered.

"For instance, the university –"

"Okay," Mel broke in. "I'm a *liberal* Liberal, and we're scarce out here. But you can't just put the blame on Social Credit; that's too easy. You hear that the government interferes with the university. That isn't true. The university isn't handicapped by outside interference; it's handicapped by mediocre leadership. The Alberta government has really been pretty good about things like appointments and book censorship."

Ironically, it was Mel's numerous visits to eastern Canada that introduced him to the image of Alberta as a backward province. "I used to think of Alberta," he said, "as a frontier where all kinds of exciting things were being done. I used to think we were making progress, social and political. Then I saw we're standing still. The press in Alberta has renounced its function as critic. The only thing they attack is the C.B.C. – the opposition. Basic issues, like dishonesty in the local government, get better coverage in the Toronto papers than they do here. People have lost interest. They don't go to sessions of the legislature, for instance. The people who should be leaders won't touch politics. Look, I've lived in Edmonton all my life. I was thirty years old before I met a person who admitted that he votes Social Credit. The whole province is involved in this hypocrisy. Everyone laughs at the Social Credit Party for being anti-welfare and anti-intellectual and anti-C.B.C. and anti-medicare and anti-government. But the business people and the church-goers and the press vote Social Credit. The wealthy don't want any social change; they don't want any shift in the power structure, and they know Social Credit won't rock the boat."

"Is there any hope?" I asked.

Mel had started out to show me the manuscript of a child's history of western Canada that he was soon to publish. "They say Diefenbaker ran seven times before he won an election." He smiled, opening the manuscript. "Look at it this way: Edmonton is booming, and this time it isn't only real estate. It's theatres, graduate schools, artists, ideas. A young photographer came in for help just this morning: there's a shortage of garrets."

Edmonton is a cultural boom town. This was brought home to me most intensely by a woman who grew up in Illinois. Miss Alison White came to teach at the University of Alberta in 1955, and her course in children's literature quickly became popular both in the university and in the city. In 1961 she became a Canadian citizen. "It's not that I reject the United States," she said. She had been playing the Prelude to Bach's English Suite number 3; she sat at her piano, surrounded by paintings from Australia and her library of rare children's books, by pictures of an Illinois childhood, by antique glass and silver. "I'm what they call a New Canadian. I prefer Canada as a home. Maybe it's because we're all fugitives here." She touched gently a lovely green polar bear done by an Eskimo carver. "And I like to live in a cosmopolitan city."

Established artists as well as the young are finding Edmonton a provocative and congenial place in which to work. The artistic accomplishments range from Lionel Thomas's bronze-and-water-sculpture in front of City Hall to Jack Shadbolt's exciting mural for the Edmonton International Airport. And the work of the university painters is nationally known: the humour and fantasy and inner life of Norman Yates, the eccentric and antic carnival spirit of Harry Wohlfarth, the dream façades, sophisticated and abstract, of Jack Taylor.

Robert Goulet left Edmonton to seek fame, but the pianist Marek Jablonski has stayed, as have the composer Violet Archer, the conductor Brian Priestman, the famous teacher Dr. Jenny Le Saunier, and the brilliant *Journal* critic Anne Burrows.

Theatre offerings range from those of the middlebrow Citadel Theatre through the Walterdale Playhouse to the experimental work of Studio Theatre, from musicals and the Russian classics to Wilfred Watson's violent antiplay, *Oh Holy Ghost* DIP YOUR FINGER IN THE

BLOOD OF CANADA *and write,* I LOVE YOU. Writers like Rudy Wiebe and Henry Kreisel are giving to the West a sophisticated literary tradition; Sheila Watson, whose *The Double Hook* may be the finest novel yet to appear in Canada, teaches at the university.

The poet Ted Blodgett, huge and bearded, speaks table-talk that becomes poetry when he is on the subject of Edmonton: "It *isn't* a city; it's a theatrical performance. It is something invented by the *Edmonton Journal.* . . . I think it's the altitude; the altitude affects the light. . . . There are no natural boundaries here. I love it. I feel lost. . . ."

But the Janus-faces of Edmonton – its poets and its politicians, its ten churches on 96th Street and its whores on 97th, its Klondike dream and its hungering for a proper (yet enjoyable) tomorrow – meet in the shared and rich details of the present.

Edmonton is a policeman in a buffalo coat, the swirl of snow squinting his eyes. It is the town-crier in his long white curls, crying us on to a new extravagance. Edmonton is the dust and the girls at the corner of Jasper and 101st; it is a hike up a ravine trail when the buds burst green on the balsam poplars. It is a raft race on the North Saskatchewan in the heat of July. It is the flowers and the accents in the city market on a Saturday morning. It is the gulls beating westward at sundown. It is students drinking coffee in the Tuck Shop, a Chinese supper in the Seven Seas. It is Art Evans's daily column in the *Journal.* It is listening to good music on CKUA.

Edmonton is the young financier who told me at a cocktail party that in the middle of the previous night he drove his date 140 miles to show her a small town, and then wept at the dark silence of remembered grain elevators.

And Edmonton is for me a green stone polar bear looking out from the window of a high-rise apartment to the spruce-flecked ravines by the river, to the gold of the visible forest at the city's edge. It is my host in a revolving restaurant telling me over lobster Newburg that Edmonton is all systems go, baby; it's the heartbeat of a nation. It is a ten-cent malt in the basement of the Bay. It is a valley that on a January morning might shelter ten thousand buffalo. Edmonton with its high towers illumined at six o'clock on a winter's night is a blue-green vision of a city, hung from the stars above a black chasm.

THE YELLOWHEAD ROUTE

A ride of two miles took us to Jasper's, where we arrived exactly fifteen days after leaving Edmonton, two of them days of rest and a third lost by the obstruction of the Athabasca. It is hardly fair to speak of it as lost however, for there was no point at which the delay of a day was so little unacceptable to us. The mountains of the Jasper valley would have repaid us for a week's detention.
> – Rev. George M. Grant, *Ocean to Ocean:*
> *Sandford Fleming's Expedition Through Canada in*
> *1872*

This pass, known by the several names of the Leather, Jasper House, Cowdung Lake, and Yellow Head Pass, had been formerly used by the voyageurs of the Hudson's Bay Company as a portage from the Athabasca to the Fraser, but had long been abandoned on account of the numerous casualties which attended the navigation of the latter river.
> – Viscount Milton and Dr. Cheadle,
> *The North-West Passage by Land*

Actually, the Yellowhead Route has been considerably improved in the last century and a half. Today the road from Winnipeg to Vancouver via Saskatoon and Edmonton is 1,665 miles long – only 100 miles more than Highway No. 1. Its highest point is 3,711 feet above sea level, considerably lower than either Kicking Horse or Crowsnest Pass. As a result its greatest snowfall is only 152 inches, compared with 343 in the Rogers Pass area. But the fact remains that this highway is not up to the engineering standards of the Trans-Canada Highway through Regina and Calgary. Together the two roads make a unique but demanding Great Circle Route that embraces half a nation.

Highway 16, Alberta's section of the Yellowhead, begins on Main Street in Lloydminster, for Main (or 50th Avenue) is the fourth meridian, and that is the border between Saskatchewan and Alberta.

Lloydminster, a prosperous and attractive town, thrives on agriculture and oil. This is where the famous Barr colonists, nearly two thousand settlers from England, established their headquarters camp in 1903. But the story of their struggle with a strange new land is a Saskatchewan story. And the log church those brave people completed in 1904, St. John's Minster, is preserved on the Saskatchewan side of the border; its gentle English exterior proportions and its forbidding interior are hard to forget.

North of this town a short drive is the equally famous Frog Lake. The country to the north is Cree country. And to the Woods Cree in 1885 came two distinguished leaders. One was the Reverend Henry Bird Steinhauer, a Methodist missionary, an Ojibway Indian with a Pennsylvania name, a scholar proficient in Hebrew and Greek who helped translate the Bible into Cree. The other was Chief Big Bear, a Plains Cree who was by occupation a warrior and hunter. He had spent a lifetime fighting the Blackfoot.

When the Riel Rebellion broke out in the early spring of 1885, the spirit of Big Bear was for a short while victorious over that of the Reverend Steinhauer. Five bands of Indians in the vicinity of Frog Lake were caught between their loss of an old way of life and the necessity of accepting a new one. On the night of 1 April, they gathered to feast and dance. Messengers came from Louis Riel, and with their messages came hope for the revival of the past. The young men grew reckless. At dawn, wearing full warpaint, they entered and took possession of the tiny settlement of Frog Lake; they ordered the whites to proceed as prisoners to the Indian encampment. The Indian agent, Thomas Quinn, resisted. Wandering Spirit, married to the sister of the agent's wife, ordered him to obey. Again the agent resisted. Wandering Spirit shot him dead.

Eight more men were killed in what was to be known as the Frog Lake Massacre. Two women and one man were taken prisoner. And one man, warned by a friendly Indian, had time to escape and spread the alarm.

The name of Big Bear struck terror throughout the Northwest; within a matter of days the Indians and Métis were in control of most of the North Saskatchewan. But the Canadian government was quick to mobilize an army of five thousand troops and four hundred horses. The other two leaders of the rebellion, Poundmaker and Riel, after dramatic initial successes in Saskatchewan, were forced to surrender. Big Bear and his Cree began to retreat. And after fighting against artillery with hunting rifles, they too began to recognize the futility of resistance. On 2 July, three months after his first victory, evading all the columns of soldiers sent out to find him, the old chief walked in almost alone and surrendered to one of the few Mounted Police who weren't out looking for him. Big Bear went to the white man's jail; eight Indians were hanged for the nine murders at Frog Lake.

West of "Lloyd" is the little town of Kitscoty, where one of Saskatchewan's leading writers, Edward McCourt, grew up on a homestead. All along here the country opens periodically, presenting from the top of a low rise a textbook picture of the parklands. At Vermilion I turned north on No. 41 and drove toward the region that is fast becoming Alberta's "lake country." There are many old log buildings along the way, some of them carefully roofed and chinked and still in use. Here I have seen the remains of log houses that were built in the Ukrainian style, with thatched roofs. But now the grandsons of those settlers are looking at the plans of summer cabins.

Crossing the North Saskatchewan, I found the land more rugged; I stopped briefly at an attractive campsite on Kehiwin Lake, near the Kehiwin Indian Reserve. This is the fringe of the lake country. Its principal towns are Lac La Biche, Cold Lake, Bonnyville, and St. Paul; its principal highway is No. 28, leading out from Edmonton. This is also a land of tempting back roads; all along No. 28, arrows point north to places that invite with such intriguing names as Floating Stone Lake. But this time I dropped in on an old fisherman on Moose Lake: Mr. H. R. Almost.

Everything was as I remembered it: the cleaning table was sloshed clean, the woodpile was where it belonged and just as big as ever, the paths were barely holding their own against the grass and trees. The old boats leaked just a mite, as they had years earlier. Mr. Almost's perfect Ontario accent ("calm" rhymes with "ram") hadn't changed in the slightest. We sat down on an old bench where we could see the lake's sandy bottom, the reeds, the open water – and I happened to mention that nothing seemed to have changed.

Mr. Almost shook his head grimly. "I used to always like to hear the birds singing in the morning. It's seldom you hear them now."

He gave me a catalogue of the birds he has loved and lost. There used to be three or four brown thrushes up in the trees singing in the morning. Now none. There used to be two or three pairs of orioles, two or three of phoebes. One pair of each is all he sees now. A gull flew over; where he sees one, he used to see forty. In the past there were all kinds of mud-hens (coots); he hasn't seen one in a year. Where once he counted twenty-three night-hawks feeding in an evening, he now sees none. The few arctic terns that used to visit have vanished. And in a few years, he added, even the ducks will be gone.

Mr. Almost blames the indiscriminate spraying of crops and trees for the disappearance of birds. He is saddened by the silence of his mornings and evenings, and he sees worse to come: "The spray is going into the ground. The vegetables are going to fetch it up from the ground, and we'll all be eating it. We *are* eating it."

I drove away, noticing a summer world of clover and bees, of glowing fireweed and bright fields of rape. In the town of Spedden two lovely little churches stand domed against the landscape; in the churchyard of one, a farmer was bailing hay. It was then I decided to stay on No. 28 as far as Smoky Lake.

Outside that town is a graveyard of the Greek Orthodox Church; a forest of white crosses stands out brightly from a distance. This time I dropped in to chat with two old men who were busy putting a new coat of latex paint on the tall cement crosses.

I especially like the three-barred Eastern crosses, each with the third bar slanting down to the right. I could not read the inscriptions: they were in the Cyrillic alphabet, hand-lettered in the wet cement while the cross was being made. Artificial flowers were attached to many of the crosses, colourful against the scattering of tall jackpine and new spruce. The graveyard overlooks the gentle valley of White Earth Creek. More recently, families have taken to using English on conventional headstones, and I read the names Zukowsky, Makarenko, Cebuliak, Boychuk. Here, also, a few Indian children lie buried.

Intrigued by these reflections of a Ukrainian culture, I drove south to Mundare, on the highway I had set out to explore but had strayed from in Vermilion. The Basilian Fathers (of the Ukrainian rite) maintain in Mundare a cloistered monastery: a novitiate for the whole of Canada. Across from the long hedges and old wooden buildings of the monastery stands the Ukrainian Catholic Church of St. Peter and St. Paul, a lovely church badly in need of a coat of paint. Next to the church stands a museum maintained by the fathers; it specializes in Ukrainian national and religious traditions and customs. Most prized among its treasures are books of the liturgy dating back to the sixteenth and seventeenth centuries.

Finally, next to the monastery itself, stands a grotto. Built by Father Bodner and his students, beginning in 1933, it has become a stopping place for people of all faiths. As many as five thousand gather here on the feast-day of Peter and Paul – the 29th of June or the next Sunday thereafter. The trees, the walks, the flowers, the Stations of the Cross, and the scenes from the life of Christ suggest a European heritage. The sculpture, unfortunately, is too often of the mail-order variety; the light-studded cross at the top of the grotto seems more vital and indigenous.

I continued westward. Elk Island National Park is for me the biggest surprise on the Yellowhead Route. I grew up within a hundred miles of that park and never once paid it a visit. The park is only twenty-five miles from Edmonton, yet I know few Edmontonians who have explored it; they go to Banff and Jasper.

The preserve was begun in 1906 when five local businessmen became concerned that the elk in the Beaver Hills were about to become extinct. The glacier-formed hills stand two hundred feet above the surrounding area; the plentiful beavers that gave the hills their name were wiped out by 1870 (and reintroduced in 1922). This area, expanded to include some of the aspen parklands typical of the region, became a national park in 1913. The game count of 1966-67 showed a population of 664 moose, 337 elk, 148 deer, 588 plains buffalo, and the largest herd of woods buffalo in the world – 35 head. Today the aspen is closing in on the grazing meadows to such an extent that it may be necessary to stage a prairie fire of the sort that kept the meadows open in years past.

The seventy-five square miles of the park are completely fenced to keep in the animals. All around is farmland that has been or is being stripped of trees: in 1967 the smoke from places where farmers were burning brush and clearing land was, on occasion, a blue haze over Edmonton. Today the park constitutes the principal green area near that city; in a matter of minutes the Edmontonian can begin to know the birds, animals, and plants that once characterized the entire vast parklands area.

I met a Swiss photographer who had come from Jasper and Banff to Elk Island. In the mountains, he lamented, the wild animals have become so tame and used to tourists that he got few good shots. In Elk Island, to his delight, a bull buffalo performed magnificently, snorting and tearing up the sod while his cows looked on in admiration.

The park is full of surprises. Recently a woman exploring a black-spruce bog found four varieties of orchids that weren't listed as being present in Elk Island. Wolves became extinct here in 1890, black bears in 1910, but twenty-six mammals still inhabit the immediate area. Birdlife includes seven kinds of woodpeckers and, recently, a few great blue herons. Heavy stands of white spruce grow on the islands in Astotin Lake – the kind of spruce that covered much of the vicinity perhaps five hundred years ago.

Many of the services and functions of a national park go unnoticed by the casual tourist. I met a young naturalist who makes scientific specimens of all the birds found dead in the park. A porcupine had just been hit by a car; he went to a refrigerator and brought it out, and carried it to his work table. I had an opportunity to study its protective hairs and its quills. As he cut it open, incidentally laying bare a lovely roast, I saw how everything from the condition of its teeth to the contents of its stomach would be information useful to future students of our wildlife.

Highway 16, passing through Edmonton, does little justice to that impressive city. At the risk of encountering a lot of traffic I like to swing south on Jasper Avenue and proceed along 16A onto Stony Plain Road. On Jasper you get one last glimpse of the river that dominates the eastern half of the drive. West of Edmonton the forest soon wins out over the farms; the Athabasca watershed begins at the crossing of the Pembina River.

Albertans like to call this section of road the Evergreen Route. Edmontonians in a hurry to get to open water on a Friday night drive out to the hilly country and places like Wabamun, Seba Beach, Lake Isle, Lake Eden, Jackfish Lake, Edmonton Beach, Lac la Nonne, Nakamun, Sandy Beach, Devil's Lake, Alberta Beach on Lac Sainte-Anne – or even as far as the Brazeau Dam. In the dim past of Edmonton, a lake called Drunken Lake was notorious as a place where traders corrupted Indians before beginning to dicker for furs. Sceptics now insist it would take a dozen archaeologists armed with dozens of cases of rye to decide which lake originally earned the name. A camp along here called Camp He-Ho-Ha only heightens the mystery.

West of the Pembina toward Chip Lake, muskeg replaces the occasional prairie. In Edson you become aware that the mountains are out west of you; the scent of muskeg and spruce is everywhere, and the high, clear, sunny air makes a man throw out his chest.

This exuberance led early settlers to call Edson the "Gateway to the Last Great West." Two exuberant railway companies, the Grand Trunk Pacific and the Canadian Northern, decided almost at the same time to use the Yellowhead Pass; in places their two road-beds were only a few yards apart. Both companies defaulted in the payment of interest guarantees in 1917, and both were taken over by the federal government to become the Canadian National Railway.

Today Edson is central in the provincial government's attempt to eradicate rural slums; the area is too high in altitude for successful wheat farming. But I have ridden out of Edson in a jeep, into the back country over abandoned loggers' trails, and come home with a creel full of rainbows. I've sailed on hidden lakes, gone swimming, picked berries, all the time keeping an eye open for the grizzly that one summer killed the man who was hunting him.

Hinton, west of Edson, is the first pulp-mill town in Alberta, as anyone can tell by the stink. The plant, operated by a subsidiary of the St. Regis Paper Company of New York, pollutes the air of Jasper Park when the wind blows from the wrong direction. Hinton itself is divided into two towns, upper and lower; I prefer the upper for its view of the nearby Rockies and the approach to Jasper. Hinton is a natural setting for Alberta's forestry school.

Since most of Alberta's major roads run through mountains or farmlands, visitors are surprised to learn that something like sixty percent of Alberta is forest. Unfortunately, most of the forests have been burned by fires at least once in the last sixty years; some have been burnt again and again until the soil and the seeds that might produce new forests are gone. Even today, however, the young forests are central to Alberta's watershed management, to her immense store of wildlife and fish, and to both her logging industry and her fame as a beautiful natural world. And now the use and preservation of these forests has become a field of study for young Albertans.

In Hinton I visited the forest technology school; I was especially fascinated by a recently acquired fire-simulator. In past years an average of 240,000 acres went up in smoke each year in Alberta; with the smoke went twenty-seven million dollars in forestry products, not to mention the loss to hunters, trappers, fishermen, and tourists. Here in school the men who will fight future fires get their basic training. Five overhead projectors focus through a common lens onto a screen. The teacher can change wind direction, flatten out the smoke, picture charred or burned areas; he can introduce a bulldozer putting in a fire line: he can incorporate sound effects such as a helicopter, a fire pump, an aircraft. The students have radio and telephone contact as they give and receive orders; the instructor can cut off that contact and see how a student reacts.

It would be nice if the instruction ended with the simulator; but even as I visited the school, 315 fires were burning to the west of us in British Columbia. A blue haze hung over most of Alberta. I watched a student doing experimental work in a greenhouse; an instructor helped me read an aerial map. But only when I visited a look-out man did I begin to understand how specialists come to grips with the reality that is a green but dry summer forest.

Gary Van Duzee is the man who operates the Athabasca Lookout, just north of Highway 16 west of Hinton. His look-out is on a hill high enough that he doesn't have to climb a tower; there is simply a cupola on top of his living quarters. His living-quarters are one large room divided by a short wall into a U-shape. On one side of the partition is his bedroom, on the other his elaborate radio equipment. The end of the room is his kitchen; a ladder leads up from the kitchen to a trapdoor and the glass cupola above.

When I drove up the hill to visit Gary, I found him out in front of his white wooden home; he was summarizing sky conditions and reading instruments that record temperature and humidity; this is also a weather station, at least from the middle of April into November.

Gary, a twenty-two-year-old bachelor, had arrived at his post in April to find it buried in five feet of snow. Since it is located at 5,187 feet above sea level, traces of snow linger into June, and the first trace of winter snow appears in August.

As we walked up to his look-out, his dog following, I noticed he had been at work building log and stone walks and attempting to establish a small rock-garden. During a period of high fire hazard he has to be in his cupola most of the day; when the hazard is low he goes up for an hour or two, then comes down for an hour.

Gary Van Duzee is a Calgary boy; his grandparents brought his old Dutch name to Alberta when they came as homesteaders from the United States. When he finished high school, Gary first went into the Princess Patricia's Canadian Light Infantry ("What I enjoyed most was parachuting"), then after two years took his discharge and entered the forestry service.

I had wondered who would like such a job. Gary was neatly shaved when I met him; I was certain I'd be tempted to throw away my razor. Handsome, dark-haired, with dark, bright eyes, he was dressed in shorts, a light shirt, and hiking boots, though a chill wind was blowing. "I like this better than hot weather like eighty-five degrees," he said.

He is quiet, versatile, and obviously both independent and reliable, as a man must be on such a job. He is the salt of the earth, as the saying has it. "Treat an outfit right and they'll treat you right," he assured me. And later he said, "Being up here makes a weak believer a strong believer."

Lightning has struck his look-out twice. For a while two bears took to bothering him, one of them standing three feet at the shoulder. But neither has showed up recently. He had started out as a hunter in this kind of country, but now he prefers to photograph the animals he has come so much to respect. He especially enjoys hiking, and when his two-week vacation comes in the fall, he likes to backpack into the mountains west of his look-out – and west of all roads.

We went up the ladder to see where he planned to go next.

From northwest to southeast the mountains marked the limits of his view, the Boule Range, then the Fiddle Ridge. Brûlé Lake lay blue and still in front of Boule Roche. Between us and the lake the new Alberta Resources Railway was a sand-coloured gash through the forest. We could see northward for fifty miles, past tiny lakes to where the railway disappeared into a green world of spruce and pine. To the south the Athabasca flowed out of Brûlé Lake and eastward to Hinton and the smudge of smoke that marked the site of the mill. To the south, across the river, pulpwood cutters have cut out long strips, leaving between them strips of trees that will help with the reseeding.

Gary showed me how he takes a reading on a telltale wisp or column of smoke, then gets a reading from another look-out and pinpoints the fire. He has to be in regular communication with the men at Huckleberry or Adams Creek or Luscar or Obed.

Those men, at least, are far away. Gary doesn't like crowds. "This is pack-horse country," he said, indicating a distant meadow where he had recently spotted elk and moose. "But now they're building too many roads. Especially that road to Grande Cache."

We crawled back down to his small kitchen and went out into the chill but sunny air. I noticed four drawings on his walls, sketches of old men and of dogs. I asked about them.

"My girl in Edmonton does them. Now she's doing a dog-team on the barrenlands for me." He hesitated. "I write her some poems once in a while."

Many a young writer has thought of becoming a fire look-out. I asked Gary about this. He'd never written a word in his life and hadn't wanted to, until the scenery and the girl from Edmonton, who liked canoeing, moved him to take up his pen.

Driving down off his quiet hill, I entered onto a newly construct-
ed road. Trucks roared by, with dust and gravel flying. A bulldozer
clanked toward me. Gary Van Duzee's premonition is correct: the road
to Grande Cache will forever alter his pack horse country.

Three mountains signal the entrance to Jasper National Park. Folding
Mountain, outside the gate, is a long slope, a folded-rock formation
known as an anticline. Roche à Perdrix is a sharper slope; two climbers
have recently died below its summit. Beyond that peak is Fiddle River
campground, in a stand of spruce beside a rocky river; it's an excellent
place to stop to rest or to study complicated geological formations.
Roche Miette is a cliff: it stands as a guardian of the gate. And its
name, so legend has it, derives from a voyageur named Miette who
climbed up and sat with his legs dangling over the two-thousand-foot
perpendicular face of rock.

At the foot of Roche Miette you get your first glimpse of Pyramid
Mountain: directly ahead and touched with snow even in August, its
pyramid peak and its reddish rock make it a landmark, for it stands to
the north of Jasper town.

Now the road follows the Athabasca River, with its gravel bars
and silvery driftwood, its islands with willow and scattered spruce; the
milky green of the silt-laden river offers a sharp contrast to the darker-
green water on the south side of the road.

Talbot Lake, remnant of a postglacial lake that once filled this
valley, is dark green, patterned more sombre by the growths of plantlife
on its floor. Reeds and patches of dead trees heighten the effect of its
being a remnant of something past. It ends abruptly on your left and
Jasper Lake is visible on the right: here blowing sand raises dunes
beside the glacier-fed waters.

The milky lake is ringed with hard, grey, barren mountains, and
now it's obvious you've passed through a gate – through the cliffs of
limestone on either side of the water, Roche Ronde to the north,

Roche Miette to the south. These mountains change with the season, the day, and the hour. To drive along here at midnight is to enter a world of stilled lakes where spruce stand like hooded ghosts, where the mountains are pale and unearthly. To come here in the winter is to leave the harsher flatlands and enter into a snow-covered pass that is strangely warmed by Pacific air.

Then the peak of Mount Edith Cavell comes into view, with its layering of snow and rock; before reaching it you are in Jasper town. The totem pole, carved on the Queen Charlotte Islands by a Haida chief, Simon Stiltae, and brought here in 1915, becomes a pivot for a ring of mountains. As you face the way the Raven faces, you see on your left the Colin Range, grey and gaunt, dominated by the sleeping face of Roche Bonhomme. Directly ahead are two mountains, the wooded slopes of Signal Mountain in contrast to the rock of Tekarra. And to the right, snow-covered and still quite distant, is Mount Edith Cavell.

I talked to a man who stopped to see the totem pole and has never left. Werner Beilard, an immigrant to Alberta from Germany, thought he knew mountains. He visited Jasper and liked it; he took a temporary job; then he found himself writing civil-service exams so that he could get a permanent job.

For a few years now he has worked as an assistant technician at the fish hatchery. This too is worth a visit, to see the pools in which thousands of trout feed and to look at splake, the cross produced when eggs from eastern brook trout are fertilized by lake trout. From here the park lakes are stocked with two and a half million fish each year. Rainbow and cut-throat are planted in the spring, eastern brook and splake in the fall. To get to the higher lakes the men use helicopters, making sure that no fisherman is likely to find a lake that isn't worth a try.

Werner is kept busy the year round, protecting the tiny fish from their natural enemies. In the winter, lynx, great horned owls, a bird called the dipper, and mink steal fish. In the summer the osprey and the kingfisher come here, after the robins have done a little stealing to feed their voracious young. Fish otters have shown up on occasion. And one winter Werner trapped fourteen mink here and released them at Talbot Lake.

The area within a few miles of Jasper town abounds in lakes and canyons and rivers, in plant and animal life. But for those who, like the voyageurs of old, must press on to greater dangers, there is an easy seventeen-mile drive to the edge of the park, to the border of Alberta and the top of the pass. And as you begin your long descent to the Pacific, there waits ahead of you that stately peak Mount Robson, resplendent at 12,972 feet and the highest peak in the Canadian Rockies. It completes the procession of mountains that guides the stranger through Yellowhead Pass. It gives a startling beauty to the northwestern corner of Jasper Park. But by a divine error that is hardly forgivable, the mountain itself is to be found in British Columbia rather than in Alberta.

5. PEACE RIVER: THE ROAD NORTH

The going was easy at first, even for seven greenhorns, though the sky was overcast. Rain began to fall during the early afternoon, and they camped at Mile Twenty-one. But they were resolved to be as tough as the homesteaders who had preceded them by fifty years: next day they started at dawn and rode thirty-two miles. The old trail had almost disappeared into the returning muskeg and forest, rain continued to fall; when they reached the confluence of the Berland and the Athabasca, their horses were in tough shape.

Two boats met them; though it was May, the continuing cold weather meant the river was low and treacherous. They said goodbye to John Hackett and his string of horses, crossed the river, and found trail boss Joe Groat waiting with two new wranglers and twenty-three fresh horses. They had 190 miles left to cover.

On the morning of the third day it was the riders who were in tough shape. Seven business and professional men from Edson, they were commemorating the opening of the Edson-Grande Prairie Trail into the Peace River country by riding to Grande Prairie. And they were so stiff and sore they could just barely help each other into their saddles.

To make matters worse, while breaking camp they discovered their whisky was missing. It had gone back to Edson with the first pack train. They camped that night on Marshhead Creek, stiff and thirsty, too tired to play their usual game of poker on one of the pack boxes.

On the fourth day the sky cleared; a bush plane circled low over the riders; a message came tumbling out of the sky. Back in Edson, the tragedy of the misplaced whisky had been discovered. The message read: "Have booze and cameras. Can meet at abandoned Marshhead airstrip. White for yes. Red or blue for no."

Seven weary gringos and two wranglers did everything but strip off their jockey shorts in order to make the answer clear.

"Fine," the trail boss said. "But the pack train must go on. We can't delay."

They were six miles beyond the airstrip. Whoever went back to rendezvous with the plane would have to ride an extra twelve miles. The silence was unbearable to a lawyer in the group.

"Twelve miles, twelve bottles," Knobby Sommer said. "I'll go back."

"You'll need an undertaker," Jingo Joy said. 'I'll go with you."

Mounted on Double Diamond and Mohawk, the two men turned around. Sagebrush Soltys, Cordite Cheisa, Tumbleweed Topott, Bushman Brown, and Gallopin' Grant pushed on. When the volunteers caught up with the train that night, two pack-animals were down in the muck. And the long-abandoned trail had become so vague that even the part-Indian veteran Joe Groat wasn't sure where he would find the Little Smoky River. They waded into the muck and water to unload the two horses, led them to safety, and without so much as start-ing a fire to dry their socks, they opened four bottles of their newly recovered whisky.

On the fifth day they found the Little Smoky. But while they were wading across a beaver dam, one of the horses snagged on a beaver cutting. Before a wrangler could get to the pack horse, she began to struggle. Someone stepped off his horse into the blood-red mud. But already it was too late. The mare was dead by the time they had freed her of her pack. A subdued group of riders set up their tents that night on the Waskahigan River.

Next morning they were awakened by a wrangler. They'd have to do without still another horse. Outside their tent flaps, a new colt frisked in the wet grass. One of the mares had foaled during the night.

Joe Groat looked at his bewhiskered crew. "Okay, you fellows. If we lose another horse, we'll have to shoot a rider."

That prospect somehow cheered the men forward. On that sixth day they rode hard; now they were more at home in the saddle than on the earth. Toward evening the lead horse went through a patch of spruce, and shied at the sight of a truck parked in a clearing.

The seven greenhorns had ridden over the worst part of the old trail. Ahead of them was a dirt road. The truck was loaded with fresh food and cold beer. Concerned wives had sent in clean sheets. Messages of encouragement came from hundreds of admirers. The Provincial Archives of Alberta wanted pictures and a full report.

The seven latter-day pioneers relaxed. They had only an easy three-day ride to make now, and they'd be sitting down to a huge reception dinner in the thriving little city of Grande Prairie.

THE LAND OF TWELVE-FOOT DAVIS

A Beaver Indian legend has it that if you drink Peace River water, you're certain to return. The truth is, however, that with the Swan Hills standing athwart a direct route from Edmonton to Peace River, the problem has always been to get there in the first place. Early travellers had the choice of circling either to the left or to the right of the Swan Hills – the blank white heart of any map of Alberta.

The Edson-Grande Prairie Trail was the western route. The second choice was even more difficult. On that route the first task was to get to Athabasca Landing: the Athabasca Trail ran for one hundred miles north from Edmonton. Travellers rode on oxcarts or wagons, or, in the wintertime, on sleighs. Warburton Pike, an English traveller, launched onto the trail thus in 1889:

> On the morning of the fifth day I reached Edmonton, a pleasant little
> town scattered along the far bank of the North Saskatchewan. . . .
> Finding that I had no time to spare if I wished to catch the steamer
> down the Athabasca river, I left again the same evening, after buying a
> supply of flour and bacon. I changed the buckboard for a wagon, having
> for driver a French half-breed who had spent his early life on the prairie
> in buffalo-hunting. . . .

Athabasca Landing was the chief jumping-off place for traffic down the Mackenzie. But it was also the beginning of a water route into the Peace River country.

Alberta is a land-locked province, yet her four great rivers give her a long and fascinating history of water transportation. Sternwheelers like the S.S. *Midnight Sun* ran upstream from Athabasca Landing to the mouth of the Lesser Slave River. Passengers rode freight wagons over a sixteen-mile portage, then boarded the S.S. *Northern Light* for the passage across Lesser Slave Lake. Then, if they persisted, they rode a wagon another ninety miles to Peace River Crossing, where they could board still another steamer. The Catholic mission operated the *St. Charles* on the Peace. The Hudson's Bay Company owned the *Peace River*. But the grand old mistress of that 575-mile stretch of good water was the S.S. *D.A. Thomas*.

The Welsh capitalist Baron Rhondda (that is, Mr. D.A. Thomas) had her built for his Peace River Development Company; he was especially concerned to exploit the coal-fields of Hudson Hope – a dream that collapsed with the beginning of the First World War. The sternwheeler was taken over by the Lamson, Hubbard Company, an American fur-trading concern that kept her until 1922. She was 167 feet long with a beam of 40 feet and carried two hundred tons of freight. Her twin stacks belching smoke, extra wood piled on her low bow behind the flagpole, passengers loafing on the long passenger-deck, her big wheel churning the water white: she was a floating hotel. In 1924 the Hudson's Bay Company took her over; the big steamer had a notorious appetite for wood, and she lived up to it always, keeping a large crew of men busy cutting, stacking, and loading fuel. In 1930 the Bay ran her down the Vermilion Chutes, where the river is nearly two miles wide and drops thirty feet in one mile, principally over a fourteen-foot ledge of rock. The famous pilot Louis Bourassa was in the pilot-house; the only damage was the loss of half of the sternwheel. The old queen was taken down the Slave to Fort Fitzgerald and dismantled, because her boilers were more valuable than her reputation. When I worked on the river portage at Fort Fitzgerald in 1948, we were using her big old wheel-house as the grandest outhouse in a province that boasts a superior collection.

The water route north, along with the Edson Trail, fell into disuse with the completion of the Edmonton, Dunvegan, and British Columbia Railway along the south shore of Lesser Slave Lake and as far west as Grande Prairie in 1916. The flood of homesteaders began, and has not yet ended.

I flew north from Edmonton to Peace River, over the Swan Hills, in seventy minutes. I borrowed the car of a friend who had gone moose hunting in the jeep he had towed up Highway 43. Looking at a road map I was caught again in the magic of those Peace River names: Dunvegan, Teepee Creek, Bear Canyon, Bad Heart, Valhalla Centre, Friedenstal, Wapiti, Blueberry Mountain, Driftpile, Faust, Winagami Lake, Grouard Mission. The old and the new come into focus best at Dunvegan, where a magnificent suspension bridge crosses the old waterway. But I had something else in mind.

There is, along the eastern edge of the Peace River country, a group of towns in which a considerable percentage of the inhabitants are French-speaking – the towns from McLennan west, little farm towns such as Donnelly, Falher, Guy, Girouxville, Tangent, Eaglesham, Codesa, and Jean Côté. I visited two men in the area, a retired homesteader and a young farmer.

The sign outside Falher read: "Bienvenue à Falher, Honey Capital of Canada." Father Giroux and Father Falher, before the First World War, brought into this area many French Canadians who had been working in the textile mills of New England. Flavius Plourde is eighty-three years old – "I'm pretty near an old man now," he said, laughing, his face free of wrinkles and almost beatific in its radiant good humour. He invited me into the modest house where he has lived alone since the death of his wife.

He was married in 1908 to a girl from the Gaspé; he himself was then living in Dame-Du-Lac on Lac Temiscouata, Quebec, and he worked first as a sportsmen's guide in the hunting country around the lake. But he had a fever to be off and wandering, and the young couple went to Rhode Island.

By 1912 they were travelling west to the fabled Peace River country with a group of fellow *Canadiens* who were leaving the States and the mills for the promise of new land and a freer life. The Plourdes travelled the old route into the country: a trip that began in earnest at

Athabasca Landing. The winter ride from there to Grouard lasted three
and a half days, if you had an excellent team.

M. Plourde was modest about his excellent command of English.
As a result we struck on a delightful way of communicating: we looked
at his lifetime collection of photographs and snapshots.

He led me to the old buffet in his dining room. On the dining-
room table were a collection of fossils and rocks he has picked up in
this region, and a bouquet of flowers made of foam rubber by a little
niece. He explained that he and his wife had no children. The first pictures were of cousins: one family with eight daughters, another with
two priests to its credit. He showed me two photographs of the big old
house in which he was born in Quebec, a house much larger than any I
have seen in the Peace River country. He showed me a picture of his
father's sawmill, then of his father: a photograph taken one hundred
years ago, the father stiff and lean and young behind a magnificent
beard.

Flavius Plourde was a very handsome young guide with a dark
moustache, and women obviously delighted in being photographed
with him. He has pictures of a beautiful woman sharing a canoe he
built, others of a very stout dowager from Philadelphia who shot a
moose and posed with Flavius and the antlers. He has pictures of himself calling moose, with Sugarloaf Mountain in the background, more
of a hunting lodge.

Then he brought out a large and carefully posed photograph of a
group of men and women standing beside a train in Duluth,
Minnesota. "Which is me?" he challenged, laughing. Flavius Plourde
stood young and confident beside his young wife, in a group of pioneers
who were leaving Rhode Island and Massachusetts for new homes in
the wilderness.

The next picture was of only a few of those men, sitting on the
bow of a river-steamer. Flavius counted – only he and one other man
were now surviving. But the exploits of each were fresh in his mind:

that man became mayor, that man went on to British Columbia, that man was pinned under a truck at 5:00 P.M. and was found dying the next morning at nine.

M. Plourde homesteaded three miles north of Falher. The country was mostly bush, with a little prairie. He used an axe and a plough and oxen, and he has snapshots of his homestead shack with four people standing proudly in a row before its low door; he has a picture of his log barn, of the first calf born on his homestead.

"Gee whiz," he said, for we had hardly begun, "I got lots of pictures."

And he has: he and his wife in a cutter, the horse covered with frost. A four-horse team breaking land. His stock and a straw pile. His geese. The best team of horses he ever owned. A bull team pulling a threshing machine, with horses pulling the stationary engine: the first threshing outfit in Falher. Men threshing out of stacks, with snow on the ground. A threshing crew, including one Indian, standing in a ragged line. Four men sawing wood with a tractor and a saw. His wife feeding her chickens. The water barrels on a wagon used before they used "roof water." A binder and three-horse team in a wheatfield.

To go shopping they drove a team on the ice to Grouard. Grouard was sixty miles distant, and the trip one way took two days. He showed me a picture of sleigh dogs lined up in the old mission and Indian settlement of Grouard. ("The railway passed it. It's all gone now.") He showed me pictures of his first car, a Pontiac, and of a trip he and his wife took to Banff.

He has saved some old postcards: pictures of the Gaspé, of a log drive, pictures of the lake and town he left behind in Quebec. But here in this new country he finds time for old pleasures. Mounted and hung above the dining-room door is the head of a moose he shot in 1934, next to a newspaper photograph of John Kennedy. Flavius has a cabin on the Little Smoky River. His guns hang on a rack made of deer's hoofs. He showed me pictures of his hunting trips; a fly tent along the

Smoky, strings of fish in front of grinning fishermen, two men with a bear on a pole so they could carry it out of the spruce forest. "I like to go in the bush and see lots of things," he said, and to do just that he had been to his cabin the previous evening. "Down there I saw bear tracks, and two deer." And right then he insisted we interrupt our picture-gazing and go outside to see the robin's nest on his back porch, the wasps' nest above it on the wall. "So many wasps this year," he said. "I don't know what it means. Maybe a mild winter."

Inside again, we had to have a drink of water from the Little Smoky. He brought out a jug from his pantry. "It's good water," he said. "Clear. And it has a mineral in it." We drank mightily, and the water was good; I had learned that in the Peace country water is always a concern.

After we had finished looking at another album of pictures, I went out into the street; the schoolchildren were passing by. As they strolled along they talked easily, now in French, now in English, now in French.

Flavius has been retired for many years. I drove out to visit a young farmer near the town of Guy.

It was a September day and harvest was in full swing; Guy Tokarz (he was named after his home town) hardly had time to eat or sleep. Fortunately for me, he did stop for coffee, and seeing two trucks parked in the farmyard, I hoped I might catch him taking a break.

Guy came to the farmhouse door when the dog began to bark. The comfortable house has a large sunny kitchen; we sat down around the table, Guy and his brother and father and mother and I. Guy was sitting, but hardly relaxing; he spoke rapidly, moved rapidly as he distributed cups and spoons.

The Tokarz family is Polish in origin; the children learned Polish in their home, French in school, and English from some of their neighbours. Guy spoke Polish to his mother; he spoke French to his father and brother, English to me.

Albert Tokarz, born in Poland, had worked for five years in a French factory; then in 1928 he came to Canada to homestead. He had read in Europe that in the Peace River country you could "pick up money every place."

His first job was pulling out and picking up stumps – grubbing, as the expression has it – for ten hours and one dollar a day. He worked for two years before he could bring his wife from the Old Country to join him. Meanwhile, he was clearing the jackpine off his own land as well as working out. He turned his first furrows with horses and a walking-plough, and he spoke English to give me a lecture I heard once a week in Alberta: "A young fellow now won't lift an axe. You can't even hire him to sit on a machine. When I first came here –"

But Albert's five sons are a refutation of his favourite thesis. Four of them farm. Guy helps his father look after 960 acres as well as attending to a farm of his own. He had just finished harvesting five hundred acres of his own crop – "small seed" as he called it – the alfalfa, creeping red fescue, red and alsike clover that make this region prosperous. "Listen," Guy said, finding a bottle of rye in a kitchen cabinet and pouring straight shots for me and his father, "you've got to be working fifteen hundred to two thousand acres or it isn't worth the trouble." Albert Tokarz and I drank to each other's health. The boys had too much work to do.

Mrs. Tokarz was picking up our coffee cups. But Guy, as busy as he was, couldn't resist the opportunity to talk farming. "The way it's set up, a little farmer can only get a little loan; a bigger farmer can borrow seventy thousand dollars –"

"When I was young, one dollar a day." Albert Tokarz set down his empty shot glass. "I broke my leg one winter, when we had sixteen head of cattle. My wife hauled water sixteen miles with a team, all the way from the Smoky River. There was an old Indian trail, no road."

"No water here," Guy explained, "yet Dad wants to raise cattle. We drilled four dry holes. All we have is rain water and the cistern. . . ."

The talk wandered on, with the intensity characteristic of large families, where you have to assert yourself to be heard. But finally the younger brother reminded us that harvest wasn't over. The old man nodded but didn't move. Mrs. Tokarz discreetly took away the bottle of rye. . . .

Back on the hard-surfaced road, I began to appreciate the landscape more than I had. On my first trip into the Peace I arrived at night; the sky was dark but clear, the earth was black and unbelievably flat. I might have been looking out at the sea, had I not been able to recognize in the distance the lights of two towns and, nearer at hand, the lone lights of isolated farmsteads. Talking to M. Plourde and the Tokarz family, I had begun to understand that these flat, square, open fields were only recently covered with forest. I realized I had seen few cattle. The only water was in dug-outs or cisterns or in the rivers – and it was hard to talk to anyone without quickly mentioning water.

Now, having begun to understand at least a little the mystery of that land and its river, I drove directly to the wooden statue of Twelve-Foot Davis and, leaving my borrowed car, I climbed on foot the sacred hill.

Twelve-Foot Davis is both real and legendary: in the Peace River country you are quickly told by a proud tale-teller that he was illiterate, had a squeaky voice, and stood only five feet two inches in his moccasins. Henry Fuller Davis earned his name in the Cariboo gold rush, chiefly by arriving too late. The most promising claims had been staked. But the Little Diller and Tontine, two neighbouring claims, young Davis noticed, were farther apart than they ought to be. He did some careful measuring and promptly filed on a twelve-foot strip that lay unclaimed between. Out of his discovery he made fifteen thousand dollars. And he thereby won his enduring nickname.

He earned his enduring reputation on the Peace. Twelve-Foot used his gold-field earnings to become a trader on the Peace River, establishing posts at Dunvegan, Fort Vermilion, and Lesser Slave Lake. By the time he died, he had become famous for his integrity and generosity in general, and for his pumpkin pies in particular. Twelve-Foot died in September of 1890 while on his way back from Edmonton to Fort Vermilion. He was first buried, I am told, at the Anglican mission on Buffalo Bay, Lesser Slave Lake.

Italy has its quarrel about Dante's bones. The Peace River has its difficulties too. According to the legend of Twelve-Foot, some of his friends and acquaintances were lamenting his death in a Peace River beer parlour when one of them mentioned how he had so much loved to stand on a hill above the Crossing and either watch for approaching riverboats or look out toward the most enthralling view in the country: the fork where the Peace and the Smoky rivers meet, where Alexander Mackenzie wintered in his Fork Fort in 1792, before completing the first overland journey across North America. As the historic discussion continued, one beer led to another, and it was finally and unanimously resolved that Twelve-Foot should be buried on the spot he had so loved during his long life.

Without further delay these men went out and harnessed a team, drove a wagon to Lesser Slave Lake – a hundred miles each way on today's modern roads – and transported their friend and hero to an appropriate resting-place.

I am also told you can get a better view of the forks from Judah Hill, across the valley. But the view from Twelve-Foot's impressive grave is one of a roof of sky, of a long valley of rivers, islands, and forest converging on the town below your feet. Turning from the view to the simple marker, you cannot help but be moved when reading: "H. F. DAVIS Born in Vermont 1820 Died at Slave Lake 1893 (sic) Pathfinder Pioneer Miner and Trader He was every man's friend and never locked his cabin door."

THE MACKENZIE HIGHWAY

Mile Zero, like mukluks or weak coffee, is a Canadian institution. Mile Zero of the Mackenzie Highway is a stone marker in the farming town of Grimshaw, Alberta; the road, most of it gravel, runs 626 miles to the north. It ends on the far side of Great Slave Lake in Yellowknife, the new capital of the Northwest Territories.

The bus parked outside the depot in Peace River had a windshield that seemed to have been hit by shrapnel; another passenger remarked that a man could make a fortune in the north by inventing a cast-iron car window.

I rode in the company of two high-school drop-outs. It was September and they had only in the past ten days made the heady decision that they'd had enough of this education stuff. They were going north for the first time in their lives, to work on a seismograph rig at Rainbow Lake. They were to join Party Seven, which they took to be a good omen; there would be from sixty to one hundred men in the isolated bush-camp.

These two boys, eating chocolate bars, leaning across the aisle to talk to me, said little of the homes they had just left, little of the countryside outside the bus's windows: the flat square farms edged by forest, the log buildings here and there beside new granaries, the patches of newly broken land still rough with stumps, the signs of past forest fires, the brilliant sunshine on the yellowing leaves. Like the other men on the bus, they talked mostly of money.

The younger of the two, slender and blond, had spent the summer working in a grocery store in his small home-town. "Can't make much money smashing groceries," he explained to his stout, dark-haired companion. "No unions in Alberta," he went on. "In British Columbia a store clerk makes more than a department manager here. They wanted me to run produce." The second boy had driven a delivery truck in Edmonton for the summer. At the end of the summer, he explained somewhat proudly, he was five hundred bucks in the hole.

They began to exchange the words of wisdom they had received from acquaintances who worked in the oilfields: "The secret to hanging onto your money is, don't cash your cheques." I agreed that that had the ring of sound fiscal policy. "And no gambling," the blond boy continued. "There's always somebody in those games better than you are." The stout boy had been trying to interrupt: "Oil rigs pay more than seismograph, but you get more hours on seismograph." I learned that they had been promised an eighty-hour week as minimum. "You've got to get out of the town where you were born or you'll never make it," the stout boy explained, adding that if he ever got out of the hole he'd never go into debt again in his life.

We stopped in the town of Manning for coffee. We were joined in our restaurant booth by a young fellow who had been north and was now going back to Zama Lake from a ten-day holiday that had cost him twelve hundred dollars. The dark boy groaned. We talked money again: the newcomer, having ordered coffee for all of us, asked directly, "How much overtime you getting?"

The two boys who had not yet seen their first job were wondering if they should quit and go with another outfit, when the waitress brought the big spender a sandwich. He looked at it, then at the waitress: "How far did you have to run to catch it?"

The blond boy resumed his story of the grocer who sold supplies to the oil camps during the Swan Hills boom: a quiet country storekeeper made enough in five years that he could retire for life. The newcomer was not to be outdone so easily. "I worked with a guy who once robbed the jewellery store in Fort McMurray. He went in with two kitbags and filled them with rings and watches and stuff like that. Took everything to Vancouver and sold it to a fence for twenty thousand dollars. He didn't have to work for four months."

At this point I learned that all three were working for well under two dollars an hour. The dark-haired boy rather pathetically announced he'd heard that if a guy went to barbering-school and then went north. . . . "The nearest barber to High Level is 122 miles. . . . The fella up there at Zama was doing a head every five minutes, but three drunks one night were so mad at the haircuts they got, they ran him out of camp."

The bus driver was carrying out boxes of freight, so we knew it was time to go. As we headed into the dust the old veteran of twenty informed his two greenhorn friends: "They killed a lot of men up here on these roads last winter. One transport company lost three drivers in one week. They keep it out of the papers."

Manning is in the lovely valley of the Notikewin River; quickly we dipped down off the rich flat farmland into the valley of the Hotchkiss; then, north again, we dropped into the truly beautiful deep valley of the Meikle, the spruce trees dark green, the aspens like beaten gold, the bushes russet and brown and red.

The river valleys are rugged; above them the country seems tamed, by the sawmills, by the men out picking up roots and rocks or burning the windrows of bulldozed brush. But now and then the bus topped a low rise: the immensity of the country in a moment dwarfed the road and the farms, for the long, wide, shallow valleys run from horizon to distant horizon, and seem to be full of nothing but virgin forest.

We had another twenty-eight miles to go to High Level when the two new boys began to collect their gear; they'd been on the bus for twelve hours. The old veteran made a great show of seeming to doze off as the two greenhorns approached their adventure.

Rainbow Lake, first developed by Banff Oil Limited, now produces the cheapest oil in North America. Earlier exploration led to the conviction that somewhere in the area was a Devonian reef holding immense quantities of oil and natural gas. In 1965, Banff Oil, at fifty-seven hundred feet below the muskeg, hit a big pool. A new Alberta town has been laid out at Rainbow Lake; it expects shortly to have a population of forty-five hundred new citizens.

High Level, on the Mackenzie Highway, is a boom town, for it is the jumping-off place for the oil fields at Rainbow and Zama. At the peak of activity, 110 seismic crews were in the bush near High Level; 4,000 men were getting their supplies through this town; they cut over 16,000 miles of seismic line through the surrounding forest in their successful search for oil. Fifty to fifty-five oil rigs were being serviced out of what had earlier been little more than a bus stop.

The usual boom lasts seven or eight years. But High Level has a chance of surviving its own success. The Great Slave Lake Railway came to High Level in 1963, and this may, in the long run, prove more significant to the town's continued growth than the presence of oil. The G.S.L.R., called "The Eskimo Line" because it employed many of the skilled Eskimos who were earlier trained to work on the DEW line, was the first railway into the Northwest Territories. Completed to Hay River and Pine Point in 1965, it was intended primarily to haul out concentrated lead-zinc ore.

The town is located within the 31,976 square miles of the Footner Lake Forest, largest of the eleven forests in Alberta. Because of the railway, a huge sawmill is taking timber out of the valley of the Chinchaga River and the beautiful Watt Mountain area – the line of hills to the west of town.

Most important, three brand-new grain elevators dominate the skyline: High Level is the most northerly bulk-grain shipping-centre in North America. In one year fifty thousand acres of homestead land were made available by the completion of surveys; there were three applications for each new homestead.

We drove out of the usual northern dust and stopped in the usual northern mud. A car was waiting to take my young friends to the landing strip and an airplane; they were told they'd be out in the bush and at work within an hour.

Owen Jordan was the first man I met in High Level. He is a living part of the story of the town's growth, for Owen filed claim here on a homestead in 1958 "to get away from the public."

Owen, like many men in the north, is what is affectionately called "a Saskatchewan refugee." He was a farmer and survived the Depression. As he put it, "We moved so often in Saskatchewan that when we backed the wagon up to the house, the chickens turned over on their backs to have their legs tied."

A quiet-spoken man, he remembered fondly the delight he and his wife had taken in their north-country homestead. But in 1960 he traded off some property he owned farther south and ended up owning the café, garage, grocery store, and ten cabins in High Level – "a settlement of thirty people around a gas pump in the bush." On his first day of business it was twenty below zero, and four oil stoves "went on the hummer" in the cabins. "It was all outdoors plumbing, and that was wicked too."

But Owen had acquired more than a business; he had got hold of a dream. The road north fascinated him; he wanted to build a worthy stopping-place. He sold the café and service station and he "wore out about fifty pencils" designing what he wanted to build. "I was told I was ready for the bughouse when I put up a big hotel on the Mackenzie Highway."

By 1964, the hotel complex represented an investment of $400,000. In 1965 the first oil well blew in at Rainbow. There hasn't been a vacant room in the hotel since November of 1965. The hotel has the most northerly beer parlour in Alberta; now it employs one man just to haul in beer. The hotel sells as much as three thousand dollars worth in one day. Owen Jordan himself has retired: to a new home on a new street in High Level.

Just east of this new town is an area that is held by some historians to be the oldest farming area in Alberta. Fort Vermilion's history is old enough to be somewhat vague; the first fort on that stretch of the river may have been "The Old Establishment" that Alexander Mackenzie noted as he was going upriver to his winter camp in 1792. There was a Roman Catholic mission at Fort Vermilion by the middle of the nineteenth century. The Anglican mission was established in 1879. But up until very recently, Fort Vermilion has been accessible only by boat or plane; I couldn't resist the new road.

In High Level I boarded a relic of a bus, along with a full load of Métis families, Mennonite girls who had been to Peace River to do some shopping, and a scattering of Indians (there are fourteen reservations within one hundred miles of High Level). The forty-seven mile drive took two hours and forty minutes, for the bus hardly careered around a sharp bend through the hanging dust without either someone stepping out into the middle of the road or a passenger lurching to his feet under a heap of packages to cry out that we had just gone past his destination. Every gate, every corner, every creek, every reservation was a potential bus stop. I sat with five different passengers in the course of the ride, and during these visitations I was treated to phrases in Slavey, Cree, French, and English – all of them in the soft musical voices of northern peoples.

My last companion on that short ride was John Lizotte, a Métis farmer aged eighty-two. He got on at Lambert's Corner, sat down beside me, his round, sad old face almost disappearing inside his too-large windbreaker collar as he plopped down, and immediately he explained how it used to take him four hours to walk out here from Fort Vermilion to visit his friend. He was no enemy of progress, John Lizotte. He gave me the latest news about his friend, whom he assumed I knew – for the friend was a distant cousin to the trader who was shot out in the bush by a debt-ridden trapper only last winter, and he was certain the whole world knew of the incident.

And then I did recall – not John's friend, but John's father. I remembered reading that back in the nineteenth century the Hudson's Bay Company brought in a Michael Lizotte from Quebec to run a farm at Fort Vermilion. Young John had started work on his father's farm at the age of twelve, using oxen and a walking plough. He spoke of the flour mill of that time: "It made flour the colour of mud." Back in his father's day, he went on, the traders didn't want a man to leave home. There was no road. And there wasn't a big government ferry carrying people across the river.

The settlement of Fort Vermilion is a typical north-country settlement; it runs for something like two miles along the high bank of the Peace River. Half a mile out in the water is a long, narrow, deserted island; beyond the island is another half-mile of water. On the rocky shore beneath the settlement were the usual boats and kickers, and a float plane tied to a tree. Among the trees were two sleigh-dogs, loud and invisible. And facing the road is a fascinating and disorderly assembly of buildings – a post office, little cafés, stores, mission buildings, government buildings, and those sturdy old two-storey whitewashed log houses that won't ever be built again.

I had come out to visit a wilderness settlement; I had not bothered to bring along a sleeping bag. The search for a bed became a rather epic undertaking. I went from the town's modest and full motel into the best café; it was run by a family recently arrived from Hong Kong, and they had hardly enough sleeping space for themselves.

Next I saw a sign that advertised the weekend's movie; in Fort Vermilion a child can still see a movie for twenty-five cents. Perhaps I could sleep somewhere in the theatre.

While I did not meet with success at the door of the building that was supposedly the local movie palace, my inquiry led me into a delightful conversation with its owner, Ernest Rivard. An aristocratic-looking, bent old gentleman, he explained that I was having a lark compared to what he had endured. He came west from Montreal at the age of twenty-one, intending to stay for one year and then go home. In Peace River he and another fellow were grubstaked by a trader and sent

down river to trap for the winter. They left Peace River in a scow with
a year's supplies aboard; the trip took eight days and almost ended the
venture, for they ran into heavy ice floes. "Cold," he said. "We didn't
dare sleep – the ice could sink the scow like that." He snapped his fingers. Fortunately, a chinook blew in, and they managed to get as far as
Fort Vermilion. His face lit up in a smile. "Lots of fun then. No cars,
just horses and dogs. Lots of good times and everybody was happy. Mail
came once a month – by dogs, then by a team of horses. Two months in
the spring with no mail at all."

"Did you get home that spring?"

"It was forty years before I got home."

"Don't discourage me," I said.

We talked a little longer, especially of the days when the grand
old sternwheeler the *D.A. Thomas* came steaming around the bend to
land passengers and freight. I tried to bring up the subject of places to
sleep once more. "And dogs," Ernest went on. "Dog teams everywhere
in the winter. Hundreds of dogs tied up and barking all summer – there
are only a few left now. The power toboggans came." He was proud of
the settlement. "We grew wheat here before they grew it in
Calgary...."

While we talked, the wife of the owner of the motel sent word
asking if I still needed a place to stay. She had located a friend who was
playing host to six stranded visitors; there was certain to be room for
one more. Shortly a car arrived to pick me up; and shortly I knew I was
indeed beyond the confines and mores of what passes for civilization.
My hosts had already prepared a room and bed for me; they insisted
that I make use of their car; they insisted that I plan to have breakfast
with them.

Lloyd Northey is a bush pilot; he and his wife and his sons came
into Fort Vermilion nine years ago, and today he operates a fleet of four
planes, flying for Indian Health (there is a hospital in Fort Vermilion),
for tourists who want to catch thirty-pound trout, and especially for the

oil outfits. Parked in his yard he had a twenty-eight-man bush-camp unit: two bunk-houses, a cook-house, and a wash-house. The camp would be moved into the bush as soon as the muskeg was frozen. Meanwhile I had a room in one of the bunk-houses all to myself, and the comfort seemed downright extravagant.

I borrowed the Northeys's car to visit the experimental farm. A substation of the Beaverlodge experimental centre, it has been in operation since 1908. Even in that year, forty-four thousand bushels of grain were grown in the district, much of it ground into flour in the local mill. Because of the foresight shown then, the experimental farm has been a shaping influence in the development of this vast area.

Today the preliminary soils reconnaissance suggests optimistically that nearly six million acres north of the town of Manning will prove to be arable. The records kept since 1908 reveal some remarkable developments. For instance, in the forty years from 1918 to 1958, the total annual precipitation rose from eleven and a half to fifteen and a half inches, the mean annual temperature rose from twenty-six degrees to thirty degrees, and the period free from a killing frost (twenty-eight degrees) grew from 80 days to 114 days. The shortest growing season on record is 22 days, the longest 148 days. The lowest temperature recorded was seventy-eight degrees below zero in January 1911. The highest was 103 degrees in May 1912.

Mike Rudakewich, the young district agriculturalist, believes that the area will prosper with the solving of certain problems. Farmers are experiencing considerable difficulty in finding water. The area is ideal for mixed farming, but farmers have hesitated to go into livestock because of the shortage of water, the long market haul, and the distance from improved breeding-stock. The nearest veterinarian is three hundred miles away, so if you have only one sick cow it's cheaper to let the cow die than to attempt to bring in the vet.

In spite of all this, Mike optimistically points out that this is the fastest-growing agricultural district in Alberta. And Mike, who graduated in agricultural engineering from the University of Alberta in 1964, is persuasive not only because of his enthusiasm and knowledge; his father, he told me, went into the Hines Creek area of the Peace River country in 1929 – at a time when the pessimists were saying that homesteading anywhere was futile. Today in the British Columbia section of the Peace country the super-farm has become both a fact and a portent of the future. One corporation, controlled out of Nebraska, is farming forty-one thousand acres.

Two-thirds of the people in the Fort Vermilion area are of some Indian background; the Slaveys, especially, from here and the region to the north and west, have won renown as forest-fire fighters. The district around Rocky Lane is a Ukrainian settlement. And the La Crete area is almost entirely Mennonite.

I had heard that a number of Mennonite families were leaving Alberta for Bolivia and the British Honduras; one travel agent alone claimed to be handling the emigration applications of 159 persons. I asked Mike about this.

He insisted first that they are among the best farmers in the area; they go into mixed farming, they grow lots of vegetables for home use, and they are able not only to repair but to build specialized machines such as root-pickers and brush-cutters (in this country, replacements for broken parts might be two hundred miles away). He explained that only a few are leaving; there are 250 Mennonite families farming in the La Crete area alone. Some of them, he added, don't like such things as pension plans and health plans and income tax. More of them feel that the provincial government is using its schools to break down their rather austere religious beliefs. And finally, some of them have had three crop failures in a row.

Mennonite religious belief, deriving from the Anabaptist movement of the sixteenth century, seems to encourage a close contact with the agricultural frontier. It rejects the use of force, including military activity. The Russian Mennonites of North America have come in

recent years to frown on the use of alcohol and tobacco. Life in an isolated farming community, then, seems ideally suited to the practice of
their firm religious principles. The Mennonite writer Rudy Wiebe,
while a graduate student at the University of Alberta, wrote his first
novel, *Peace Shall Destroy Many*. In his story of a rural community in
northern Saskatchewan during the Second World War, he captures
both the spiritual struggle of a group of Mennonites and the intimate
day-to-day experience of anyone farming in the western provinces.

In thinking of those Mennonites who are leaving the north of
Alberta, I could not help wondering how many were simply responding
to that old North American impulse to be off to the simpler, freer,
more elemental frontier. "They seem to be a nomad lot. Good farmers,"
Owen Jordan had remarked in High Level. "When they get a little
money, off they go," Ernest Rivard had said on the riverbank above the
Peace River, after showing me his power-boat. Both Jordan and Rivard
were themselves men who had wandered and finally settled on the
frontier; perhaps they were well qualified to understand.

Early the next afternoon I returned to High Level. I remembered, but
did not repeat, my trips up that long road to the Northwest Territories.
Today a much-improved gravel highway leads to the riverboats and the
fishing fleet of Hay River, though the town still experiences its old tendency to be flooded in the spring, to sink into the permafrost in the
summer. And much of the northbound traffic no longer goes into Hay
River; it turns off at Enterprise, to complete the 626-mile drive from
Grimshaw into Yellowknife.

The big new ferry, the M.V. *Johnny Berens*, named after an outstanding riverboat pilot who worked for many years on the old sternwheeler the *Distributor*, carries traffic across the Mackenzie River just
above Fort Providence. The river is narrow here, only forty-five hundred feet, but the ferry offers an experience that is unique, for the disappearance of the steamboats means that there are almost no opportu-

nities for a tourist to travel on the Mackenzie River or on Great Slave Lake. During the winter, road traffic crosses the Mackenzie on an ice-bridge. During break-up and freeze-up there is a period when the road is closed.

It continues around onto the north side of Great Slave Lake, crossing the north-west arm of the lake at Frank Channel, via a modern steel bridge. The old trading settlement of Rae is only a few miles off the road. Yellowknife is a town of forty-five hundred people, and, new as it is, it boasts a museum of the North. Here are more bush planes and helicopters than anywhere else in the country. Here is Canada's most productive gold mine. Here the rocks and the lake and the jackpine together, on the edge of the barrenlands, create a landscape that may well make Yellowknife the most appealing capital in Canada.

6. ATHABASCA: THE RIVER NORTH

I was working on the M.V. *Richard E.* for the season. We were pushing three loaded barges down the Slave River. It was late in a sunny afternoon, and late enough in the fall that the river was low. I climbed up to the pilot-house to see a log cabin that had nearly slid into the river. The current, eating away at the shore, had tumbled a trapper's cabin off the bank and next spring the ice and flood waters would carry it down to Great Slave Lake. The mate joined me, for he too was loafing away an hour, waiting for the cook to let us into the galley for supper. "Let's go," the mate said. "I'll beat you in a game of crib."

As we started for the door the pilot at the wheel said, "Take a look at this."

We were pushing downstream around a bend. As I say, the water was low, and straight ahead of us a long spit of sand reached out into the broad river. Out on the sand, and not yet aware of our approach, a dozen buffalo were bent to the water and drinking.

For something like two minutes I saw Alberta as it must have been before the first rifle cracked death into a buffalo's heart. The decaying cabin fell behind. The water was so smooth it wore fewer ripples than the sand itself. The buffalo went on drinking, reflected where they drank. The forest behind them was a green wall tinged here and there a golden-yellow.

Then an old bull looked up and saw us. He waited as if we must change our minds and turn away. Then he snorted. A dozen buffalo, kicking up sand and bucking, galloped, roared along the spit, crashed into the forest, and in a flash were gone.

On the Muskeg Flyer to the Oil Sands

Today William McGillivray and Katherine Stewart, daughter of
Alexander Stewart, Chief Factor, were joined in holy wedlock by
Captain John Franklin, R.N., Commander of the Land Arctic
Expedition
> – Fort Chipewyan, Hudson's Bay Company
> daily records, Wednesday, 23 May 1827

The boatmen on the river break through this crust in order to collect
the underlying tar, which they boil down and use for pitching their
craft. Some parts of the banks are rendered plastic *en masse* from being
over-saturated with the asphalt, and in warm weather they slide gradu-
ally down into the bed of the river, incorporating the boulders and peb-
bles in their course.
> – Dr. Robert Bell, 1882

I rode the Muskeg Flyer from the Dunvegan Yards in Edmonton north
to Fort McMurray. For the first 127 miles, from Edmonton to Lac La
Biche, it is just another ride through rich farmlands on a dinky, rickety,
empty, slow, and obsolete train. And then, at the storm-blue railway
station in Lac La Biche, where sweet peas riot up the walls, it is transformed.

The muskeg and forest win out over farms at Lac La Biche; the
town itself speaks of poverty and the raw frontier. As in many northern
settlements, the few buildings are scattered far and wide and at random
across the landscape. And the beautiful lake is largely ignored; only the
lovely old wooden hospital is happily located.

From here no highway runs parallel to the railway tracks.
Through 172 miles of forest this railway, for a dozen Indian and Métis
settlements, is the only connection to each other and the outside.

In Lac La Biche the hoghead (engineer) put another passenger-
car onto the end of the train. It was partitioned in half; the back end

was the caboose, and there the conductor and rear-end brakie lived in a kind of rough luxury, with bunks for sleeping, a coal-stove for cooking, and lots of space for desks and radio equipment and teapots. The front half of the car was for passengers. Two antique coal-stoves reminded me that autumn was not likely to last forever. The kerosene lamps above our seats were filled and ready for night. And now the empty car filled rapidly: four rather drunk young fellows from Edmonton going up to work on a seismograph rig, six Métis women and their children, four or five teenage Métis, four or five older whites and Indians, including a very ancient Indian and his sick wife.

The train pulled out of Lac La Biche at two-thirty, only a little behind schedule. I found myself sitting with a retired railway section-worker, a man called Steve who described himself only as a White Russian, and an Indian trapper who went only by his last name, Janvier. They proved to be wonderful travelling-companions, for Steve knew every mile of track, Janvier knew the bush around it.

Even as the train started we were talking of bush pilots, of load-ing wood on the old river-steamers, of a man who made and lost a for-tune prospecting for uranium. This was the north I remembered, for on my first trip in with a bush pilot we were forced down by weather at Lac La Biche, and we sat for two days talking, drinking, and watching the sky. The train was hardly out past the last pasture at Big Bay when the brakie sat down beside Steve and they began to swap yarns.

They took pride in the colossal failures of this preposterous old Northern Alberta Railway. They talked about the time the engine ran out of fuel on an uphill grade. They remembered being delayed for so long in Lac La Biche that a passenger found an automobile, drove into Edmonton for something he had forgotten, and got back in time to catch his train. For many years the hoghead, the conductor, and the two brakies ran traplines along the track. They'd stop at the various creeks and ravines and lakes on each trip, and to speed things up each man was assigned specific traps to check. In the blueberry season they'd stop and pick blueberries for their families and friends. Yet this same crew was irritated when, in 1928, an old Indian flagged down the train because he was out of matches and needed a light for his pipe.

Now the train makes a top speed of forty miles an hour. Those days it averaged ten or twelve. In the spring the track would be under water for miles through flat country, as the original builders, to ensure themselves an adequate profit, had done little more than lay tracks across muskeg. The road-bed was so thin that during a forest fire the muskeg burning under it often twisted and warped the steel rails.

With a road-bed such as this, the engine developed a nasty habit of jumping off its track. When this happened, the crew simply dragged out the necessary equipment and put the engine and whatever cars might have followed back where they belonged. But this tended to consume a certain amount of time. Steve claimed that one trip took twenty-three days. After the first week, however, he assured me, the company fed the passengers free of charge.

A trip that took one week was hardly worth comment. One winter two passengers were in a hurry, so they hired two dogteams and beat the train from Fort McMurray to Lac La Biche.

Yet this train had its days of glory too. Before the advent of bush flying, all the riverboat captains and missionaries and traders and government officials used this route to get into the Mackenzie area. The train trip, with luck, was only a thirty-hour run, and in those days sleeping cars and an excellent dining car were provided.

Across the aisle from us, a young Métis mother was breastfeeding her baby. There were children everywhere; a mother set a plastic pot on the green cushion facing her and a little boy bravely mounted it, in spite of the swinging and lurching of the train.

We stopped at one of the little settlements. None of them has sidewalks. No cars come to the station; at best a jeep might show up. People jumped off the train to gossip in Cree and English with local friends, waiting for the warning whistle to blow. The settlement was made up of scattered shacks and log cabins, horses, garbage piles, a ragged little church. Once there had been a lumber mill here, but the country was logged off and the mill had been dismantled and taken away. Two young whites in dress shirts and beards, teachers, were playing soccer with a group of Indian boys beside a small school. I am told that many of the teachers in the north are adventurous young people from Britain.

The train restored to me my sense of space. The forest simply went on and on. Afternoon was turning to evening. The noise increased by the hour as the Métis drank brew and the four young whites littered the car with empty beer bottles. A fight broke out briefly, but was quelled before the women could decide whether to scream or go watch.

"A quiet trip, this one," Steve said. He was flipping through a catalogue he had borrowed from one of the women. The conductor came through lighting the kerosene lamps.

We stopped in the wilderness beside a railway work-train, a crew that was laying new ties. The railway gang had been in the bush since early spring, and as the four boys got off, some of the young men from the work gang came into the train, trying to buy a bottle of whisky. A tall blond boy, intense and quiet, stopped to say he'd pay fifteen bucks for a twenty-six. I couldn't oblige but he sat down and talked on. He'd saved eighteen hundred dollars on this job, and was planning to go outside in a few weeks and buy a new car. He was from McLennan he said. "You ever been in the Peace River country? I'm going back there." On the knuckles of his right hand he had scratched, with a ballpoint pen, the four letters H-A-T-E. He left and I went outside to scrounge a cup of coffee from the railway workers.

When I returned to my seat, Steve and Janvier were sharing a bottle of beer, passing it back and forth between them. The White Russian, short, with intense blue eyes, was doing most of the talking. Janvier, dark and tall, squinting his only eye, kept nodding his head.

The next stop was his. I left them and went to the front of the car to watch the poker game.

The conductor had earlier set up a table; now two Métis men were playing, with a boy of nine or ten and an elderly Indian woman. Five or six young people, their children finally asleep, were watching, I watched too; the boy and the Indian woman seemed to be winning.

Janvier got off at Chard to go twelve miles east to the Chipewyan reservation. Steve had promised to tell me of the adventures and generosity of Father Mercredi, an Indian priest who lived for years at Chard. I went back to my seat; Steve had dozed off, so I left him and returned to the game.

The train, appropriately, does not go quite all the way into Fort McMurray. It stops three miles short, beside the Clearwater River at a place called Waterways. It was nearly midnight when we got in; the conductor said they could find me a bunk in the railway bunk-house. But I was eager to see the Fort McMurray I hadn't visited since 1950. I called a taxi from the railway station and rode to the brand-new Peter Pond Hotel.

Peter Pond is the enigmatic hero of this country; in 1778 he came out far to the west and north of any previous trading post and built Pond's House, on the Athabasca River, north of the present Fort McMurray and forty miles from where the river enters Lake Athabasca.

Pond was born in Connecticut in 1740; he entered the American fur trade, then transferred to the Canadian northwest in 1775, possibly because he disapproved of the American Revolution. His character is much debated upon. He has been called "a violent man of unprincipled character" and "an intrepid trader who had remarkable intelligence and spirit." His detractors say he was implicated in at least two murders. His defenders claim he was attacked by Mackenzie and others because he was American, while his associates in the North West Company were all Scots from the Orkney Islands, men who were close friends as well as associates in business.

Whatever the case, today in Fort McMurray Pond's name is attached to a new hotel, a new school, and a new shopping centre.

I was awakened by the crowing of roosters. I pulled back the heavy draperies: across the street, facing my hotel room, was a row of old shacks and log houses. A Métis who had tried to give up trapping for the agricultural life was raising chickens. But his chickens had become as obsolete in Fort McMurray as his traps. Again he was one step behind, as he could see by looking across his little garden. The Peter Pond Shopping Centre very nearly surrounds a small, sturdy mission church built of hand-hewn logs. The HÔPITAL SAINT GABRIEL is now across an alley from HANNIGAN'S BURGER KING. A brand-new oil town is being built right on top of an old trading post and river terminus, complete with a pizza joint for the swingers and a Gospel Church for the displaced. In 1950 I heard mostly the barking and howling of sleigh-dogs here; now the dogs are gone, and the roosters cannot hear themselves for the roar of earth-moving machines, the endless pecking of hammers on new buildings.

I remembered a day in the Arctic, in the town of Inuvik, when I asked an old Eskimo in a parka and mukluks what he most disliked about that new town. I expected him to criticize the liquor laws, for he had lamented the effect of alcohol on his people. But he only pointed toward the dusty road and said, "Listen." And for the first time that day I heard the unceasing roar of motors.

It is noise that marks Fort McMurray as a boom town; caterpillars crawl up and down the streets, and trucks are everywhere on the move.

A woman going to work one morning counted eleven new foundations being put in around her house. That night she counted eleven houses. This is a prefab town. The five hundred newest houses are among the most attractive I have seen in a housing project anywhere. They are handsomely situated, for the town is ringed with forested slopes. Here the Hangingstone and the Horse rivers add their beauty to the confluence of the Clearwater and the Athabasca.

These new houses are largely for the personnel involved in extracting oil from the oil sands of Alberta. The biggest of these deposits, located along the Athabasca River, has been a temptation and a problem to industry for well over one hundred years. This deposit is estimated to contain 626 billion barrels of oil, the equivalent of half the world's known conventional oil reserves. The oil, with its mixture of sand, has been described as a blend of molasses and coffee grounds; the sand is constituted mainly of quartz, with minor amounts of mica, feldspar, and clay; the oil is thick and sulphurous, and must be upgraded before it can be marketed. Along the Athabasca, the sands, up to two hundred feet in depth and extending over an area of thirty thousand square miles, are buried by a mixture of muskeg and glacial deposit that varies in depth from zero to two thousand feet.

Over eighteen hundred test holes have been drilled since 1897, when the Geological Survey of Canada sponsored the first hole. Runs as high as 250,000 barrels per acre were assessed, with the average set at 100,000. The problem was quite simply how to separate the oil from the sand at a cost that would be competitive with conventional oil wells.

This problem baffled a series of companies; but, meanwhile, Dr. Karl A. Clark of the Alberta Research Council was working on a hot-water separation process. Oilmen became satisfied that hot-water flotation made the development of the sands economically feasible; the Alberta government gave a subsidiary of the Sun Oil Company of Philadelphia the right to mine approximately six square miles of tar sands at the rate of one hundred thousand tons a day.

Two thousand construction workers went into the north to build an extraction plant at Tar Island, and Fort McMurray, twenty miles away, began its transformation.

Today two giant crawler-mounted bucket-wheel excavators, each standing one hundred feet high, move slowly across the areas from

which the overburden has been stripped, dumping sand onto a convey-
or belt that connects with the extraction plant. A pipeline runs 266
miles south to Edmonton, where it joins trans-Canadian lines.
Synthetic crude flows at the rate of forty-five thousand barrels daily.

The exploitation of the Athabasca oil sands has finally begun,
and now exploration work has outlined other deposits, especially to
the west around Peace River, Loon River, and the Buffalo Head Hills.
Today Alberta's oil sands are known to comprise over 7,900,000 acres;
they are estimated to contain in excess of seven hundred billion barrels
of oil, three hundred billion of which are estimated to be recoverable.

Fort McMurray is, conceivably, only the first of a number of tar-
sands towns. There is salt in the area, as well as gypsum, limestone, sulphur, and coke. Gas wells have been drilled and capped within a hundred miles. The area could easily produce finished petroleum products
as well as the usual crude for export. Ultimately, I am told, petroleum
products from places like the Athabasca tar sands might not only run
our cars and surface our highways, but *feed us* as well.

Meanwhile, the population of Fort McMurray has quadrupled in
four years; the town planners are building schools and churches and
homes for a minimum of five thousand people. Meanwhile, also, a sign
on the highway outside town reads, "No Gas or Services Next 125
Miles."

The experience of this isolation is a curse to some, a heady discovery to others. A young white girl in a drugstore casually mentioned
that she's going outside to get a divorce. She hadn't known there were
so many eligible men in the world. The newcomers are under stress, but
prospering; the people here when the boom began are the people hard-
est hit.

There is, first of all, little accommodation in town that the
natives can afford. I talked to an articulate young Indian leader of the
Indian community. He listed the natives' problems. Their education in
the religious schools of the past was mostly a religious education; it

taught the Indian that he was inferior, the white superior. You can quickly teach an Indian to drive a truck, he explained; the basic problem is a lack of social, not economic skills. The Indian was used to a permissive communal life, in which all men were equal and the first concern was for people. Now he is forced to become the isolated and profit-motivated self of contemporary society. It is hard to persuade a man who has hunted and trapped over hundreds of square miles that he should take out a thirty-year mortgage on a 100 foot by 150 foot lot.

In the past, the trader grubstaked the Indian and kept him in debt, so that in fact he never handled cash. The missionaries like Father Lacombe and the Reverend McDougall sold him down the river – persuaded him to knuckle under to the encroaching whites. He simply lost his decision-making ability.

"Consider," this young man told me, "the image of the Indian we get on TV. I walked into my apartment one night and said to my daughter, 'Hello, my little Indian.' She burst out crying. 'I'm not an Indian,' she said." Her father sat down to find out what was the trouble. The little girl had been watching TV, and could not in any way identify herself with the Indians she saw.

As we talked, I noticed through the window of the office a flight of geese heading south. I pointed them out to the Indian across the desk. "Ah," he said, "it's fall again. The hunters will soon be coming up from the city."

I couldn't resist going to see what was happening to my old friends on the waterfront. A spur of the railway goes down to the shore of the Clearwater halfway between Waterways and Fort McMurray. Here at The Prairie, the Northern Transportation Company Limited, a Crown corporation, loads barges with down-river freight. Nowadays modern tugs push the loaded steel barges to Fort Chipewyan, to the uranium boom towns at the Saskatchewan end of Lake Athabasca, and out of the lake on Rivière des Rochers to where it joins the Peace to become the Slave, and then on down the Slave to Fort Fitzgerald. At "Fitz" there is another sequence of rapids. Freight must be trucked around them to Fort Smith or Bell Rock in the Northwest Territories, then be put back on barges for the fourteen hundred-mile ride to the Arctic Ocean.

I got out of the cab at the shipyards; the timberways run back from the beach for at least five hundred yards. Onto these, each fall, the boats and barges are pulled to be repaired, to be kept safe from freeze-up, from the floods and drifting ice of spring.

But now I saw that four boats had not been put into the water for this season. The highway and railway into Hay River have meant still another change in the water routes of the north. Like grebes that must die if ever they touch dry land, the boats sat in a row: the M. V. *Radium Queen*, the *Radium Express*, the *Horn River*, the *Peace*. Their brass beginning to grow dull, their bright paint peeling, they sat on ribs of wood on dry land, flat-bottomed and looking top-heavy, their running lights dark, their wheel-houses high and empty above me. A raven croaked in the trees beyond. I remembered when the *Peace* came into Fort Fitzgerald, her barges loaded to the water line with lumber for Fort Simpson, with groceries for a trader in Aklavik, machinery for Norman Wells, canoes for Resolution. Now someone had set a tin pail over her galley stovepipe to keep out the rain.

I walked along one of the thick timberways, keeping out of the mud, and went down to the river. Here the Clearwater is broad and smooth between gentle and forested banks; down river two islands conceal and mark the junction with the Athabasca.

Everything was quiet. I walked across the dock and onto the deck of a house barge, the sound of my footsteps echoing in the empty steel barge, the air smelling faintly of alkylate. I sat down on a bollard of *Radium 304* to watch the river; and as I glanced up I saw behind an island the wheel-house of an approaching boat.

She came slowly into view, pushing one barge, her freight a load of lumber. Nearby a crane was moving into position to lift the bundles of new white spruce lumber off the red deck of the barge. I watched for a long time. Finally I could read her name; she was the *Miner*, come back from a run to Eldorado Mine at Uranium City, one hundred miles up Lake Athabasca, into Saskatchewan. Now two deck-hands appeared in bright orange life-jackets; the older man came to the bow of the barge and attached one end of the heaving line to the neatly flaked-out head-line. He divided the coil of heaving line in his two hands, and as the barge came slowly nearer the moored barge he threw the line and I caught it. I pulled the head-line across the gap between us and hooked it onto the bollard; the two deck-hands began to take up the slack on a hand capstan.

I recognized the chief deck-hand. He was Napoleon Hyman, twenty-nine years a riverman. Born and raised in McMurray, he had been a fireman for six years on the sternwheelers, when they carried fifteen deck-hands; now he was chief of three on a diesel-powered tug.

"Who's your skipper?" I called.

"Billy Bird," he answered. "Hey," he added. "Where you been?"

I walked back past the stacked lumber and onto the deck of the *Miner*. She was neater and cleaner than any boat I had ever seen. Both Billy Bird and Napoleon have always believed in lots of fresh paint. I went up the ladder to the high wheel-house and got there in time to catch the skipper signing off the radio. He sat down on the high stool beside the wheel.

Captain William Bird got his first job on the river forty-five years ago. "I was bull cook for an old Chinaman on the sternwheeler *Slave River*. He's dead now. The free traders, Lamson, Hubbard, were running the *D.A. Thomas* above the Chutes, the *Slave River* from there down to Fort Fitzgerald." He put aside the papers he'd picked up. "Next I went decking on a sternwheeler for the Bay. We'd pull into the bank and load up to fifty cords of wood, packing it on our backs and fighting mosquitoes."

His life, in many ways, is a history of the river. Billy was born in Fort McMurray in 1907. His father ran scows through the Athabasca Rapids: the ninety-mile series of fifteen rapids that interrupted steamer traffic between Athabasca Landing and Fort McMurray. Business was so good that in 1911 Joe Bird moved his family to the Landing. But then the railway pushed north to Waterways and the traffic through the rapids was done. Joe, a skipper and pilot now, took the upriver steamers over the notorious rapids. And he moved his family back to where Billy was born.

Young Billy decked for his father, then under famous old Captain Alexander, who trained many a young riverman. "He was a hard old bugger," Bill said, "but we liked him."

By 1941 Bill had his mate's certificate. The old steamers on the Mackenzie, the *Distributor* and the *Mackenzie River*, didn't tempt him, for he wanted to stay near his wife and his growing family. He worked on the *Nor-Basca* pushing fish barges for a big commercial-fishing outfit (the same outfit, incidentally, that in 1961 caught a lake trout weighing 102 pounds in Lake Athabasca). In 1948 Bill got his master's certificate, and since then he has skippered the newest boats on the river.

The fur-trading routes are home to Captain Bird. His father came from British Columbia as a riverman. His father's father was James Bird, a Hudson's Bay Company factor from England who married a full-blooded Carrier girl.

Bill's family now totals four boys and seven girls. I asked him if the boys were about to become riverboat captains. "No," he said. "My boys don't take to the river. The oldest would have made a good riverman." He rested one hand on the shiny mahogany wheel.

Then we talked for a while, the gossip of rivermen. He'd been on the radio: the skipper on Great Bear Lake had taken sick and Cecil Kirkland was flying in to relieve him. "We've had good water this summer. Getting low now though; a fish barge was stuck on a bar for two days last week. . . . I guess the *Clearwater* went down since you last saw us water rats." And he talked about the *Clearwater*. A new skipper just in from Vancouver took her onto Lake Athabasca and ran into a terrible blow. She went down with all hands: should have been nine, but a deck-hand got drunk here in McMurray and missed the trip. They found one corpse – there on the North Shore: had a lifejacket ring on his ankle. The sea-gulls had got to him.

But even rivermen can't go on gossiping forever. The office ashore was waiting for the handful of papers that lay beside the compass. Bill stood up to go ashore to the office, then home to see his wife and family while the next tow was made up.

"How do you like this new McMurray?" I asked as we went down the ladder. He laughed, because I'd forgotten how to run down a ladder and instead crawled rather gingerly. But he was serious as we stepped ashore. "McMurray is finished. She's had it. I liked her the way she was." As he paused, we could hear the distant whine of engines. "I guess she's going to be quite a place. People and cars – and dust—and mud up to your arse."

I went into the galley to scrounge a cup of coffee, mostly for old times' sake. The cook of a riverboat looks on all other men as his enemies; they are determined to mess up his clean galley and eat all the food he has worked so hard to prepare. This cook was no exception to the rule; but I was joined by two other men who shared my intent. We brazened it out and were victorious.

I found myself having coffee with two disgruntled Albertans. One was a riverboat engineer, the other a ranger with the Department of Lands and Forests.

The engineer was from a small town. "To hell with this," he said, "and to hell with McMurray. And I'll tell you why. I worked in South America on the boats, and this is the same thing. *Mañana* country. Not just McMurray. Alberta. All of it. Tomorrow. Just get by today, don't rock the boat, don't rev up your engine. I'm going to British Columbia, that's where I'm headed. To Vancouver. If you've got no skill, stay in Alberta. If you're skilled, go to British Columbia. That's where the wages are. The wages draw the skills and the skills draw the industry."

The ranger had come down to the riverboat to see about shipping his household effects north to Fort Chipewyan. He was a city boy, he'd spent the first twenty years of his life in Edmonton, and he too was fed up with McMurray.

"You can have this damned boom town," he said. "It's starting to feel like a *city* here." He dumped more condensed milk into a cup of hot coffee, while the cook growled over his galley stove in a wonderful but intimidating Scandinavian accent.

"This is the best country I ever saw," the cook said. He had obviously had this exchange with the engineer before. "I've been around the world twice."

"I'm going to Chip," the young ranger insisted. "No *road* in there." He turned to me now. "If you're writing a book about Alberta, don't mention Chipewyan. That *is* Alberta. Those people in there are trappers. Fishermen. They need beaver, not tourists. Red squirrels. Moose for the winter. Caribou. One season they shipped out 240,000 muskrats. You ought to see the lake trout northeast of Fort Chip. We tagged some walleyes up there – in thirty-nine days they travelled 220 miles."

"I'm going to travel right straight to Vancouver," the engineer insisted, "as soon as I see the snowballs flying. You know something? This young kid here thinks he knows Alberta. I was a kid myself when Grant McConachie started flying fish out from Cold Lake. My *pioneering* ends where winter begins."

The ranger was undaunted. "That's when it's fun to go into Wood Buffalo Park with the Indians. The biggest park in the world. No tourists in there." He stopped. "Well, there is a road now. Right through the buffalo herds." But he went on: "If you want history, buddy, Fort Chipewyan is history. Some of the old log buildings are still standing. Mackenzie was there. Franklin was there. But it's more – it's the *spirit* of the place. The spirit is what makes the difference."

"I got pies to bake," the cook said. "If I got paid for doing what you guys do, I'd never complain about anything. One of these days mighty soon it's going to be freeze-up. I can always tell: my galley gets full of big talkers."

7. A Last Word: In Praise of Winter

December. The book is written. The year is done. I have returned to the mountains, alone this time; the snow is falling outside the window. And I am not alone. We have been sipping hot wine and chatting, five of us at a low table in front of a fire. We are all tired.

The snow-draped lodge where we skied all day, at seventy-two hundred feet in the Rockies, goes by the name of Sunshine Village. But we talk of other mountain resorts, as one does when skiing: Marmot Basin, West Castle, Pigeon Mountain, Mount Temple, Whitehorn, Skoki, Norquay, Whistler Mountain. And we talk of many feet of snow, of skiing from November into May.

The snow is falling.

We are chatting, five of us by the fire. Snowflakes knock soundlessly at the window. Two of my companions are sisters, housewives from Calgary who've come up here to rest briefly before the happy swirl of Christmas. It is only a short while until the celebration commences; my wife and two daughters have gone out to the farm where I was born. But I've been skiing all day, with fragments nagging at my mind: the mosaic colours of a poplar trunk in rain, the red of a flower called strawberry blite when it's crushed on one's fingers, the wild canary that hit my window one afternoon, then sat dazed in my hand while children gathered to cheer its sudden flight. I have three books I bought as presents that now I decide I can't give away: the flowers, the mammals, the birds of this province.

My third companion is a young priest, sent up here by his bishop to rest for two days from overwork and exhaustion. He is with his brother, a ski buff who is resting from resting. We are, we discover, all Albertans.

We talk of home and of winter. We talk of curling brooms as they dance their furious dance on sheets of enamelled ice. We talk of boys playing hockey in an open rink under the white glow of lights, their parents chilled to the marrow in the shadows, warmed by pride and fear. The ski buff remembers skating on a slough where the wind swept the ice to a sheet of glass; he remembers a fire of willow sticks and the frost turning to hot needles in his flesh. The priest, a boy on the prairies, first skied behind a galloping horse. And silently I recall my parents going to a card party with neighbours; they put kitchen chairs and blankets in the sleigh, they took a hot rock from on top of the kitchen stove and wrapped it in rags and set it in straw in the bottom of the sleigh box: the runners squeaked on the cold night.

A waiter brings more wine, then adds a log to the fire. The two sisters talk recipes: Christmas cakes and pudding, how best to stuff a turkey. The ski buff is opposed to the very existence of mince pie. I think of my young daughters watching in my sister's kitchen: cake pans of thick dark fudge, buttered plates of brown-sugar candy. And when we were children we made our own marshmallows, rolling the cut squares in saucers of burnt coconut. We made popcorn balls that glued our jaws together. We went to our cousins' kitchens and cousins came to ours. Aunt Maggie made her hard-time candy from a recipe learned on a Saskatchewan homestead. Aunt Annie remembered sugaring-off in an Ontario maple bush, and she made us taffy on the snow. Aunt Mary arrived with more cookies to add to our store of macaroons and jam-jams; and we marvelling children announced that Christmas would never come.

But then one morning we tied our little sleds to the runners of my father's sleigh and laughing together we headed west to the Battle River hills. We left the team at a fence post, and carrying an axe and ropes we plunged down into the snow-drifted valley to march in each other's tracks toward a stand of spruce trees.

Outside the window the dark evergreens on the mountain chart the course we skied all day. And even now, in the fading light, one last skier floats up to the white horizon. The priest sees him also and points him out to the others. We are silent. We are tired. Together we watch the lone figure as he disappears into the high country, invisible beyond the trees and the rim of falling snow.

We sip our hot and spicy wine.

And on the flatlands now, as evening falls, the headlights glide in long columns out of the cities; the big new cars flash out across the ice-bound rivers and the ghostly hills, where cattle bend silent to the wind. The snowploughs wink blue as they pioneer a new white land. The roads become sideroads and the sideroads multiply into streets and lanes.

And in the towns and on the farms, the old men grouch in their kitchens, their wives find still another excuse for going to the drawn blinds. A father dreams of an afternoon in the beer parlour, showing off his roaring son. A woman waits to cry a grandchild into her empty arms. In the bursting pantry the very shelves groan for tomorrow. Up in a closet corner the packages lie dark in myriad ribbons and stars. The wooden box of Jap oranges is cool in the cellar. The tree, out in the car-shed, is stiff with frost. Someone turns on the light on a porch, in a yard. The silence of a winter night drums in from a drifted stubble-field. A car hums in the distance. A faint fall of snow lifts up the glare of headlights like beacons on the sky. An old man slips out once more to read the thermometer, once more to sweep the front steps.

HIGHWAY SECRETS

Alberta, land on the mountain backbone of the continent sloping both north and east and south towards three very distant oceans. Day after day thousands of vehicles roar along the Trans-Canada Highway through Banff National Park, and just west of the town, where the road bends above the Bow River and the Vermilion Lakes across the foot, as it were, of Mount Edith, they are speeding over the first human-built habitation yet discovered in Canada.

Highway excavation there in 1983 revealed to archaeologists several hearths and the postholes of a circular structure at least eleven thousand years old.

If you know where to pause (in typical Parks Canada fashion, the place is unmarked), you recognize that these our ancestors in this place built their home to open south towards the warmth of the glorious sun. But, looking about, it is also impossible not to believe that when they gathered here around their fires eating giant bison and bighorn sheep,

the remains of whose shattered bones were also found, that they did
not appreciate the magnificence of these mountains, these rounded
opening valleys, these rivers hidden in the trees, these brilliant lakes
shifting colour at every brush of wind. It is a land to make any human
heart sing.

Who were these people, and when did they first get here?
Unquestionably they were nomads who lived by gathering edible plants
and by hunting the huge animals that have long since vanished from
the earth – at least in that size – mastodons, woolly mammoths, buffalo, bears, musk oxen, caribou, sloths, tigers, camels, wolves, bighorn
sheep, antelope. They must have been extraordinary people to cope
with such gigantic beasts, having only their own physical strength aug-
mented by fire and clubs and stone tools like hammers, spears, knives.

Even more amazing is how, hairless as they largely were, they
dealt with the climate. During the preceding million and a half years
of the Ice Age, the northern half of our continent was covered by two
immense sheets of ice – very much like Greenland or Antarctica today
– in places thousands of metres thick. Bits of it still remain: on the
islands of the Arctic Ocean, some covered with ice and some with
their meagre soil lifted high above the sea by the ice underlying them;
and in mountains of Alberta. There, along the border between Banff
and Jasper national parks, the Columbia Icefield spreads up and sprawls
between, across the tops of the mountains in many-tongued glaciers. It
is the tiny (though overwhelming) continental reminder of the ice
which once covered the whole world here. Now you can step from the
smooth comfort of your car onto rotting primeval ice; you can consider,
if you slip, a fissure yawning to accept you with complete, chilling,
antediluvian, indifference.

During the Ice Age so much of the globe's water was solidified
into ice that wide continental shelves were exposed, and so the land
connection between Asia and North America was broader than today's
Alaska.

The most widely supported scientific theory now holds that human beings came to our hemisphere from Asia via this land bridge. They were probably following animals into the unglaciated land of what is today Alaska and northern Yukon.

The question remains: when? In 1976 the wooden foundation of a village of twelve houses was discovered in a peat bog in the rainforest of central Chile; carbon 14 dating gave an age of thirteen thousand years. Two metres below that three hearths were excavated, revealing charred plants dated at thirty-three thousand years. In a cave in Pennsylvania archaeologists found irrefutable evidence of human life dating from thirteen thousand to twenty thousand years ago. If people from Asia had spread to the east coast of North America and to the very tip of the hemisphere over thirty millenia ago, when did they first arrive here? How did they cross those hundreds of kilometres of ice?

Libraries have been written discussing this question; I will summarize to the point of a certain, perhaps enlightening, absurdity. Current theory holds that the two ice sheets were rarely continuous. Along the eastern slopes of the Rockies, from the present Yukon to the central plains, either glacier would advance or retreat according to topography and the varying climate. At various times and places they might be widely separated, at others, tongues of ice might grind into each other and their meltwaters mingle to flow down the tilt of the continent somewhere into the sea.

Further, global warming between thirty to eighteen thousand years ago created a possibly comfortable land corridor between the two ice masses. The first peoples may have migrated at that time and developed millenia of civilizations in the south when for a time the ice closed the north corridor again. The fact remains that no undebatable evidence of this migration before 9000 B.C. has yet been found in Alberta. Which is not surprising, considering its nomadic civilization and the advance and retreat of uncountable glaciers which, if they did not grind stone artifacts and teeth (the only human bone hard enough to possibly survive) out of existence, would so dislocate such evidence as to make it more or less undatable.

The famous "Taber Child," infant skull bones discovered on the bank of the Oldman River in 1961, was at first analysed to be over twenty-five thousand years old. This made them the oldest human remains ever discovered in the Americas. However, by 1982 better scientific methods declared their age to be a mere thirty-five hundred years.

A haystack the size of a continent – and no assurance that a needle actually exists in it. But every year of searching adds to our knowledge. Firm dates now indicate that people ate butchered mammoths in the Bluefish Caves south of Old Crow, Yukon, fifteen thousand years ago. In Alberta, the oldest human evidence is from sites at Vermilion Lakes and on Sibbald Creek – exactly where they should be if the Ice-Free Corridor existed. These are human sites both confirmed by the best scientific evidence to be ten thousand five hundred to eleven thousand years old.

That's seventy-five hundred years before Abraham left the Euphrates valley to become a nomadic herdsman working his way to Canaan, and sixty-five hundred years before the pharaohs dreamt the great pyramids of Egypt.

If you like to time-travel backwards into human experience, drive west from Calgary (or east from Banff) and turn south off the Trans-Canada Highway onto Highway 68. After twenty-two kilometres of driving up and between crests of rocklike cockscombs into the foothills, you will discover a spot where, in one glance, eleven millennia of what is known (so far) of human history in Alberta is recognizable. The historic marker will tell you where to stop.

Fifty metres below a plateau of chinook-toughened aspen, a grassy plain carved by glaciers opens around the junction of Jumping Pound and Sibbald creeks. About a kilometre wide and three long, Sibbald Flat is surrounded by hills rising to Moose Mountain (2430 metres) in the south and the Front Range of the Rocky Mountains (over 2700 metres) to the west. In late August the peaks are already dusted with snow, and the black cattle winding across the flat towards their twilight drinking look like nothing so much as a long trail of bison, though the distant sounds of their lowing are much too tame and pastoral. In 1980, when highway construction cut down through the north shoulders of this flat, an Early Human site was exposed – ah, Alberta with its big highways, what would we know without them?

This site provided everything people needed to live: a south-facing slope sheltered from the north winds by hill and trees, which also supplied good fuel: pine, aspen, spruce; excellent water in the creeks below; massive gravel deposits for the manufacture of tools; all of this overlooking a prime grazing area for animals and warm chinook winds from the west to temper winter and uncover grasses. The spear and arrow points, the scrappers, choppers, drills, hammers, and anvil stones unearthed here begin with the same fluted techniques as the Clovis, New Mexico, discoveries dated by archaeologists at eleven thousand years ago. Here a compressed range of earth strata fifty centimetres deep moves one from prehistoric hunters to Frank Sibbald in the 1880s (his father Andrew was the first teacher on the Stony Reserve) starting his cattle herd on this summer pasture.

The site is now inside Kananaskis Country, and the markers overlooking the plain provide sketches and a verbal description of prehistoric hunter life, from preparation for the hunt to the stalking of the "furred giants" on the flat below – giants indeed, their stubby horns were two metres from tip to tip – to the close, human surround and the kill. A dangerous, vital intimacy of food as life and blood, an intimacy impossible to us moderns who will stalk these cattle now grazing this same flat in the inert, bloodless, unrecognizable form of plastic-wrapped supermarket cuts.

"Alberta," "Calgary," "Banff," "Sibbald Flat" are, of course, the European names for this land; the stories of human prehistory I have

been outlining are European as well. As one might suspect, the original inhabitants of Turtle Island – their name for what is now called
North America – have their own stories about these things. In 1798
the Miami chief Little Turtle saw five Tartars in Philadelphia and, recognizing their physiological similarity to himself, talked to the French
traveller Count Volney about such an oddity. The count showed him a
map of the world, and explained the Bering Strait theory of human
migration from Asia. Little Turtle understood so well as to grasp immediately a possible weakness in the theory: "Isn't it possible," he asked,
"that the Tartars, who resemble us so closely, came from here? . . . Why
shouldn't we have been born of this soil?" [Count Volney, *Oeuvres
completes* (Paris, 1837), p. 711-13.]

Certain it is that every aboriginal race living in Alberta has a
story of human origin beginning here, "of this soil." And the aboriginal names of the land, those that still survive or can be uncovered in
un-European memories, are the body of these stories because for an oral
people the land is, quite literally, that people's history. You come to a
river and ask, "What do you call this river?" You are told: "This is
Oldman River." And you ask, "Why do you call it that?" and if you are
to be answered, you must be told a story: the story of Old Man. And
his story expands into the story of the origin of mountains, animals,
plants, birds, of woman and child. Also, into the origin of death. As
the Blackfoot tell it, "Old Man was travelling about, south of here,
making the people. He came from the south, travelling north, making
animals and birds as he passed along . . . ." After innumerable adventures – many of them ribald, profound, or silly because Old Man certainly embodied all possible human virtues, foibles, and ignorances –

> he had come nearly to the Red Deer's River, he reached the hill where
> the Old Man sleeps. There he lay down and rested himself. The form
> of his body is to seen there yet. . . . This is as far as the Blackfoot fol-
> lowed Old Man. The Cree know what he did further north.

Old Man's Bed is labelled on J.B. Tyrrell's 1887 map of northern Alberta. Across the Red Deer River, south of Drumheller (and the to me ironically named Royal Tyrrell Museum of Palaeontology) rise the Wintering Hills. If you look carefully as you drive south towards them on Highway 56, and you can unclutter yourself of European presuppositions, you will recognize Old Man's Bed on their northern slopes. The highway, of course, cuts right through it.

Travelling these Alberta highways in the summer of 1992 with Robert Kroetsch, looking at what is so obviously here now, talking to people, trying to see what once was, history and prehistory – to get back, even before these last few human seconds of time here in relation to the gaunt minutes of glaciers (ten thousand to two million years ago), the hours of dinosaurs (60 million to 120 million years ago) and those fantastic Burgess Shale creatures imprinted across the tips of the present Rocky Mountains (indicating a time when those seemingly immovable masses were flat sea bottom 460 million to 530 million years ago) – trying to open every sense to this beautiful land, a residual rage simmered over in me again.

Rather more: a resident, not residual, rage. Who can forget that effete epitome of English cultivation, so handsome (in profile) Rupert Chawner Brooke writing so lyrically in a passing train window his *Letters from America* (1916):

> Canada is a country without a soul. . . . A European can find nothing to satisfy the hunger of his heart. The air is too thin to breathe. He requires haunted woods, and the friendly presence of ghosts. . . . For it is possible, at a pinch to do without gods. But one misses the dead.

He should have been more than pinched. Even Earle Birney, born here, living his youth in Morningside and Banff, writes so smartly stupid in 1962 – by age fifty-eight one would expect a poet to have thrown away his European telescope:

we French and English never lost
our civil war
endure it still
a bloody civil bore

The wounded sirened off
no Whitman wanted
it's only by our lack of ghosts
we're haunted

As it happens, Robert Kroetsch is not one of those Canadian writers Birney may be poeting about – "them able leave her ever." Kroetsch has never been one of the "wounded sirened off," no matter where in the world he has lived, and to travel through Alberta with him lending his eyes out is to recognize, unforgettably, that we are not haunted by a lack of ghosts; we are haunted only by one-eyed ignorance.

Our enormous haunting heritage is everywhere around us, available to any resident or traveller. The shale skeletons in the rocks of Moraine Lake; the dinosaur bones of the Red Deer valley; the Okotoks Erratic; the Early Human site on Nose Hill – Old Man's nose, of course – where, as seen from below, the tall houses of Calgary sail into space like ships into the sea; Head Smashed-In and Old Woman's buffalo jumps; the Majorville Medicine Wheel; Writing-on-Stone rock art in the Milk River Badlands; the forks of the Red Deer and the South Saskatchewan rivers; the Peace Hills and the Medicine Lodge Hills, The Nose (Old Man again) in the Neutral Hills, the Ribstones – I am barely beginning a list that, to tell, would utter stories to fill a library of books, and I am still centuries away from the immigrants whose coming altered Alberta as much as the retreating glaciers with their individual and amazing stories.

My own family was one of them: my parents and siblings arrived in Didsbury on 4 March 1930 after a CPR journey from St. John, New Brunswick, the *Metagama* from Bremerhaven and a stateless refugee camp at Moelln, Germany, via Riga and Moscow from that small Mennonite farm village their ancestors had built on the plains fronting the Ural Mountains near Orenburg, USSR. The names alone of the places where they waited, sometimes for months and prayed to leave, tell a story repeated uniquely by over a century of people fleeing the world to find this province.

Let me tell you, when he travels, story teller Robert Kroetsch keeps both his eyes and both his ears open; both nostrils too. This book, *Alberta*, which first appeared twenty-five years ago to great acclaim in Canada's Centennial Year, tells many of our stories, ancient and new. In 1967 our land was poised on the edge of its second century, seemed about to leap forward, at last, into confidence. By 1970, of course, we had the first of several Quebec crises, and the eighties would discourage everyone with so much talk that not even the United Nations' assertion that we lived in the best, most liveable of all the world's countries would convince us to believe a word most of our politicians said.

But to travel with Robert Kroetsch in 1992 – no matter what history will record about this Canadian year – is to travel with a writer. Whenever I looked up, there he was, standing with his white head bent and scribbling words into a notebook. After some days I mustered the courage to peek: only one or two words drawn very large, and to me unreadable, per page. Never, I noticed, more than four. Old Man's perfect number. As our journey continued I began to sense I had rented too small a car; every drug store we glimpsed on the horizon was raided for more notebooks until I knew I should have arranged for one of those half-tons with cab we were always meeting, if any vehicles at all, our backseat now piled so high with paper tangled so lightly by his ineffable words of memory they would soon be invading the trunk.

We achieved a climax, of sorts, in Lomond, a two-elevator town (population 177) on what was once short-grass prairie near the Bow River southwest of Brooks. In the ubiquitous "Chinese" prairie cafe.

The only occupant was the owner, reading a weekly newspaper, and when Bob told him we were travelling writers he beamed in recognition. O, he said, a writer had come in yesterday, he thought he would write a book about Lomond, and the day before there had been two, they were both writing books about something as well. Bob and I looked at each other with a wild surmise (as the poet has it); the climax came as he handed us the menu.

"Must be easy, write a book," he smiled at us. "Everybody's doing it."

Rudy Wiebe
Edmonton, October 1992

INDEX

McDougall, The Reverend John Chantler, 207
McDougall United Church (Edmonton), 195
MacEwan, John Walter Grant, 145
McGillivray, William, 267
MacGregor, James G., 222
McIntyre Ranching Co. Ltd. 1894, 13-15
McKay, Arthur Fortesque, 13
Mackenzie, Sir Alexander, 33, 252, 258, 271, 281
Mackenzie Highway, 256-57, 263
Mile Zero, 253
Mackenzie River, 53, 263-64, 278
Mackenzie River, 278
McLean, Archie J., 186
McLennan, Alberta, 246, 270
Macleod, James Farquharson, 59, 156
McLeod River, 129
Macleod Trail, 187
McLuhan, Marshall, 212
McMahon, Frank and George, 192
McNaught, Euphemia and Isabel, 41-44
Magrath, Alberta, 167
Majorville Medicine Wheel, 294
Makarenko family, 231
Maligne Lake, 97-98, 112
Maligne River, 99
Mandel, Ed, 19
Mandel, Eli, 222
Mann, William Edward, 214
Manning, Alberta, 254-55, 261
Manning, Ernest Charles, 76, 79, 212-14
Manyberries, Alberta, 59
Many Spotted Horses, 142
Marmot Basin, 192, 283
Marshhead Creek, 242
Martha Cohen Theatre (Calgary), 7
Martz Hardware (Heisler), 46
Mary Vaux, Mount, 112
Masque, 182
Matheson, Cathy, 27-29
Mathur, Ashok, 4
Mavis family, 72
May, Wilfrid "Wop", 211

Mazankowski, Mr. & Mrs. Donald, 45-46
Medicine Calf, 142
Medicine Hat, Alberta, 69, 134, 145-48, 150, 153, 174
Medicine Lake, 97
Medicine Lodge Hills, 294
Meikle River, 255
Mennonites, 153, 258, 262-63, 294
Mercoal, Alberta, 127
Mercredi, The Reverend Father Patrice, 271
Métis, 33, 67, 70, 127, 204, 229, 258, 268-72
Meyer, George, 174
Michener, Roland, 60
Midnight Sun, 244
Miette, Roche, 238
Miette Hot Springs, 95
Mile One Draw (McLeod River), 129
Mile Three swimming hole (McLeod River), 129
Milk River, 3, 294
Milk River Ridge, 13
Milton, William F., Viscount, 207, 227
Minehead, Alberta. *See* Robb
Miner, 277
Minnewanka, Lake, 83
Mistaya River, 87
Mitchell, 149
Mitchell, Victor, 182
Mitchell, William Ormond, 142, 173
Mitsuing, Ray, 6
Mix, Tom, 186
Mona Lake, 99
Moose Lake, 229-30
Moose Mountain, 290
Moraine Lake, 294
Moravians, 60
Morley, Alberta, 39, 159
Mormons, 59-60, 138, 166-67
Morningside, Alberta, 202-4, 293
Morrison, Archie, 73
Mountain Park, Alberta, 128-30
Mount Royal College (Calgary), 178
M Ranch, 5

Tower of Babel, 85
Towers, Mr. & Mrs. Gord 45
Trans-Canada Highway, 18, 85, 138, 140,
   143, 187, 227, 287, 290
Treaty No.7, 142
Trochu, Alberta, 60
Trochu, Armand, 60
Troyer Cattle Co., 45
Trunk Road. *See* Forestry Trunk Road
Tuck Shop (Edmonton), 225
Tunnel Mountain, 82, 84
Turcott, Garth, 163
Turner Valley, Alberta, 174
Turner Valley oil field, 188
Turtle Mountain, 11, 157
Tweed, Tommy, 149
Twin Butte, Alberta, 165
Tyrrell, Joseph B., 293
Tyrrell Museum. *See* Royal Tyrrell Museum

– U –

Ukrainian Cultural Heritage Village, 30
United Farmers of Alberta, 77-78, 191
University of Alberta, 60, 66, 79, 147, 179,
   182, 193, 218-24, 262
   Clinical Sciences Building, 221
   Health Sciences Centre, 220-21
   Medical School, 221-22
   Pembina Hall, 220
   Students' Union Building, 219-20
   Studio Theatre, 224
University of Calgary, 1, 7, 139, 178, 182,
   187
University of Lethbridge, 154
Unwin, Mount, 112
Upper Waterfowl Lake, 87, 89

– V –

Valhalla Centre, Alberta, 246
Van Duzee, Gary, 235-38
van Herk, Aritha, 1-2, 4-5, 8-12, 40
van Herk, Maretje, 2
Vauxhall, Alberta, 17
Vermilion, Alberta, 229

Vermilion Lakes, 287, 290
Vermilion River County, 64
Veteran, Alberta, 26
Victoria, Queen, 60
Victoria Glacier, 85
Viking-Kinsella oil field, 206
Vinson, Tom, 102-6, 109-11, 113, 116
Vinson, Tommy, 108-9
Volney, Constantin-François de
   Chasseboeuf, Comte de, 292
von Holland, Ted, 196-99
Voyer, Sylvain, 222

– W –

Wabamun Lake, 59, 233
Wah, Fred, 1, 4
Waiparous Creek, 200
Wales, Edward, Prince of, 173
Walking Eagle, 222
Walter, Edna Viola. *See* Campbell, Mrs.
   George
Walter, John, 210
Walter, John H., 69-70
Walterdale Playhouse, 224
Wanderings of an Artist, 222
Wandering Spirit, 228
Wapiti Campground, 93-94
Wapiti River, 246
Ward, Smoky, 22
Ware, John, 76, 145, 185
Waskahigan River, 243
Waterhole, Alberta, 60
Waterton-Glacier International Peace Park,
   166
Waterton Lakes National Park, 165-66,
   174, 187
Waterways, Alberta, 271, 275, 278
Watson, Sheila, 225
Watson, Wilfred, 224
Watt Mountain, 256
Weadick, Guy, 185-86
Weeping Wall, 93
Weller, George, 46
Weller family, 49